ZEALOTS FOR ZION

ROBERT I. FRIEDMAN

ZEALOTS FOR ZION

Inside Israel's
West Bank Settlement
Movement

RANDOM HOUSE

NEW YORK

Library of Congress Cataloging-in-Publication Data
Friedman, Robert I., 1950-
Zealots for Zion : inside Israel's West Bank settlement movement / by
Robert I. Friedman.
p. cm.
Includes index.
ISBN 0-394-58053-2
1. West Bank—Politics and government. 2. Jewish-Arab
relations—1973- I. Title.
DS110.W47F75 1992
956.95'3—dc20   91-51030

Manufactured in the United States of America
9 8 7 6 5 4 3 2
First Edition
Book design by Victoria Wong

4285

To Christine

Unto thy seed I give this land.

—God's promise to Abraham
recorded in the Book of Genesis

The sun will be turned into darkness and
the moon to blood before the great and
terrible day of the Lord shall come.

—Joel 2:28–32

Author's Note

This book is the product of my Middle East reporting, which began in 1977. Unless otherwise noted, I conducted all the interviews, with the exception of those with Yoram Hazony and his circle of friends in the settlement of Eli.

Acknowledgments

I would like to thank the following organizations and individuals for their support: the Dick Goldensohn Fund; the Foundation for Middle East Peace and its founder, Merle Thorpe, Jr.; the Fund for Investigative Journalism; the Shefa Fund; Danny Rubinstein of *Ha'aretz;* Michah L. Sifry of *The Nation;* Janet Aviad of Peace Now; Yosef Cohen of *Kol Ha'ir;* Michael Caruso of *Vanity Fair;* the editors of *The Village Voice;* and Robert Silvers of *The New York Review of Books,* where this project began. Finally, I would like to thank my editor at Random House, Jason Epstein, without whose patience and encouragement this book would not have been possible.

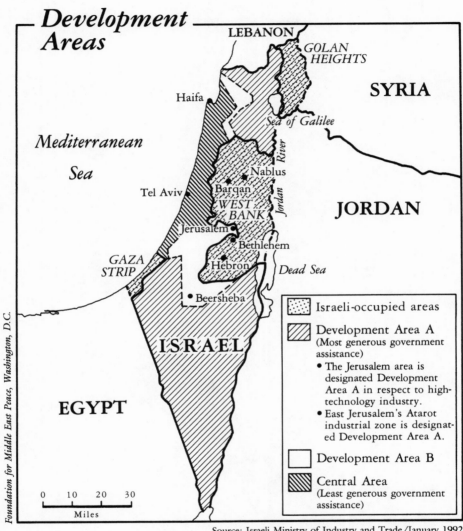

Development Areas

LEBANON

GOLAN HEIGHTS

SYRIA

Haifa

Sea of Galilee

Mediterranean Sea

Nablus

Barqan

Tel Aviv

WEST BANK

Jordan River

JORDAN

Jerusalem

Bethlehem

GAZA STRIP

Hebron

Dead Sea

Beersheba

ISRAEL

EGYPT

Israeli-occupied areas

Development Area A
(Most generous government assistance)
• The Jerusalem area is designated Development Area A in respect to high-technology industry.
• East Jerusalem's Atarot industrial zone is designated Development Area A.

Development Area B

Central Area
(Least generous government assistance)

0   10   20   30
Miles

Foundation for Middle East Peace, Washington, D.C.

Source: Israeli Ministry of Industry and Trade/January 1992

West Bank

Mediterranean Sea

Jenin

Nablus

Ariel

Tel Aviv

West Bank
(Israeli occupied —
status to be determined)

ISRAEL

Ramallah

Jericho

Jerusalem city limits
unilaterally expanded
by Israel, June 28, 1967;
annexed by Knesset,
July 30, 1980.

Jerusalem

Ma'ale
Adumim

Bethlehem

Efrat

Hebron

Kiryat Arba

JORDAN

Jordan River

D e a d

S e a

	1949 Armistice Line ("Green Line")
- - -	1967 Cease-fire Line
▲	Israeli settlements

0   5   10 Miles

Gaza Strip

Gaza

Mediterranean
Sea

ISRAEL

Khan Yunis

Rafah

EGYPT

SINAI

▲	Israeli settlements
▨	Palestinian refugee camps
▧	Palestinian residential areas

0   1   2 Miles

Foundation for Middle East Peace, Washington, D.C.

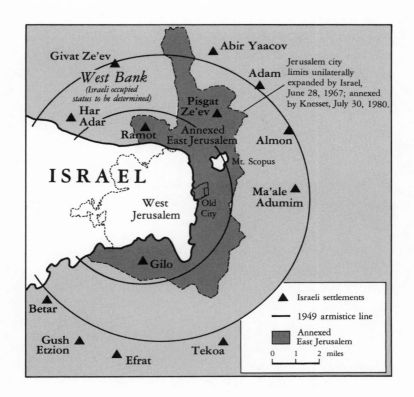

Givat Ze'ev

West Bank
*(Israeli occupied
status to be determined)*

Har
Adar

Ramot

ISRAEL

West
Jerusalem

Abir Yaacov

Adam

Jerusalem city
limits unilaterally
expanded by Israel,
June 28, 1967; annexed
by Knesset, July 30, 1980.

Pisgat
Ze'ev

Annexed
East Jerusalem

Almon

Mt. Scopus

Old
City

Ma'ale
Adumim

Gilo

Betar

Gush
Etzion

Efrat

Tekoa

▲ Israeli settlements

—— 1949 armistice line

▉ Annexed
East Jerusalem

0   1   2   miles

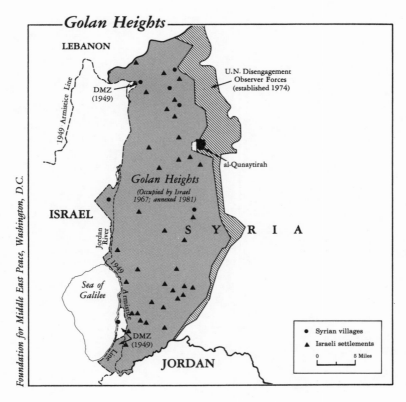

Golan Heights

LEBANON

1949 Armistice Line

DMZ
(1949)

U.N. Disengagement
Observer Forces
(established 1974)

al-Qunaytirah

Golan Heights
(Occupied by Israel
1967; annexed 1981)

ISRAEL

S   Y   R   I   A

Jordan River

1949 Armistice Line

Sea of
Galilee

DMZ
(1949)

JORDAN

● Syrian villages

▲ Israeli settlements

0   5 Miles

Foundation for Middle East Peace, Washington, D.C.

Contents

Introduction

Early in the summer of 1990, Bob Silverman, a thirty-year-old U.S. diplomat based in West Jerusalem, drove his armor-plated Mercedes to the West Bank Arab town of Hebron, the site of fierce clashes between Palestinians and ultranationalist religious settlers who had moved into the town's ancient Casbah with the avowed aim of turning the city into a Jewish domain. Silverman's job was to track the growth of Jewish settlements in the Israeli-occupied West Bank and Gaza Strip for the State Department, which calls them "an obstacle to peace." As Silverman was taking photos of a Jewish housing development of low-rise stone-hewn apartment blocks near the crowded Arab vegetable market, an armed settler wearing a knitted prayer cap lunged at him and tried to wrestle away his camera. Silverman, dressed in a conservative blue suit and tie, identified himself as a U.S. diplomat. The settler waved a pistol, calling Silverman a "dirty American bastard." Israeli soldiers lounged nearby. Soon, swarms of settlers emerged from their homes and formed a human wall around Silverman, taunting him and preventing him from leaving the area. Only when an Israeli officer intervened was the young American allowed to go.

The United States immediately lodged a protest with the Israeli government, and Philip Wilcox, the venerable U.S. consul in West Jerusalem and the former head of the State Department's Israel Desk, sent a tart cable about the incident to Washington. Furious State Department officials privately vowed that Israel's $3.5 billion in annual aid would be cut in direct proportion to the amount of money it was spending on settlements in the occupied territories. Frustrated with Israel's failure to provide data on settlement-building activity, the United States finally resorted to using spy satellites to conduct its own survey.

The increasing tension over the settlement issue set the stage for a bitter battle over Israel's request in spring 1991 for $10 billion in U.S. government loan guarantees to absorb the vast exodus of Jews from the Soviet Union. The U.S. guarantee would enable Israel to borrow money from commercial banks at lower interest rates than it normally would be able to obtain. The United States would have to repay the loan should Israel default. The Israeli government, which felt so confident about securing the loan guarantees that it included the first installment of $2 billion in its 1992 budget, was stunned when Secretary of State James Baker asked Congress on September 4, 1991, to delay the bill until after a Middle East peace conference that was scheduled for October 1991 in Madrid.

Although the pro-Israel lobby fought hard for immediate passage of the loan guarantees, the Bush administration linked the request to a settlement freeze, as well as to Israel's continued good-faith participation at a regional peace conference. Administration insiders said that President Bush believed that if the United States did not impede Israel's settlement drive, the Arab lands Israel occupied in the June 1967 Six-Day War would soon be completely absorbed into Israel, foreclosing the possibility of Middle East peace.

The United States, like most other countries, views Israeli settlements as illegal under the Fourth Geneva Convention of 1949, which bars occupying powers from moving citizens to occupied land. This convention has been interpreted in UN resolutions as forbidding Israel from altering the demographic composition of the territories it has seized, either by expelling Palestinians or moving Jews there. Although U.S. policy on Israeli settlements has been consistent since the Johnson administration, only Jimmy Carter and George Bush have seriously challenged the Israelis on the issue. "It is against our policy for these settlements to be built," said President Bush in Kennebunkport, Maine, shortly before the Madrid peace talks began. "We're not giving one inch on the settlements."

The conflict between the two allies was over more than West Bank settlements. After its victory over Iraq, the Bush administration envisioned a New World Order in which Israel and the Palestinians would end their hundred-year war. Israel's past role as a "strategic asset" against communism in the Middle East was obsolete. The United States had new obligations to the Arab world after the Gulf War, which meant finding a more evenhanded approach to solving the Arab-Israeli dispute.

But Israeli prime minister Yitzhak Shamir had his own dream: the continued colonization of the occupied territories in his quest to realize "Greater Israel." Already, Israel has acquired a vast foothold in the lands occupied since 1967, where more than 100,000 settlers live in 144 settlements (excluding those in East Jerusalem), built at a cost of more than $15 billion—a huge sum for an economically hard-pressed nation that depends on billions of dollars in annual U.S. aid. By 1992, Israel had expropriated more than 50 percent of the land of the West Bank—the core area of the biblical Land of Israel and home to one million Palestinians—and 34 percent of the Gaza Strip, where 750,000 Palestinians live packed together in refugee camps as miserable as any in the world. Nestled amid Gaza's squalor are nineteen Jewish settlements protected by ten-foot barbed-wire fences, land mines, and Israeli soldiers. West Bank Jewish settlers use four times more water per capita than the Palestinians, who have to get permission from the military to dig wells. According to a confidential State Department report prepared in 1990, the Israelis have not allowed the Palestinians to dig a new well on the West Bank in more than a decade. "What is happening in the occupied territories is the systematic dispossession of a people from their land," a senior U.S. official in Israel told me. "The settlements are a lunatic enterprise."

But for Shamir and his ruling Likud party, there was nothing lunatic about reclaiming the land of ancient Israel for Jews who are persecuted and may have nowhere else to go. In 1991, the Israeli prime minister declared that he wanted a "big Israel" to accommodate a "big immigration" from the Soviet Union. Some four hundred thousand Soviet Jews have arrived in Israel since the massive exodus began in 1990, and the country is anticipating perhaps a million more. The Shamir government claimed it was not sending the new immigrants to the territories, but their presence in Israel squeezed the housing market, inflated rents, and impelled many native Israelis to consider moving to settlements with their generous, government-subsidized mortgages, free land, and tax abatements.

The settlements are not only affordable, but many are also attractive suburban housing developments that would not look out of place in Phoenix or Orange County, California. Just a few miles east of Jerusalem, along the road to Jericho, in a brown, barren lunar landscape of enormous boulders and talcum-powder-fine sand, miles of ridges have been covered with three- and four-story apartment complexes made of glass and shimmering white stone. The settlement is called Ma'ale Adumim, and with fifteen thousand people it achieved city status just before the outbreak of the Gulf War. According to plans released by the Shamir government, Ma'ale Adumim was to be linked to Arab East Jerusalem some fifteen kilometers away by a solid block of Jewish housing projects. Palestinian neighborhoods in East Jerusalem are already boxed in by a web of new Jewish housing complexes built on expropriated Arab land. Near Nablus in northern Samaria, lush green hills dotted with hundred-year-old olive trees have been bulldozed and replaced by communities of squat single-family homes with red-tile roofs and small gardens. They look like Potemkin villages, but their names—Eli, Shilo, Ofra—come from the Bible, as do the reasons the deeply religious inhabitants give to justify their presence there.

"From the Mediterranean Sea to the Jordan River there will be no Arab state," Matityahu Drobles, co-chair of the World Zionist Organization's settlement department and author of a detailed plan to colonize the occupied territories, told me in his office at the Jewish Agency in Jerusalem when I visited him in the winter of 1991. The WZO, which is funded by donations from world Jewry, works closely with the Israeli government to encourage Jewish settlement in the territories. "Judea and Samaria are part of the Land of Israel," said Drobles, using the biblical names for the West Bank. "If we want to achieve Jewish sovereignty, we have to settle. Those who have the power here will prevail—and we have the strength. I read the Bible. It doesn't talk about the borders of England. But *Eretz Yisrael* [the Land of Israel] is in the Bible. According to the Bible, I have the right to the East Bank of Jordan too. For my generation the West Bank is enough. As for the next generation, the East Bank is their problem."

Drobles, who moved to Israel from Argentina, told me he planned to settle hundreds of thousands more Jews in the West Bank and the Gaza Strip in the next few years, erasing the 1967 borders and absorbing the territories completely into Israel proper. "The problem is finding jobs for Jews who live in the territories. I need factories, and investment capital from America."

Despite U.S. opposition, settlement activity went full bore after the Gulf War. Sensing that the impending negotiations with the Arab world would jeopardize the status quo in the occupied territories, the Likud government decided to strengthen its grip by expanding existing settlements, establishing new ones, and investing heavily in infrastructure. Between June 1990 and January 1992, Housing Minister Ariel Sharon spent more than $1.6 billion to settle Jews in the territories, breaking ground on at least thirteen thousand new homes there.* Israel's 1992 budget called for spending one fourth of all industrial investment and two thirds of all housing money in the occupied territories.

In brazen contempt of U.S. policy, Israel erected three new settlements on the eve of visits to Jerusalem by Secretary of State James Baker, who had flown to the region to start Middle East peace talks following the Gulf War. Two† more settlements were established in the wake of the Madrid peace talks, while ultranationalist settlers accelerated their acquisition of Arab housing in East Jerusalem—often by illegal means—exacerbating tensions in the city and threatening to derail the peace process. "Nothing has made my job of trying to find Arab and Palestinian partners for Israel more difficult than being greeted by a new settlement every time I arrive [in Israel]," an angry Baker told a House Foreign Affairs Subcommittee in May 1991. "I don't think there is any bigger obstacle to peace than [Israel's] settlement activity that continues not only unabated but at an enhanced pace."

The socialist Labor government of Levi Eshkol began building Jewish settlements in the occupied territories just three months after Israel's victory in the June 1967 Six-Day War. Labor, which publicly declared that it would barter much of the land Israel had occupied for a peace treaty with its Arab neighbors, confined its settlement program largely to the Golan Heights, the northern Sinai, the Gush Etzion block near Bethlehem, and the lightly populated Jordan River Valley. The settlement movement grew rapidly, however, after the right-wing Likud party defeated Labor in 1977. While most of Labor's settlements were built with security considerations in mind, the Likud proclaimed that Jews had the God-given right to live anywhere in *Eretz Yisrael,* the biblical Land of Israel, including in heavily populated Arab areas. While the Labor party tried to hermetically seal Arab areas inside a wall of Jewish settlements, Likud's plan was to move into

---

*The Israeli government spent more than $3 billion on settlement expansion between 1990 and 1991, according to the *Report on Israeli Settlement in the Occupied Territories,* a bimonthly publication of the Washington-based Foundation for Middle East Peace.

†According to Peace Now, nine settlements have been built since the Gulf War, two that the Shamir government acknowledged and seven others that have been built next to existing settlements. The government claimed these sites are suburbs of established settlements and not new developments.

their very midst—with the intent of making life untenable so they would eventually quit the land and flee. In September 1977, Ariel Sharon, then Likud's minister of agriculture, unveiled a master plan* calling for the settlement of two million Jews in the occupied territories by the end of the twentieth century. The Likud argued that it was no less valorous to create a Jewish majority on the West Bank than it had been for the Zionist pioneers to do so along the Mediterranean coast during the 1920s and 1930s. Such Jewish settlements would impose a Jewish majority on the West Bank and make it impossible for Israel to relinquish the territory without expelling hundreds of thousands of Jews—an action that no Israeli government, no matter what its ideological inclination, could carry out without risking civil war.

For Likud's settlement policy Israel has paid a high price: its good name. As the Palestinians refused to surrender quietly to Shamir's colonial pursuits, the vaunted Israel Defense Force (IDF), or Israeli Army, was turned into a brutal army of occupation that enforces curfews, demolishes homes, and breaks the bones of young Palestinian stone throwers.† More than one thousand Palestinians have been killed by Israeli soldiers and settlers since the *intifada,* or uprising, began in December 1987, and the casualty count continues to rise relentlessly. There have also been more than 119,000 serious injuries to Palestinians, 66 expulsions, 120,000 trees uprooted, 2,050 house demolitions and sealings, and vast prison camps have been erected where, on any given day, 14,000 Palestinians are being held— almost one percent of the Arab population of the territories. According to the IDF, some seventy-five thousand Palestinians were arrested during the first three years of the *intifada,* of whom thirty thousand were never charged with any offense.

B'Tselem, an Israeli human-rights group established in February 1989 by prominent Jewish lawyers, doctors, academics, and Knesset members, concluded in a carefully documented study that some forty-five hundred detainees had been subjected to various forms of torture since the onset of the *intifada.*‡ The case of Wa'il, a twenty-year-old Hebronite arrested in May 1989 for *intifada*-related crimes, was typical. "In the evening, there was another interrogation session," B'Tselem reported. "Lying on his

---

*The plan was called "A Vision of Israel at Century's End."
†The "break the bones" policy was authored by then–Defense Minister Yitzhak Rabin at the onset of the *intifada.*
‡At least six Palestinian security prisoners have died as a result of torture, B'Tselem reported.

back, with his hands tied, Wa'il was hit and kicked on the testicles, strangled twice round the throat for up to a minute, and beaten on the head with a metal bar covered with rubber. He was then placed in the 'banana position': tied on a stool, with head and legs bent over on either side, he was beaten on the stomach. At 11:00 P.M. he was brought back to the closet." "The closet" is a small, dark, coffin-like tomb where detainees are held for extended periods, often bound and hooded. The hood is often soaked with water or sometimes urine. Variations on this sequence continued for the next month, during which time he was not allowed to shower or change clothes. After thirty-six days of confinement, according to the report, Wa'il was charged and tried for throwing stones, and sentenced to five months' imprisonment.*

The report caused an outcry among the Israeli right, which denounced the document as anti-Israel. "I haven't read the B'Tselem report," fumed Shlomo Goren, Israel's former chief rabbi. "I don't know them and don't want to know them. They betray the people of Israel and the state of Israel; they're serving our enemies. Since they're traitors, they weren't created in the image of God."

Such attitudes are not uncommon in Israel, where some Orthodox rabbis have called Palestinians descendants of the ancient Amalekites whose extermination is mandated by the Bible, and where other religious leaders have declared that Jewish blood is purer than the Arabs'. "It should be recognized that Jewish blood and a *goy*'s blood are not the same," Rabbi Yitzhak Ginzburg told an Israeli court after thirty of his yeshiva students rampaged through the West Bank town of Nablus, shooting to death a thirteen-year-old Palestinian girl in July 1989. "The people of Israel must rise and declare in public that a Jew and a *goy* are not, God forbid, the same. Any trial that assumes that Jews and *goyim* are equal is a travesty of justice."

Despite such racism, Israelis have not abandoned democracy, which as practiced in the Jewish state is still robust and freewheeling. Peace Now, which was formed by Israeli reserve officers, many of them decorated combat veterans, held massive demonstrations protesting the Likud government's settlement policy. And some of the country's best writers, such as Amos Oz and David Grossman, steadfastly have catalogued the sins of occupation and the collateral damage it does to Israel's soul. No one in Israel, not even on the right, any longer believes in the myth of the benign

*Pp. 55–56 of March 1991 report.

occupation. Israelis have seen too many horrors. At least half the nation wants to end the occupation, trade land for peace, and even negotiate with the Palestine Liberation Organization, according to polls. As for the argument that holding the territories gives the tiny country strategic depth, Israeli liberals contend that occupying the West Bank did not prevent Iraqi Scuds from slamming into Tel Aviv. And even if Israel felt it prudent to maintain "effective military control of the West Bank as a defensive buffer zone, [it] does not require Israeli political rule over 1.8 million Palestinian Arabs," wrote Major General Shlomo Gazit, the former head of Israeli Military Intelligence and one of a legion of former generals and security chiefs who have advocated relinquishing political control of the territories and have conceived various plans for doing so. "We would not like to dominate another people against their will," said former Labor party leader Shimon Peres shortly before the June 1992 Israeli national elections. "It's a moral issue. It's a political issue. Throughout our history as a Jewish people, we have never dominated other people, and whoever dominated us disappeared from history. We don't want to copy that."

Israel did not set out to be a right-wing apartheid state-in-the-making, where Palestinians would be held in Bantustans—if they were not expelled. It began as a giant rescue mission and human-reclamation project. Modern Zionism's founder, Theodor Herzl, had observed that anti-Semitism was virtually a congenital disease among nineteenth-century Europeans, a condition that seemed only to worsen as Jews were integrated into Gentile society. The lesson of history, Herzl concluded, was that wherever Jews were a minority, they would be persecuted. The remedy was to carve out a home for Europe's Jews in the land from which they had been expelled some two thousand years before, but had never forgotten.

For many young pioneers from Eastern Europe's ghettos who had dreams of turning Palestine into an exemplary society, Zionism became a utopian venture, where Jews would experience a national, spiritual, cultural, physical, and material rebirth, and in the process transform Jewish civilization into "a light unto the nations." At the same time, the Jewish homeland would be a life raft where persecuted Jews, protected by their own government and army, could live like normal people in "a nation like any other." More than a reaction to anti-Semitism, Zionism was a Jewish national liberation movement that adhered to the principles of nineteenth-century liberalism and democracy.

The Zionist movement found an early benefactor in imperial Britain, which had taken Palestine from the decaying Ottoman Turkish Empire at the close of the First World War. On November 2, 1917, the British issued the Balfour Declaration, which promised to support a Jewish national home in Palestine but said "that nothing shall be done which may prejudice the civil and religious rights of existing non-Jewish communities in Palestine. . . ." Implicit in the Balfour Declaration, however, was Britain's support for eventual Jewish independence in Palestine. The problem was that Palestine had a large Arab majority population that had not only lived there for many generations, but, by the early twentieth century, had its own aspirations for self-determination as well.

At first Jewish leaders believed that the Arab community would be grateful to the Jews for bringing them modern science and technology. Instead, the Arabs repeatedly clashed with the Jewish settlers, and took dozens of lives. The violence worsened as Jewish immigration into Palestine increased and Jews began to purchase land from absentee Arab landlords, dispossessing thousands of angry and frightened Arab peasants. Nevertheless, during the early years of British rule in Palestine, British officials worked closely with the Zionists, helping them to set up their own institutions of self-government. In response to escalating Arab violence, however, the British issued a white paper in June 1922, declaring that the Balfour Declaration never meant to create an independent Jewish state in Palestine.

In 1936, as Jewish emigration from Nazi Germany increased, the Arabs of Palestine revolted against British Mandatory rule and Zionist colonization. For three years, British troops fought fierce battles with Arab guerrillas, inflicting heavy casualties. By the time the rebellion was crushed, the Palestinian community was so enfeebled that it could no longer seriously challenge the Zionist quest for statehood.

Following the Arab Revolt, Ben-Gurion and the other Jewish leaders decided that, in view of continuing Arab enmity, the Palestinians would not peacefully accept a Jewish state and would not willingly become its citizens. Zionist leaders considered several ways to solve the "Arab problem." Many Zionists hoped that financial incentives would entice the Palestinians to leave. In June 1938, during a daylong executive meeting, the Jewish Agency, the governing body of the Jewish community in Palestine, overwhelmingly endorsed, in principle, the mass transfer of Palestinian Arabs from proposed Jewish areas of a future Jewish state. "It is the most moral [thing to do]," said Menachem Ussishkin, who advocated transferring sixty thousand Arab families to Arab countries. "We will not be able to begin our political life in a state in which Arabs will constitute 45 percent [of the population]."

Ben-Gurion also considered transferring the Arabs to make way for a Jewish state. "We must expel Arabs and take their places," he wrote to his son Amos on Oct. 5, 1937. "And if we have to use force—not to dispossess the Arabs of the Negev and Transjordan, but to guarantee our own right to settle in those places—then we have force at our disposal."

The mainstream Zionist organizations, meanwhile, had shown remarkable patience in the face of increasing Palestinian terrorist attacks. The Haganah, a quasi-underground Jewish self-defense force affiliated to the Jewish Agency headed by David Ben-Gurion, developed a policy called *havlaga*, or restraint. The policy rested on Ben-Gurion's belief that the British, and not the Jews, should respond to Arab provocations. However, the much smaller right-wing terrorist undergrounds—the Stern Gang, led by Yitzhak Shamir, and the Irgun, by Menachem Begin—carried out acts of indiscriminate terror against the British Mandatory government and Arab civilians, such as putting bombs in Arab marketplaces and on Arab buses. In the single month of July 1938, for example, the Irgun killed seventy-six Arabs in terrorist bombings.

The same ideology that spawned the Stern Gang and Irgun has shaped the Likud party today. The party of Shamir and Sharon is the descendant of Revisionist Zionism, a movement that played a small role in the creation of the Jewish state and remained at its margins until Menachem Begin came to power in 1977. While many of the pioneering Labor Zionists were socialist utopians who believed that physical labor on Jewish soil could revitalize and even elevate the Jewish spirit on the road to a kind of secular messianic redemption, Revisionists, who were mostly small shopkeepers, believed that political power and military might alone could cure the ills born of the diaspora. While the Labor Zionists drained Palestine's swamps, built the kibbutzim, absorbed new immigrants, and created the institutions of the army and the state (subsuming a people already living on the land along the way), the Revisionists built little more than an ideology based on the principle of "Conquer or die." They envisioned Israel as a powerful ghetto-state surrounded by an iron wall of bayonets and tanks.

The Revisionist movement was founded by Ze'ev Vladimir Jabotinksy, one of the most charismatic and controversial figures in modern Zionism. Adored by his disciples, who hailed him as the Garibaldi of the Zionist revolution, he was denounced by many other Jews as a fascist; Israel's first prime minister, David Ben-Gurion, once called him "Vladimir Hitler." As early as 1906, Jabotinsky had established a Jewish self-defense corps in Odessa. During the Arab riots in 1920, he organized another Jewish self-defense brigade in Jerusalem. In 1923, in Riga, Latvia, he founded Betar, an international paramilitary Jewish youth movement, whose members wore brown shirts and marched in torchlight parades. (Moshe Arens, Israel's former defense minister, headed Betar in America, while one of its most infamous members was the late Brooklyn-born rabbi Meir Kahane.)

Jabotinsky enjoyed tremendous support among Eastern Europe's pogrom-plagued Jews. Although he was a cosmopolitan, bourgeois intellectual, his emphasis on developing Jewish military might attracted a number of trigger-happy zealots, some of whom were drawn to Mussolini and Hitler, and most of whom were opposed to liberal democracy, which they felt had castrated Zionism. Like many right-wing Israelis today, Jabotinsky advocated granting Palestinians living in a Jewish state civil, but not political, rights. His preference, however, was a Jewish state devoid of Arabs. "We should instruct American Jewry to mobilize half a billion dollars in order that Iraq and Saudi Arabia will absorb the Palestinian Arabs," Jabotinsky wrote to a supporter in November 1939. "There is no choice: the Arabs must make room for the Jews in *Eretz Yisrael*. If it was possible to transfer the Baltic peoples,* it is also possible to move the Palestinian Arabs."

Opposed to Palestine's socialist-dominated Jewish Agency on a host of issues—ranging from immigration policies to relations with local Arabs— and intensely displeased with their go-slow "acre after acre, goat after goat" diplomatic approach to securing a Jewish homeland, Jabotinsky broke away from the main international Zionist body and formed an independent Zionist organization, the Revisionist movement, in April 1935. His followers subsequently formed the Irgun and the Stern Gang, which waged a terrorist war against the British and the Arabs. At the outbreak of the Second World War, the Irgun halted its terrorist campaign against the British for the sake of defeating Hitler. But Shamir's Stern Gang not only continued to attack the British (though most of its targets during the war

---

*On August 23, 1939, Nazi Germany and the Soviet Union signed a treaty of nonaggression. In a secret protocol affixed to the pact, the two dictatorships carved up their respective spheres of influence in Eastern Europe. The Soviet Union received the Baltic States, Finland, and parts of Poland. By 1941, the Soviet Union had transferred more than one million Balts and Poles to Central Asia and Siberia.

were Jewish-owned banks), it even sent emissaries to Beirut in 1940 to hold
secret talks with German officials from the Third Reich about forging an
anti-British coalition.* Many years later, during an interview on Israeli
Army Radio in September 1991, Shamir justified the Stern Gang's extreme
methods. "Terrorism is a way of fighting that is acceptable under certain
conditions and by certain movements," he said, adding that while terrorism
was appropriate for Jews fighting for their homeland, it is not for Palestinians who "are fighting for land that is not theirs. This is the land of the
people of Israel."

In 1944, the Irgun resumed its revolt against the British, who pressured
the Jewish Agency to curb the Jewish terrorists. Meeting in secret session,
the Jewish Agency voted to wage an anti-Irgun campaign called the Season.
Specially trained Haganah squads kidnapped Irgun members and turned
them over to the British. The Season ended in May 1945, along with the
the Second World War, but the antagonisms it created still smolder in
Israel.†

On November 29, 1947, the United Nations partitioned Palestine into
a Jewish and a Palestinian Arab state. The West Bank, a large chunk of the
Galilee and Gaza, as well as portions of the Negev, were to go to the
Palestinians. The plan left one hundred thousand Jews in the Arab state,
and four hundred thousand Arabs in the Jewish state. Jerusalem and
Bethlehem were to be separate enclaves under international control. (The
East Bank of the River Jordan, part of the original Palestinian Mandate, had
been carved off by Winston Churchill in 1922 to form Transjordan.)

Ben-Gurion accepted the partition plan. The Palestinians and the Arab
states did not. On May 15, 1948, the day after Israel was founded, five
Arab armies invaded Palestine with the declared intention of liquidating the
Jewish state. For the Palestinians, the war was a disaster. By the time it was

*Shamir, one of three men who jointly headed the Stern Gang, opposed the group's secret talks with the
Nazis. In an interview with Dan Margalit published in *Maariv* on Jan. 31, 1992, Shamir explained, "I didn't
believe in it [the secret talks]. I knew very well what the Nazi Movement was. In the year before I
immigrated to Israel [1935], I was a student in Warsaw. I encountered many anti-Semitic students and the
Nazi atmosphere in the streets. For them [the Nazis], the persecution of Jews was a very deep ideological
issue. I didn't believe that one could arouse in them an understanding of shared interests with the Jews,
with any Jews."

†According to an article by Danny Rubinstein and Nachum Barnea in *Davar* on March 19, 1982, "The
Haganah archives contain the names of 40 Jews who were killed by the Irgun or LEHI [the Stern Gang]
. . . in the course of their underground work or in the context of settling personal accounts." This figure
does not include Jews killed in terrorist acts aimed at the British or Arabs such as the Irgun bombing of
British headquarters at the King David Hotel in Jerusalem in 1946 in which 91 people, including 17 Jews,
lost their lives. Ben-Gurion, who was in Paris when the King David was bombed, told a reporter from *France
Soir*, "The Irgun is the enemy of the Jewish people."

over, Israel had conquered large areas that had been assigned to the Palestinian state. But Israel's victory was not complete. Egypt had occupied the Gaza Strip, and Jordan had annexed the West Bank, including East Jerusalem—evicting all Jews from the Old Walled City's ancient Jewish Quarter and desecrating Jewish holy places. By war's end, some 600,000 to 760,000 Palestinian refugees had fled or been expelled from Israel. Undoubtedly, many Palestinians had fled to neighboring Arab countries to wait out the war, hoping to return as victors. The Jews had nowhere to run. After June 1948, it was Israeli government policy to prevent the return of the Palestinian refugees, not only out of concern that they would be a fifth column, but also because a large Arab minority would dilute the Jewish character of the state. Arab homes were turned over to Holocaust survivors, making a Palestinian return all but impossible. Consequently, the Palestinian refugee problem became one of the most intractable components of the Arab-Israeli conflict.*

After the war, the socialist Labor government of David Ben-Gurion forcibly disarmed the right-wing underground groups, then hounded their members into the political wilderness. Ben-Gurion had feared a putsch by the Irgun. In June 1948, the Irgun arms ship *Altalena* was fired upon and sunk by the Palmach† off the coast of Tel Aviv as thousands of Israelis watched. The commander of the Jewish forces on the beach was Yitzhak Rabin. Menachem Begin, who was on the ship, barely escaped with his life. The battle cost the Irgun fourteen dead and sixty-nine wounded.

Thereafter members of the Stern Gang and the Irgun rallied around the Herut party founded by Begin. Herut metamorphosed into the Likud party after it was joined by several smaller parties. In 1977, Likud won a stunning upset victory over the enfeebled Labor party, ending an epoch in Israeli politics.

Likud was propelled into power by Sephardic or Oriental Jews, who began arriving in Israel en masse primarily from North Africa and Iraq in the early 1950s, and who were treated with paternalistic contempt by the reigning Ashkenazi, Eastern European–dominated Labor party. Though Begin is an Ashkenazi Jew, he was an anti-establishment outsider who brilliantly projected the Sephardim's fears and insecurities onto the PLO and the Palestinians in the territories.

---

*The Stern Gang assassinated UN mediator Count Folke Bernadotte in a Jerusalem suburb in September 1949. Bernadotte had been working on a plan to repatriate tens of thousands of Palestinian refugees.
†The Palmach was the elite corps of the Haganah.

The Likud coalition also found an important ally in the religious movement called Gush Emunim ("the Bloc of the Faithful"), which became the vanguard of the settlement movement. Religious Zionism had been a generally moderate movement until the Six-Day War—a momentous event that awakened the long-dormant spirit of nationalist Judaism. Suddenly, the Temple Mount in East Jerusalem, where the temples of King Solomon and Herod once stood, and ancient holy cities like Hebron, were in Jewish hands for the first time in two thousand years. Gush Emunim's rabbis proclaimed that settling the biblical Land of Israel, including Judea and Samaria, otherwise known as the West Bank, was part of the divine process that would inexorably lead to the End of Days and the Redemption of Mankind. Thousands of Orthodox Jews answered the call to settle the occupied territories. Dressed in blue jeans, plaid shirts, and brightly colored knitted yarmulkes, with an Uzi slung casually over one shoulder, the religious settlers believed that they were completing the job of nation-building begun by the socialist pioneers at the turn of the century. Gush Emunim presented a tough, muscular image of religious Judaism that hadn't been seen since the destruction of the Second Temple by the Romans nearly two thousand years ago—a disaster brought on by a similar militant hysteria.

"Israel's success in the Six-Day War unleashed a mood of intoxication that invigorated the [religious and secular] Right," wrote David Biale in *The London Review of Books*. "From their point of view, the Six-Day War completed the process of national formation begun during the 1948 War of Independence. Far from being a war of self-defense, the 1967 campaign, as seen by the Right, liberated the national patrimony and secured the true historical boundaries of the Jewish state."

But Shamir and the settlers faced the same problem that Herzl and the early Zionist pioneers confronted—the land they wished to colonize was not vacant. Much of pre-1967 Israel was built atop the ruins of Palestinian society; when Israeli armies occupied the West Bank and the Gaza Strip in 1967, they took over the Palestinians' place of refuge too. Now the West Bank and the Gaza Strip, the remnants of historical Palestine, are the focus of Palestinian national aspirations.

For decades, Israel had no one to talk to about peace. The PLO sought what it considered absolute justice—the eradication of "the Zionist entity." Except for Egypt after the Camp David settlement, the Arab states remained implacable foes. It was only belatedly that the PLO recognized Israel in 1988. It now seeks, as do many Israelis, the repartition of historical Palestine into two states—one Palestinian on the West Bank and the Gaza Strip with East Jerusalem as its capital, and one Jewish. After forty years of self-destructive policies, unrelenting terrorism, and enormous casualties suffered in its wars with Israel (as well as with Syria and Jordan), the PLO sued for peace—triggering panic in the Likud, made worse by the willingness of Arab countries to talk directly to Israel at summits in Madrid, Washington, and Moscow.

For Shamir to have surrendered the occupied territories as George Bush and James Baker wanted him to do would have been to betray his fifty-year-old dream of Greater Israel. To give up the territories would not have threatened the existence of Israel, as the hard-liners on the right maintained, but it would have led to the collapse of the Likud and the ideology that it inherited from Jabotinsky.

Shamir wasn't about to let that happen. "The sole guarantee of our survival and future," he declared after the Gulf War, "is a generation of faithful, powerful, and strong Jews in Israel, a generation that will never give up on any suffering and downtrodden Jew—even if he must be brought from afar, from the deserts of Ethiopia or the streams of Russia . . . one that will never abandon even a clod of the soil of the Land of Israel, even if it must be watered with a sea of sweat and tears." On the eve of the Madrid summit, a defiant Shamir pledged to build more settlements. "All the territories of *Eretz Yisrael* must be settled by Jews, more and more," Shamir shouted, pounding his fist on the table at a meeting of Likud party activists. A few days later, Israel Radio quoted Shamir saying to Likud supporters in France, "If someone thinks that it is possible to pressure Israel [to make concessions] . . . the answer will be that we will always remain faithful to our ideals, to Zionism, to Jerusalem, and to *Eretz Yisrael*."

The Labor party's astonishing victory in the June 1992 Israeli national elections sent the Likud and its right-wing allies into a frenzy. Their bitter adversaries—the men and women they had self-righteously denounced as "traitors" and "PLO supporters"—were, for the first time in fifteen years, called on by the people of Israel to form a government. The dream of *Eretz Yisrael* so ardently pursued by Begin, Shamir, and Sharon had been emphatically rejected. The Labor party had campaigned on a land-for-peace platform and a promise to stem the flow of funds to the "ideological" settlements built by Likud and Gush Emunim in the Palestinian heartland. Labor party leader Yitzhak Rabin also stated that the Palestinians would be allowed to set up a democratically elected, self-governing authority in the territories—the precursor, many believe, to an independent homeland. Not only does this imperil the settlement enterprise, but it represents a potentially catastrophic theological defeat for Gush Emunim, which believes the Messiah won't come if any part of *Eretz Yisrael* is relinquished.

Even before the 1992 elections, militant settlers had vowed to plunge Israel into a civil war if the government tried to trade land for peace with the Arabs. "An Israeli withdrawal from the territories would be a terrible blow to the settlers," wrote Yehoshafat Harkabi, former chief of Military Intelligence and a professor of Middle Eastern Studies at the Hebrew University in Jerusalem. "Their world would collapse. It is readily comprehensible that there is almost no limit to what they would be prepared to do to prevent this. For them, withdrawal in the wake of a peace treaty is certain spiritual defeat. . . . For them, the Zionist enterprise loses all justification without the territories. Consequently, they identify withdrawal from the territories with the destruction of Israel." Already *Alef Yud,* a settler newspaper, had warned that concessions would lead to "mutiny in the army, an armed uprising . . . and finally—Jew fighting against Jew." More alarmingly, perhaps, radical settlers threatened to blow up East Jerusalem's Dome of the Rock Mosque, the third-holiest site in Islam, to torpedo the peace process. On the day after Labor's victory, *Maariv* reported that a group of settlers was stockpiling weapons in preparation for the coming Armageddon. The fear of mayhem was so great that a reporter for Israeli television asked a top aide to Rabin if civil war between Jews could break out. "I would like not to even think about such a situation," Reserve Brigadier General Binyamin Ben Eliezer replied gravely.

This is a book about the settlers and their controversial enterprise. Whatever its future, the settlement movement has changed the geography and character of Israel. Far more than a massive construction project, it is a marriage of Jabotinsky's militant secular nationalism and Gush Emunim's messianism. Revisionism and militant religious nationalism, both marginal Zionist ideologies for the first two decades of Israel's history, had combined to set the national agenda of the Jewish state. The settlement enterprise has polarized Israel, divided the American Jewish community, and created a widening rift between Israel and its prime benefactor—the United States. Likud was on the verge of fulfilling its historical quest for

Greater Israel. And if Labor falters and Likud returns to power, there may be no turning back. The heirs of Jabotinsky and of the Zealots who fought the Romans will have triumphed over the liberal Zionist idea, the Palestinian Arabs, and the nascent peace process. Four million Jews will then permanently rule two million hostile Palestinian Arabs, and Belfast will seem like Disneyland.

ZEALOTS
FOR ZION

CHAPTER 1

The Rise of the West Bank Settlement Movement

A mound of weathered stone on a terraced ridge north of the West Bank town of Hebron marks the spot where King David established his first royal throne some seven years before he conquered Jerusalem. For the Jews of Kiryat Arba, the fortified settlement created in 1969 by forty Orthodox families under the leadership of Rabbi Moshe Levinger on the parched Judean hills, the remnants of that throne symbolize the four-thousand-year Jewish roller-coaster ride through history: majestic temples and the Wailing Wall, Exile and the Promised Return. For Hebron's Arabs, who have lived under Israeli rule since the Six-Day War more than two decades ago, the symbolism is quite different.

The Palestinians of Hebron believe that the Jews have returned to Palestine to renew their Davidic kingdom on Arab soil. They fear that Zionism will spread across the Middle East, ultimately subverting and destroying the Arab world. The settlement looming over Hebron, the Israeli soldiers patrolling its streets, the Israeli prisons holding their rebellious sons, sustain these fears. Not surprisingly, they and their fellow Arabs are obsessed with finding a way to uproot and destroy the menace they see in their midst. The Jews are equally determined to stay.

Rabbi Moshe Levinger, the father of the settlement movement, is Israel's Ayatollah Khomeini—a black-bearded zealot willing to martyr himself for the right of the Jews to rebuild an ancient civilization on the occupied lands of the West Bank and Gaza. More stubborn even than Shamir, more passionate than Begin, more extreme than Sharon, Levinger has done more than anyone else to build the kingdom of Greater Israel. A living example of *mesirut hanefesh,* an Orthodox Jewish expression for complete devotion to a cause, Levinger has by force of will and with enormous courage and charisma empowered a mass movement. To look at Levinger, with his gaunt face that sometimes seems possessed by dreams thousands of years old, one can hardly believe that he is one of the most significant figures to emerge from modern Zionism since Israel's strong-willed first prime minister, David Ben-Gurion. But Shimon Peres, Yitzhak Rabin, Menachem Begin, and Yitzhak Shamir have all learned to take this thin, intense man seriously. When Levinger defied the Israeli government and founded the Jewish settlement in Hebron on Passover 1968, there were virtually no Jewish civilians living on the West Bank, which had been captured by the Israeli Army in June 1967. Today, there are 144 settlements and 100,000 settlers in the occupied territories, excluding East Jerusalem, and the numbers are surging dramatically, fed by immigrating Soviet Jews and tens of thousands of secular Israelis who have been attracted by generous government subsidies and lower taxes.

In Rabbi Levinger's view, it is God, and not Herzl, who was the first Zionist. And it is His laws, not the laws of the state, that matter most. First and foremost, according to Levinger, is God's commandment to transform the Land of Israel into a holy nation—one that would be ruled according to *Halacha,* Jewish religious law, the Torah. Necessarily, such a sacred mission rules out political compromise. "Even if the Arabs wanted to compromise, *we* couldn't," Rabbi Levinger has declared. "If someone were to come to another person's house and want to take his house or sleep with his wife or take his children, he couldn't compromise on that! It's our country, and it's our destiny to live in our land as a 'nation of priests.' "

Levinger lives by rules that were written during the age of the prophets. He has the power not only to sabotage peace negotiations, but also to ignite an apocalypse of biblical dimensions should an Israeli government attempt to remove the settlers from their West Bank homes. Yet former Israeli housing minister Ariel Sharon calls Levinger and his wife "true heroes of our generation." And in a poll taken in 1990 for the Israeli newspaper *Hadashot,* Levinger topped the list of the most influential men of the past decade. But he has also been called "Israel's foremost religious fascist" by *The New Republic,* hardly an Israel-bashing magazine. And Israeli novelist and liberal intellectual Amos Oz has called Levinger the high priest of a "cruel, obdurate sect, [that] emerged several years ago from a dark corner of Judaism." Levinger's "ultimate goal," declared Oz, "is not to wipe out the Arabs but rather to wipe out the State of Israel and proclaim in its stead the Messianic and insane Kingdom of Judah."

Together with several hundred armed followers, Levinger now lives in the center of Hebron, a poor, drab, working-class city of eighty-five thousand fiercely nationalist Palestinian Arabs. Nowhere on the West Bank is Islamic fundamentalism as strong or as inhospitable to outsiders as in Hebron, where there are no bars or movie theaters and where many Palestinian women wear long gowns and cover their heads with scarves. Likewise, there is no place in the occupied territories where Jewish fundamentalism is as uncompromising. Indeed, for many Orthodox Jews, Hebron is a city that inspires almost as much passion and commitment as Jerusalem.

Anat Levinger, a pretty twenty-one-year-old settler who is married to one of Rabbi Levinger's sons, invited me to visit her small two-bedroom flat in the Beit Hadassah building, the hub of Jewish communal life in Hebron. To enter the twelve-family Beit Hadassah complex, one must pass through an opening in a wrought-iron fence, which is surrounded by half a dozen bored Israeli soldiers. The walls were festooned with posters of Rabbi Meir Kahane, the militant Jewish Defense League founder who was assassinated in New York in November 1990. Levinger, who attended Kahane's funeral in Jerusalem, has inherited much of the slain rabbi's flock.

Anat, whose parents immigrated to Israel from North Africa in the 1950s, had lived in Beit Hadassah for about a year. She was wearing trendy Birkenstock sandals, a purple blouse, black slacks, and a head covering that glittered with silver stars. I remarked that it must be dangerous to live in such unfriendly surroundings. "In Tel Aviv it's dangerous too," she said, smiling sweetly. She added, however, that the settlers have as little to do with the Arabs as possible. "I try not to buy food from Arabs. They need money, and they might use it to buy bombs. But sometimes if I need to make something for dinner in a hurry, I buy from them." She stood to peek out a window at the narrow road outside, which was crowded with Arab men in checkered kaffiyehs and long, flowing robes. "The city *is* dirty, and it *is* dangerous. Sometimes I look out at the filthy streets, and I get depressed. But the Jewish people need to live here. God will take care."

Like an Old Testament prophet, Rabbi Levinger dispenses eye-for-an-eye-style justice in Hebron. As far as he is concerned, any act of Arab defiance—whether a stone hurled at a passing Jewish car, an argument between Arab and Jewish shoppers, or simply a malevolent glare—brings dishonor to the people of Israel if it goes unpunished. When Levinger's American-born wife, Miriam, accused a Palestinian boy of flirting with her fifteen-year-old daughter, she called the Israeli Army and had the boy arrested. "I don't want any romances," she said. "I want my children to remain Jewish." And when Levinger's thirteen-year-old daughter was teased by Arab girls after she told them they couldn't play near her house, Rabbi Levinger became uncontrollably violent.

That was when Abdul Rahman Samua found out what it's like to be the object of Rabbi Levinger's wrath. Samua lives in a dung-colored stone house built during the Crusader era near the Beit Hadassah building on al-Shuhada Street—"the street of the martyrs"—named in honor of Palestinians killed by Israelis during the *intifada*. A small, round man with a soft, childlike voice, he owns a tiny vegetable stall in the *souk*, a grimy warren of meat, fruit, and vegetable shops that winds through the heart of the city. One afternoon in the spring of 1988, he closed the metal shutters on his shop and walked the few blocks home for lunch and a nap. Suddenly, Samua was jolted awake by screams. He came out of his bedroom to find Rabbi Levinger standing in the middle of his living room beating his wife and children while three armed settlers watched. "Levinger had his hands around the neck of my [seven-year-old] daughter and tried to kill her," Samua told me matter-of-factly in Hebron. When his nine-year-old son intervened, the rabbi punched the child in the eye, then twisted and broke his arm. Samua's wife, a big woman, scooped up her daughter, holding her tightly. "Levinger beat my wife on her back with his fists. It all happened in a matter of seconds."

Alerted by the commotion, an Israeli soldier stationed on Samua's roof scrambled down a ladder, entered the home, then quickly called for backup. (Soldiers have been posted on Samua's roof since May 1980, when Palestinian terrorists, hurling grenades and spraying automatic-rifle fire, cut down six young yeshiva students in front of Beit Hadassah as they were returning from Friday-night Sabbath prayers at a nearby synagogue.) By the time a jeepload of Israeli soldiers pulled up in front of Samua's home, Levinger was shouting for someone to fetch his pistol. Levinger's daughter and a pack of her friends, teenage girls in white blouses and black skirts, stood in the front doorway, egging the rabbi on. The Samuas' television had been kicked in, and the dining-room furniture had been smashed into kindling. Levinger refused to budge, calling one Israeli soldier who tried to shove him outside "a PLO agent." *"This is my house!"* screamed Levinger. *"This is my house!"*

The army finally negotiated a retreat. Levinger agreed to go if soldiers locked the Arab family in a bedroom so he wouldn't suffer the disgrace of being evicted from a Palestinian home in front of its owner. Levinger told the press, "I won't behave like Jews in the *galut* [diaspora] who say it's raining when a *goy* spits on a Jew. I won't let that happen in Israel." Yisrael Medad, a New York–born settlement leader from Shiloh on the West Bank and a friend of Levinger's, explains, "The fact that an Arab insulted a Jewish child after we've ruled Judea and Samaria for twenty-three years was for Rabbi Levinger simply intolerable. It was an assault on Jewish sovereignty and honor."

Palestinians also have a keen sense of honor. But Samua told me that he was afraid to press charges. It was only upon the urging of Israeli military officers who investigated the incident that he agreed to bring Levinger to trial. "About eight months later, the Israelis sent a police car to my house and drove me to a Jerusalem court," recalled Samua. After a brief trial, Judge Yoel Tsur acquitted Levinger on assault charges and on charges that he insulted an Israeli soldier. (The judge dismissed testimony from the Samua family, saying they were "interested parties.") In dismissing the testimony of the soldier who was the first to enter Samua's home—and who corroborated much of the Arab family's account—the judge ruled that once he left his rooftop post, he was no longer officially on duty. Tsur also acquitted Levinger of trespassing, ruling that when he barged into Samua's home, it was as a neighbor visiting a friend. The state prosecutor appealed to a three-judge appellate court, which, in an extremely rare action, overturned Judge Tsur's ruling. It criticized him for blatantly disregarding evidence and convicted the rabbi of assault.

Levinger was sentenced to four months in jail on January 14, 1991, the day the world counted down the hours to the Persian Gulf War. When the sentence was read, Levinger bounded over the defense table, shrieking that the court was a tool of Yasir Arafat. His attorney, David Rotem, dragged him outside. The rabbi was sentenced to an additional ten days for the outburst. Sometime later, Samua said, he was closing his shop when three burly settlers wearing knitted yarmulkes and brandishing clubs beat him unconscious.

Rotem, who admitted to me that he was "extremely embarrassed" by Levinger's behavior in court, attempted to explain his client's actions during an interview one afternoon in his Jerusalem office. "Rabbi Levinger," Rotem began in his basso profundo voice, "doesn't wake up on Sunday morning at eight A.M. and decide, Well, today I'm going to assault an Arab or call soldiers names. He gets up on Sunday morning and decides, Now I'm going to do something very important for the state of Israel." The problem, says Rotem, is that when he believes the honor of Israel is sullied, he sometimes loses control. "What motivates him? Judaism, Zionism, and the state of Israel," Rotem says, answering his own rhetorical question. "He has no other interests. Not money, not property. The guy doesn't have a penny. His wife has an uncle who has been lying in a Jerusalem hospital for more than two years. Rabbi Levinger visits him every day. He feeds him, he cleans him. He's not a rich uncle. Rabbi Levinger is not waiting for an inheritance. It's just the way he is."

Understandably, Rotem doesn't like to talk about Levinger's dark side. His attempt to portray Levinger as a victim of his own love of Israel is a way of deflecting questions about a client whom he admires—but whose behavior is increasingly difficult to defend. No doubt Rotem also believes that an assimilated Jewish writer from the diaspora, like me, could never understand the roots of Levinger's Zionist passion. Perhaps Rotem is right. But I could see that Levinger's passion had turned increasingly ugly. There was the time when the rabbi let loose Doberman pinschers on Arab demonstrators. And there was that wild afternoon when he gunned down an Arab shoe-store owner in a fit of hysteria. But more about that later.

One November morning in 1990, I knocked on Rabbi Levinger's door at 8:00 A.M., hoping to speak to a man who has a notoriously low regard for the Western media. He seldom grants extended interviews and never talks about his personal life. The Levinger family lives in a housing complex made of white stone built next to the Arab wholesale vegetable market in Hebron, filled with loading docks, muddy, unpaved roads, and noisy traffic. Levinger flung open the door with a thump and asked what I wanted. He had a pistol strapped on his hip and an Uzi slung at his side. He was wearing a rumpled white dress shirt, a worn blue jacket, and dark trousers. No one in Israel has a reputation for being pushier than Levinger, so I think he appreciated my chutzpah. He agreed to an interview later that day.

We met in the corridor outside the intensive-care unit of Share Zedick Hospital in Jerusalem, where Rabbi Levinger goes nearly every day to feed and bathe his wife's uncle. "He's not good," Rabbi Levinger said, taking a seat next to me on a blue plastic chair. "He's an old man." Aside from that personal remark, Levinger was aloof. He never looked me in the eye. I asked him if he thought Prime Minister Shamir possessed the will to face down Bush and Baker. His eyes grew cold and hard. "All through our history millions of Jews around the world prayed every day to return to *Eretz Yisrael.* Every *siddur* or prayer book that was ever written said we wanted to come back. America can't force us to leave. Judea and Samaria is the heart of the Jewish people."

The interview was vintage Levinger—long on rhetoric and short on substance. After all the trouble I went through to meet the rabbi, he said little of interest and was irritable throughout the interview.

I met Rabbi Levinger again in April 1991 during Passover in the Cave of the Machpelah—the final resting place for Abraham, Isaac, Jacob, and their wives. Abraham had bought the cave from the Canaanites for four hundred silver shekels some four thousand years ago. The cave is now in the bowels of a great sand-colored stone fortress, which was built by the Muslims—who also revere the patriarchs—during the Middle Ages. Levinger was sitting at a wooden table in a musty dark chamber called the Hall of Jacob, bent over a Hebrew prayer book, apparently deep in meditation. Actually, he was dozing. He had been released the day before from Eyal Prison in central Israel, where he had served ten weeks of his four-month sentence for assaulting the Samua family. The rabbi had been released early for good behavior.

Levinger awoke from his nap and walked in a leisurely way outside to an open courtyard, where he stood in the sun against a thick stone wall. Once again I noticed that Levinger is an extremely odd-looking man. Tall and thin, with a skull-and-crossbones face, he has an unforgettable appearance that has become part of his political persona and has been used by the Israeli left to vilify him. ("His features are so repugnant that he looks like an anti-Semitic caricature in *Der Stürmer,*" says Avishai Margalit, a professor of philosophy at Hebrew University in Jerusalem and a leader of Peace Now.) Levinger, who appeared more self-absorbed than usual, didn't seem to recognize me. (His own friends call him an "astronaut" because he is often so spacey.) But as soon as I asked him what the government should do to improve security for the settlers, he was off and running.

"Every day," Levinger began, "hundreds of stones are thrown at the army and Jews traveling the streets of Judea, Samaria, and Gaza. The government has the power to quiet the Arabs but lacks the will to do so. Perhaps we need General Schwarzkopf to silence the Arabs," he said, with a faint smile.

Levinger believes the Palestinians have no national rights whatsoever. "The Arab is interested in his rug and his house," he once told the Israeli newspaper *Ha'aretz.* "National sovereignty for the Palestinian people is a Jewish invention." To me he said, "This land does not belong to the Palestinian people. In all its history, it has belonged to the Jewish people. And because it is our place, we have to build more settlements and bring more Jews to live in *Eretz Yisrael.* The Arabs don't understand that our connection to Hebron is no less strong than it is to Tel Aviv. If diaspora Jews think Hebron is part of the 'occupied territories,' they won't move there. And if the Arabs don't stop the *intifada,* they will be transferred [the euphemism in Israel for expulsion]."

Years ago Rabbi Meir Kahane broke the taboo when he publicly called for the expulsion of Israel's Arabs. "I say what you think," he would declare, claiming to have an inside track on Israel's psyche. Now, virtually every ultranationalist politician worth his or her soapbox has concocted a formula for "transfer," and Levinger is no exception.

Rabbi Levinger broke away to greet some of the thousands of Orthodox Jews who had been arriving in chartered buses from across Israel to spend Passover at the tomb of their forefathers. Each bus was convoyed by two Israeli Army jeeps, front and rear, like scouts protecting a wagon train crossing Indian country. Most of the worshipers were poor Sephardic Jews from the increasingly drug-infested slums of Jerusalem and Tel Aviv. They came to pray, eat a picnic lunch on the cave's sparse lawn, and then return home before dark across the invisible border of fear that separates the West Bank from Israel. Like a proud proprietor, Levinger welcomed his "guests" at the top step of the huge structure before he and several dozen settlers, all bearded and armed, formed a circle in the courtyard and began to sing and whirl like dervishes in celebration of the Jewish people's deliverance from bondage in Egypt more than three thousand years ago. "The people of Israel are not afraid!" cried one of his followers.

Levinger left the Cave of the Machpelah in the company of two burly bodyguards. One, wearing a brightly colored knitted yarmulke and aviator sunglasses and carrying an Uzi snug against his hip, looked like a heavy-

weight prizefighter. I wasn't sure if the bodyguards were there to protect
Levinger from a vengeful Arab or to make sure Levinger didn't provoke a
fight and wind up back in jail. Later, I approached one of the guards, who
was resting on a bench in a shabby public park next to the cave. I asked
him what it was like protecting the famous rabbi. "He likes to talk and tell
stories about how he built Jewish settlements," he said, eyeing me suspiciously. "He likes to spend time playing with his grandchildren, and his
entire family came to his house in Hebron for the Passover Seder. He
doesn't seem to be the kind of man the media says he is. He's not going
around picking on people."

Rabbi Moshe Levinger was born in Rehavia, an upper-middle class,
predominantly German-Jewish neighborhood in Jerusalem, in 1935. His
father, Eliezer, was a neurologist from Munich who brought the family to
Palestine in 1933, the year Adolf Hitler was named chancellor of Germany.
Eliezer was a Hasid. The word means, literally, "pious one." Although
there are many branches of Hasidism, they all combine a rigorous study of
Jewish religious law with mysticism. Many are also opposed to Zionism,
believing that a true Jewish state cannot come about until the arrival of the
Messiah. The German Hasidim did not wear the long black coats and
wide-brim black hats that distinguished their brethren from Eastern
Europe. Instead, the men dressed in conventional suits and ties, hiding
their earlocks, or *payess*, behind their ears.

The Levinger family has had many geniuses, eccentrics, and crackpots.
One uncle founded the mathematics department at Hebrew University.
Levinger's aunt roamed the streets of Jerusalem in the late 1940s and early
1950s, mumbling esoteric passages from the Cabala, a collection of Jewish
mystical thought. "Everybody knew her," recalled Danny Rubinstein, the
Arab-affairs correspondent for the Israeli newspaper *Ha'aretz*, who, with
other children, followed her around. "She used to repeat, 'It's all one
connection, it's all one connection,' so we called her 'One Connection.' "

Moshe himself was a sickly child who suffered from crippling bouts of
depression and spent some of his youth in a Swiss sanatorium. In an
interview with a religious newspaper, his father, Eliezer, said his son "was
never physically strong, but even as a youngster it was apparent that he was
a person of great spiritual stature." He explained that Moshe compensated
for being "small and weak" by being "quick and diligent" in his religious
studies.

Moshe volunteered for the Israeli Army when he came of age, even though youths engaged in Torah studies are exempt from military service. For a while, he served in a reconnaissance unit, although he spent most of his time guarding border villages. After the army, he began religious studies at Yeshiva Mercaz HaRav, where he came under the spell of Rabbi Zvi Yehuda Kook, son of former chief rabbi of Palestine Avraham Yitzhak Kook and himself one of Israel's most charismatic rabbis. Kook, who like his famous father believed that Zionism was part of God's divine plan, taught that the Jewish return to Israel and the flowering of the land heralds the beginning of the Messianic Age. It was a self-actualizing kind of messianism in which one could assist the divine process simply by following God's commandments. The most important commandment, declared Kook, was settling the land, which should be secured and defended at any cost.

After becoming an ordained rabbi, Levinger worked as a shepherd on a religious kibbutz in the Galilee, just beneath the Golan Heights and the Syrian border. His beard was wild, and he was known for his sloppy appearance more than for his religious knowledge. Taciturn and humorless, he was considered an eccentric loner. He was convinced that he would witness the rebirth of the Jewish kingdom. More than that, he was sure that he would play a role in making it happen. "He believes it is his duty—a *mitzvah* [commandment] from the Torah [to rebuild the ancient kingdom of Israel]," his brother, Ya'acov Levinger, a professor of Jewish studies and philosophy at Tel Aviv University, said with an expression that combined pain and sarcasm. "This, for him, is a dogma, which he believes very deeply."

In 1959, Levinger met his future wife, Miriam, a New Yorker who was studying nursing in Jerusalem. A highly intelligent young woman, she was the daughter of Hasidic parents who had journeyed from Hungary to the East Bronx. Their neighborhood, like many in New York, was rapidly changing from a comfortable Jewish enclave of Yiddish-speaking, bagel-and-lox-eating immigrants to one dominated by poor African-Americans and Hispanics. Her father was a cantor. Two of her older brothers ran a nightclub. Miriam often visited the club, but she claims to have hated her childhood. She was terrified of street crime. "We had two bars on our street, and you always had drunks roaming the sidewalks and the gutters," she once said. "I always had the feeling that any cuckoo could come along and kill me."

Like many other American Jews who grow up with a sense of dislocation, she found herself in Israel, where she would become a settlement leader in her own right. If Moshe was an eccentric visionary, then Miriam was of true pioneering stock, stolid, tough, and pragmatic. She bore her husband eleven children and clothed and fed them, while making sure that Moshe—a man who paid no attention to personal hygiene and food—functioned properly. "My duty," she has said, "is to make it easier for my husband and to fulfill the role given to me by the Torah."

Levinger might have remained an obscure rabbi if not for the Six-Day War. The Israeli victory unlocked pent-up messianic passions in many Orthodox Jews as they were reunited with the core area of ancient Israel, the West Bank, which they refer to by the biblical names Judea and Samaria. They regard this as their historic homeland; the ancient Hebrews were people of these hills, and Jerusalem and Hebron were their most venerated cities. (The area making up pre-1967 Israel—the dagger-shaped strip of land along the coastal plain on the Mediterranean—had belonged to other peoples, the Canaanites, the Philistines, the Phoenicians.) When Israeli tanks stormed the Samarian highlands and swept into the Judean Desert in June 1967, many Jews felt that they were coming home—and that the Arabs had better get out of the way. Egyptian president Nasser had threatened to drive the Israelis into the sea; now his armed forces, along with those of Jordan, Syria, and Iraq, lay in smoldering ruins. David had slain the Arab Goliath. Jews around the world breathed a collective sigh of relief and exulted in a newfound sense of power and self-confidence.

But three weeks before the outbreak of the war, at the height of the Israeli public's anxiety, which had peaked when civil-defense workers started digging mass graves in public parks in Jerusalem and Tel Aviv, Rabbi Kook had a vision. It was Israeli Independence Day, celebrating the victory in the 1948 war, and in his holiday sermon, the seventy-three-year-old rabbi spoke of his intense longing for Judea and Samaria. "Where is our Hebron? Do we let it be forgotten? And where are our Shechem [Nablus] and our Jericho? Can we ever forsake them? All of Transjordan—it is ours. Every single inch, every square foot . . . belongs to the Land of Israel. Do we have the right to give up even one millimeter?" For his followers, the speech later was viewed as a call to settle the newly conquered lands—as well as proof that the rabbi was a great prophet.

On the sixth day of the war, as Israeli troops took the Wailing Wall—the remnant of Herod's temple—one of Kook's students climbed to the top and unfurled the Israeli flag. Soon after, Israeli soldiers in a captured

Jordanian Army jeep drove Kook himself to the Wall. "We announce to all of Israel, and to all of the world, that by a divine command, we have returned to our home, to our holy city," Kook proclaimed, as sniper fire crackled around him. "From this day forth, we shall never budge from here! We have come home!" Then battle-weary Israeli paratroopers put on tefillin, which are worn by observant Jews during morning prayers as a reminder of the presence of God, and prayed. A photo taken of the soldiers is the most famous image of the war.

Ten months later, Kook sent his pupil, thirty-seven-year-old Moshe Levinger, to resettle Hebron. He would change the political as well as the physical landscape of Israel. "The Six-Day War was of the Arabs' doing, so for me it was a sign from God," Miriam later said. "All this land where my forefathers trod came suddenly into our possession again. My husband said, 'God did His; so we have to do ours!' "

On April 12, 1968, thirty-two Jewish families moved into the Park Hotel in downtown Hebron in defiance of official Israeli government policy, which then barred Jews from moving into West Bank Arab cities. They came, they said at the time, to celebrate Passover; they never left. "When I traveled to Hebron, there awakened within me raging spirits that did not give me peace," remembered Levinger.

Levinger rented the spacious, forty-room Park Hotel from its owner, Faiz Kawasmeh, a short, trim man with a pencil mustache, whose ancestors emigrated from Iraq after the Mongol invasion in the thirteenth century. The lease was for ten days. Levinger and Kawasmeh agreed, however, that the term could be extended indefinitely. "Until the Messiah comes," Rabbi Levinger is said to have muttered under his breath in Hebrew. Soon after, a truck delivered all of the Levingers' worldly belongings, including a refrigerator, washing machine, and cartons of religious books.

Levinger's foray into Hebron had been planned in the Tel Aviv law office of Eliyakim Haetzni, an activist in the mostly secular Land of Israel Movement, an elite group of poets, intellectuals, and businessmen, many from the Labor party, who believed that the Jewish fatherland was incomplete without Judea and Samaria. The German-born Haetzni started by raising money, mainly from sympathetic American Jews. Then he took out newspaper ads seeking settlers. The response was negligible. "We saw immediately," Haetzni told me, "that there was no human material to do it but religious people, so Levinger brought his disciples."

The military authorities knew of Levinger's plan to move into the hotel, yet were all but powerless to stop him. Defense Minister Moshe Dayan, the mercurial, one-eyed hero of the Six-Day War, was in the hospital recovering from a serious accident. He had been digging for Early Bronze Age artifacts in the Negev when the cave he was exploring collapsed. Dayan, an Arabic-speaking, native-born Israeli, or Sabra, ran the occupied territories as if they were his private kingdom. Like other hawks in the Labor party, he was adamantly opposed to making significant territorial concessions, arguing that Arabs and Jews would have to learn to "live together."* But the last thing he wanted was a bunch of religious fanatics living in the middle of Hebron, stirring up the Arabs. The Hebron municipality had sent him a note, warning that Jewish settlers would poison relations and lead to violence and terrorism. However, Dayan had broken ribs, a severely strained back, and a severed vocal cord. Unable to speak and nearly para-lyzed, he was in no shape to take on the fiery rabbi.

At the same time, Shlomo Gazit, the coordinator of operations in the occupied territories, was sitting *shivah*, the seven-day period of Jewish mourning, for his father. And the military's top brass was distracted in the wake of the Battle of Karameh, a PLO stronghold a few kilometers east of the Jordan River, where Palestinian guerrillas mauled an Israeli armored column on March 20, 1968. It was the first time the PLO had whipped the Israeli Army, which lost twenty-nine dead. (The victory was a tonic for Arafat, who had earlier narrowly escaped an Israeli ambush on the West Bank, where he had been trying to set up terrorist cells.)

But even if Dayan and Gazit had not been distracted, it is likely Lev-inger's plan would still have worked. Levinger had support from within the ruling circles of the Labor government from the beginning of his move into Hebron. The deputy prime minister, Yigal Allon, wanted to see Jews return to the city of the patriarchs, where King David had established his first royal throne some seven years before conquering Jerusalem. The long Jewish presence in Hebron had ended with a vicious attack by Palestinian Arabs in 1929, in which sixty-nine Jews, many of them elderly Torah scholars, were slaughtered. The remaining Jews were evacuated in 1936 by the British Mandatory authorities, which then ruled Palestine. "Hebron is still

---

*As far as Dayan was concerned, the Jews had returned to the West Bank, never to be parted from it again. During an August 3, 1967, speech on the Mount of Olives Dayan said: "We have returned to the mount, to the cradle of the nation's history, to the land of our forefathers, to the land of the Judges, and to the fortress of David's dynasty. We have returned to Hebron, to Shechem, to Bethlehem, and to Anatoth, to Jericho and the ford over Jordan. . . . We know that to give life to Jerusalem we must station the soldiers and armor of the IDF on the Shechem mountains, and on the bridges over Jordan."

awaiting redemption," former Israeli prime minister David Ben-Gurion wrote to Levinger at the Park Hotel, "and there is no redemption without extensive Jewish settlement."

One month after the settlers occupied the Park Hotel, a deeply divided Israeli Cabinet voted to let them stay in Hebron, moving them into the courtyard of a military compound. The living conditions were terrible. Settlers slept on narrow cots and cooked on the floor on small primus stoves. One day a baby fell into a pot of boiling water while playing and was scalded to death. Finally, in 1970, after acrimonious negotiations, the government established the settlement of Kiryat Arba on the stony slopes overlooking Hebron. Soon imposing rows of stone-hewn apartment towers, ringed by barbed wire and watchtowers, rose into the clear desert air on land that had been confiscated from Hebron's mayor Sheikh Muhammad Ali Ja'abri.

It was a major victory for Levinger, who had forced the Israeli government to support a Jewish settlement in the heart of a heavily populated Arab area. "The major contribution Rabbi Levinger's group made to the future of Israeli settlement in the West Bank," wrote Israel Television's former West Bank correspondent Rafik Halaby, "was the lesson that sheer obstinacy wins out in the end."

Kiryat Arba was not the first settlement built in the newly conquered Arab lands. Though the settlement movement is now most closely associated with the Likud party, the first settlements were built by the Labor government soon after the Six-Day War, in the Sinai, on the Golan Heights, around East Jerusalem (which was formally annexed), in the Jordan Valley, and in the Gush Etzion bloc near Bethlehem, on the site of Jewish settlements that were overrun by the Jordanian Legion in 1948 with a loss of dozens of Jewish lives. Labor's policy was to build paramilitary agricultural settlements in the Jordan Valley for security purposes, while avoiding settlements in the occupied areas largely populated by Arabs— these, according to Labor doves such as Abba Eban, were to be held as bargaining chips in future peace talks. (Even Eban refused to contemplate withdrawal to the pre-1967 border, which, because it was difficult to defend, he called the "Auschwitz Line.") Labor also called for extensive Jewish settlement in the Gaza Strip; the hundreds of thousands of Palestinian refugees living there were to be moved into camps in the Sinai Desert or to cities on the West Bank. The plan was never implemented. But a plan to build massive Jewish neighborhoods in Arab East Jerusalem was begun.

The idea of ringing Palestinian population centers on the West Bank with Jewish settlements—while publicly calling on the Arabs to make peace as a prelude to an Israeli withdrawal—guided Labor party policy until 1977. Its architect was Yigal Allon, who presented the plan to the Israeli Cabinet three weeks after the Six-Day War. The "Allon plan" proposed returning the occupied territories for a "durable peace." But that was "not the preferred option," Allon wrote a supporter in April 1969. "I prefer to create an Arab autonomous unit in Judea and Samaria, which will be permanently linked to Israel," while extensively settling the sparsely popu-lated parts of the area. "Hereby we create a Greater *Eretz Yisrael* from a strategic point of view, and establish a Jewish state from the demographic point of view."

As commander of the Palmach during the 1948 war, Allon had urged Ben-Gurion to conquer the West Bank; instead, he was ordered to take the Negev. Now Levinger and his disciples were willing to settle the Hebron highlands, and if the price was the establishment of a small Jewish enclave inside Hebron, Allon was willing to be flexible. If it contradicted his own view that Jews should not live in Arab towns, it also undermined the policy of Dayan, his chief rival in the Labor party. So on the eve of Levinger's move into Hebron, Allon gave him three Uzi submachine guns and lobbied for him at Cabinet meetings. The day before Allon died in 1977, he told Israeli journalist Nachum Barnea that he regretted helping Levinger; that he hadn't understood that the rabbi was a fanatic and probably mad. "It was the classic coalition between horse and rider," wrote Barnea, "how-ever, each side thought he was the equestrian."

It was difficult for the Labor government to reconcile its pro-settlement policy with its public commitment to honor the Geneva Convention, which stated that the occupying power shall not deport or transfer part of its own civilian population into the territory it occupies. Labor politicians rational-ized that a few settlements with a handful of settlers would be a negligible obstacle to peace. On a deeper level, however, many Labor officials wanted to settle the newly conquered territory because it fired the Zionist passions of their youth.

At the same time, the question of withdrawal from the territories was largely limited to an internal debate among Israelis. Immediately after the Six-Day War, Israeli prime minister Levi Eshkol had offered to return most of the territories to the Arabs if they would recognize Israel and negotiate peace. The Arab states, meeting at a summit in Khartoum, in September

1967, responded with three emphatic no's: no recognition of Israel, no negotiations, no peace! Then the PLO unleashed a merciless war of terrorism against the Jewish state. By 1969, a public-opinion poll showed only 17 percent of the Israeli public was ready to return most of the occupied lands for a durable peace with the Arabs, compared to 78 percent who had favored doing so the year before, according to *The Jerusalem Post*.

The settlement issue grew more explosive after the 1973 Yom Kippur War, when rabbis Kook and Levinger helped form the mystical-messianic settlement movement Gush Emunim ("Bloc of the Faithful"). Gush Emunim was created, in part, as an antidote to the despair that settled over Israel after the nearly catastrophic Yom Kippur War, in which 2,700 Israeli soldiers were killed—the equivalent, proportionately, to 170,000 dead Americans, more than three times U.S. losses in Vietnam. With élan and daring that the Israelis had thought impossible, the Egyptian Army had crossed the supposedly impregnable Bar-Lev Line, a system of fortified bunkers and trenches that threaded along the Suez Canal, while Syrian armor came crashing down the Golan Heights, threatening Israel's heartland. The carefully planned attack totally surprised the Israeli Army. A commission of inquiry subsequently led to the sacking of several senior military and intelligence officers. But the nation placed the blame squarely on Prime Minister Golda Meir and her defense minister, Moshe Dayan, both of whom the commission exonerated of "direct responsibility."

The war also renewed the debate about what better served Israeli interests—retaining the occupied territories for their supposed strategic value or trading them for a peace accord with the Arabs. In Israel it was like arguing what came first—the chicken or the egg. Depression and indecision paralyzed the country's leadership.

Gush Emunim's theorists saw a golden opportunity to break through the malaise and create a redemptive movement that would revitalize the pioneering spirit of Zionism while fulfilling the Jewish people's messianic contract with God. "There was a lack of clarity in Israel after the '73 war," a founder of Gush Emunim told me. "The dominant spirit was one of depression. The Labor party didn't know what to do about the Arab territories. We stepped into the breach."

It was not Gush Emunim's messianic interpretation of the Jewish state that was new or dangerous, but rather the radical insistence that the borders were the key to Israel's redemption. For Gush Emunim, the *Halachic*, or religious, injunction to settle the land took on more importance than the principle of *Pikuach nefesh*—preserving life—the most sacred tenet of Judaism. "I tell you explicitly that the Torah forbids us to surrender even one inch of our liberated land," Rabbi Kook declared. "There are no conquests here, and we are not occupying foreign lands. We are returning to our home, to the inheritance of our ancestors. There is no Arab land here, only the inheritance of our God—and the more the world gets used to this thought, the better it will be for them and for all of us."

So Gush Emunim began what it regarded as its holy crusade to settle and build up Judea and Samaria and the Gaza Strip. Infused with a selfless dedication and an almost cosmic awareness of self and mission similar to that of the socialist pioneers who arrived in Palestine in the early 1900s, Gush Emunim captured the imagination of many war-weary Israelis: jaded young Sabras who were born long after the socialist pioneering ethos had declined and who had never before identified with political Zionism, émigrés from the corrupt and disintegrating Labor party who were looking for a meaningful ideology and lifestyle, and Orthodox Jews who decided to keep the promise. A handful of new immigrants, mostly Russian and American, also joined the fold. Gush Emunim also won important support from the right wing of the Labor party, from Begin's Herut party, from the National Religious party—where it began as a faction—and from B'nai Akiva, an Orthodox youth movement, which encourages its students to combine military duty with Torah study. One of Gush Emunim's most powerful early supporters was Ariel Sharon, who, in a crucial counterattack, led an Israeli division across the Suez Canal and encircled the Egyptian Third Army, thus becoming the hero of the 1973 war.

The first Gush settlement was established by the Labor government in the summer of 1974 at Camp Horon near the Arab village of Beit Ur the day after Yitzhak Rabin became prime minister. The settlement, a small religious agricultural cooperative—or *moshav*—of only fifty residents, was originally a shabby collection of tents, trailers, and prefabricated dwellings.

But most of Gush Emunim's attempts to settle heavily populated areas of the West Bank during the Labor government era were stopped by the army. Gush members, often led by the peripatetic Levinger, would arrive in darkness at a desolate hilltop in a milelong caravan of beat-up trailers. When the army came to expel them—as it almost invariably did—the right-wing parties would charge the Labor government with betrayal of Israel and compare it to the British Mandate government. Either way Gush Emunim seemed to outsmart the Labor government.

The most violent clash between the government and Gush Emunim occurred over Sebastia, an abandoned Turkish railroad depot near the large Arab town of Nablus. After one pitched battle between soldiers and settlers in which rocks and rifle butts were used, Defense Minister Shimon Peres flew to the site by helicopter and burst into the tent that Levinger was using as his "war situation room." Peres called Levinger a "Napoleon," and the rabbi stormed out, rending his white dress shirt in the sign of Jewish mourning—and a call for mass hysteria. The Labor party was up for reelection and was afraid to alienate its traditional coalition partners, the religious parties; Peres finally caved in to Levinger, and a settlement was established.

Nevertheless, Labor lost to Menachem Begin's Likud party in 1977. It was an earthquake in Israeli politics. The pariahs of Zionism had replaced the party that built the nation and gave it its socialist values and liberal vision. Immediately upon his election, Begin journeyed to Sebastia, by then called Elon Moreh, the settlement near Nablus that Gush Emunim had tried and failed seven times to settle extralegally before Levinger won. Holding a Torah scroll aloft, Begin vowed he would establish "many more Elon Morehs!" Begin, the former commander of the Irgun, who like Jabotinsky had called for a Jewish state on *both* banks of the River Jordan, was true to his word. Soon hundreds of virgin West Bank hills were bulldozed and replaced with hundreds, and then thousands, of neat single-family homes with red-tile roofs and small gardens—a great luxury for those coming from Israel's crowded cities. It was also an ominous warning to the Palestinians of what was to come.

But Levinger was not interested in living on a distant hill. His unshakable dream was to transform Hebron into a Jewish city. It didn't matter that Hebron had many Arab schools, where children in bright blue uniforms learned to read by reciting passages from the Koran, or that it had a highly regarded Islamic university, or dozens of mosques, not to mention auto-repair shops, kebab parlors, and outdoor cafés where men in traditional robes rubbed worry beads and drank strong, dark Arabic coffee. Levinger didn't pay attention to any of this. Instead, he wandered about Hebron, armed with old charts and maps, looking at Arab homes for the telltale markings of mezuzahs, a parchment inscribed with passages from Deuteronomy and rolled up in a tube and affixed to the doorposts of Jewish homes. Levinger did this not because he was interested in studying Hebron's Jewish past, but in order to select properties that could be seized for Jewish settlers.

Early one March morning in 1979 at 3:00 A.M., Miriam Levinger led forty women and children down the slope from Kiryat Arba into Hebron's Casbah and occupied Beit Hadassah, a derelict Jewish health clinic. "Hebron will no longer be *Judenrein*" (a German word meaning "clean of Jews"), she promised in a television interview. "Eighty percent of my family went up the chimney [at Auschwitz]. That is what makes me tick. I am fulfilling a mission for all those who died." The Begin government was thrown into a major political crisis. Though he had been elected on a pro-settlement platform, his security services warned him that it was impossible to protect a handful of Jewish families residing in the heart of an intensely hostile Arab city. Begin ordered the army to prevent the squatters' husbands from joining them, and to stop them from bringing in furniture and other household items. The government hoped that the primitive conditions would drive the women, many of whom were pregnant, back up to Kiryat Arba.

"There was a shortage of water, the sanitation was very, very bad, and one or two of the children were very sick," remembers Brigadier General Fredy Zach, military governor of Hebron from 1979 to 1981 and the deputy coordinator of the occupied territories when I interviewed him in spring 1991. "But the Levingers told me they would never move. I remember, that Hanukkah, seeing all the menorahs with candles in each window in Beit Hadassah—and I remember the light in Rabbi Levinger's eyes. He told me, 'Fredy, for me, the real holiday is seeing the menorah lit in Hebron.' I told myself, That's it. It's finished. They are going to stay here in spite of all the problems."

Zach, then a thirty-two-year-old captain, said he has witnessed two Levingers—the respected spiritual leader and the madman. Once, after Zach ordered an Arab girls' school closed because the students had thrown rocks at soldiers, Levinger demanded that the building be turned over to the settlers. "I told him, 'Rabbi Levinger, I can't give you a building on my own initiative. If you have problems, go and talk with the politicians.' He went crazy. He insulted me and called me a criminal. But a few hours later he apologized, saying 'I'm sorry, sometimes I go out of my mind.' "

Yet Levinger could also be a master of public relations. He sometimes entered Arab buildings in Hebron, wrapped himself in a prayer shawl, then called Israeli television and calmly waited for the army to carry him out in front of the cameras.

The settlers' expansion infuriated the local Arabs. Shortly before Miriam Levinger's takeover of Beit Hadassah in the winter of 1979, I had visited Fahd Kawasmeh, the Arab mayor of Hebron, who made no effort to hide his hatred of the settlers or his sympathy for the PLO. When I entered his office, one cold winter morning, the forty-year-old mayor was surrounded by a swarm of visitors and assorted hangers-on. A male servant seated me at his side and brought the customary cup of Arab coffee on an elegant gold tray.

Turning his sad, tired face to me and punctuating his remarks with the glow of the cigarettes he chain-smoked as we talked, Kawasmeh said, speaking in English, "As you know, we as Palestinians deny the right of the Israelis to settle on the land because settlement means force—the force of the government, the force of the military, the force of money. We will resist all of the forces which try to take our land.

"Gush Emunim is a society which tries to put its hand on our land, using these forces. Their goal is to make the West Bank Jewish. If you look at their settlements, you will see barbed wire around them. That wire means no Arab can enter without their permission. Soon they will build more houses inside of larger settlements needing a still larger military force to protect them. We refuse this. We refuse this system as a whole."

Even Jewish civilians living alone in Hebron without Israeli military protection would not be welcome, Kawasmeh said. The Jews had caused the Palestinians great suffering, and therefore a Jewish presence in any form would prove too psychologically upsetting. The Jews had plenty of virgin land in the Negev, he declared, and asked why they didn't go there.

Borrowing the standard Israeli argument, I said, "But don't the Jews offer employment and good health care—generally an improved standard of living? Don't Arab hands build Jewish settlements?"

"A man has to eat," answered the mayor. "And even the Jews living in the diaspora had a right to make a living."

As far as Levinger is concerned, Arabs like Kawasmeh are anti-Semites. In any case, it is irrelevant to the rabbi whether or not Arabs accept Jews in Hebron. The Jewish presence is divinely ordained, and God's commandments can not be tampered with.

Although the settlers' presence in Hebron created a security nightmare for the Israeli Army, "they believed that they were contributing to Israel's security," said Zach. "They still believe it. But for us it was not a contribution, because we guarded them, and it was very difficult." Just how difficult became apparent on May 2, 1980, a few months after I had visited Kawasmeh. At 7:10 that evening, in the Cave of the Machpelah, religious Jews were singing "*Adon Olam,*" "Master of the Universe," the final hymn of the Friday-night sabbath service. Afterward, several dozen worshipers walked the kilometer from the cave to Beit Hadassah for the Sabbath meal. As they entered the narrow street in front of the building, four Palestinian terrorists opened fire with assault rifles and hand grenades. Six young yeshiva students were killed and sixteen wounded. "It was the most devastating terrorist attack we ever faced in the territories," said Zach, who was at the scene within minutes to survey the carnage and to help evacuate the wounded.

Then Zach summoned to his office Kawasmeh, Muhammad Milhelm, the blue-eyed, American-educated mayor of nearby Halhoul, and Rajab Tamimi, Hebron's *kadi.* Zach said a helicopter would fly them to Tel Aviv for interrogation. Instead, they were flown to an airfield in northern Israel, where the men were blindfolded, driven by army jeep into South Lebanon, and dumped in an area that was controlled by a Christian Maronite militia intensely hostile to Palestinians. Zach told me that Israeli authorities hadn't a shred of evidence implicating the men in the attack against the yeshiva students. But the Begin government felt that something dramatic had to be done to sate the settlers' demands for vengeance.

The arbitrary expulsions didn't satisfy Hebron's settlers. The day after the massacre, twenty rabbis and community leaders decided to set up a terrorist underground of their own that would strike fear into the hearts of the local Arabs. "I met with Rabbi Moshe Levinger, and I expressed my view that for this kind of task pure people should be selected, people who are deeply religious, people who would never sin, people who haven't got the slightest inclination for violence," said Menachem Livni, who would head the Makhteret—the Hebrew word for underground—which would become the most violent anti-Arab terrorist organization since the birth of the Jewish state.

The foundation for the Makhteret actually had been laid in early 1979, when a group of Levinger's disciples met in a cramped apartment in Kiryat Arba to discuss sabotaging the Camp David accords and blocking Israel's scheduled withdrawal from the Sinai. After intense debates that pitted the men's obedience to the state of Israel against their messianic ambitions, they had decided to blow up the Dome of the Rock Mosque in East Jerusalem.

The third-holiest shrine in Islam, the Dome of the Rock is the site where the prophet Muhammad is said to have ascended to heaven on his winged charger. For many Gush settlers, however, the mosque—which was built over the ruins of the Second Temple—represented something quite different: Jewish impotence throughout the long and humiliating diaspora. The mosque's destruction, they had argued, would jolt the Muslim world into a homicidal frenzy, igniting an apocalyptic war between Israel and the Arabs that would end with the liquidation of Israel's enemies, the expulsion of the Arabs from Judea and Samaria, and the rebuilding of the Third Temple— ushering in the messianic kingdom of Israel. Yehuda Etzion, the conspirators' spiritual ideologue, had already purchased huge pieces of wood he thought were the original support beams of the Second Temple. Etzion told friends he planned to use them in the bulwarks of the Third Temple.

Several schemes to destroy the mosque were considered. Menachem Livni, the bearded, stern-faced commander of a reserve battalion of combat engineers in the Israeli Army, obtained aerial photos of the mosque and recruited an air-force pilot to steal a plane and strafe it. But Livni later opted for a ground attack. Squads of bomb-laden Jews were to scale the Old City walls into the mosque's courtyard. A model of the mosque was built; practice runs were timed; homemade explosives were tested in the desert. Livni calculated which way the mosque would fall after it exploded and how far the shrapnel would be catapulted. It was imperative not to harm Jews in the neighboring quarter, or to damage the Western Wall. Finally, the conspirators obtained silencers for their Uzis and tear-gas grenades to overcome the mosque's Islamic guards.

Most probably, the destruction of the famous mosque would have set off a chain of events resulting in a bloodbath for Jews around the world. The plan was eventually shelved, not out of fear of the consequences, but because avenging the murder of the six yeshiva students suddenly took precedence. Indeed, in response to the attack in Hebron, the Makhteret shifted gears and began to lay plans for the simultaneous car-bomb attacks on three pro-PLO West Bank Arab mayors who had entered office in 1976, in the last open elections Israel allowed in the occupied territories. Shock waves from those bombings still rock the Jewish state.

On the evening of Saturday, May 3, 1980, just hours after the funeral of one of the murdered yeshiva students, the inner circle of the Gush underground met in Menachem Livni's Kiryat Arba apartment to plan the attack on the mayors. The funeral had ended with hundreds of Meir Kahane's supporters rampaging through downtown Hebron, firing their weapons into the homes of frightened Arabs. (The slain yeshiva student was James Eli Mahon, Jr., a thirty-two-year-old American Christian convert to Judaism, who had served two tours of duty in Vietnam as a "tunnel rat," winning a Silver Star, a Bronze Star, a Vietnam Gallantry Cross, and a recommendation for the Medal of Honor. After the war, he was an undercover operative for the FBI, infiltrating anti-Vietnam war groups, then moved to Israel, changed his name to Eli Ha'azev, "the Wolf" and became one of Kahane's most feared enforcers.)

"We were incredibly tense after the funeral," Benzion Heineman, a prominent businessman and Gush activist who had driven from his home in the Golan Heights to attend the funeral, told me. "Livni and Etzion talked about avenging the yeshiva boys."

Three of Levinger's followers from Samaria were chosen to attack Nablus mayor Bassam Shaka: Natan Nathanson, the twenty-seven-year-old head of security for the West Bank settlement of Shiloh; Ira Rappaport, a thirty-two-year-old Brooklyn-born Jew who had a master's degree in social work from Yeshiva University in Manhattan; and Moshe Zar, a forty-eight-year-old Jew of Iranian origin who was one of the largest land dealers on the West Bank.

Of the three, Moshe Zar was the best known in Israel, where he has been dubbed "the King of Samaria" by the local Arab press. From his imposing mountaintop villa in Samaria, Zar courted powerful politicans and military officials like his close friend Ariel Sharon. His four-story stone mansion— reputedly the largest private Jewish residence in the occupied territories— was encircled by barbed wire and land mines. When I drove up a winding asphalt road that took me to Zar's front door in the summer of 1985, he stuck his balding head out of a parapet and threatened to open fire if I didn't get off his land.

Zar had good reason to be wary of strangers. Residents of the nearby Arab village of Jinsafut say they have lodged hundreds of complaints against him in a Nablus court for fraudulent land deals.

"When Zar moved here, he was very sweet, very nice, and offered us a lot of money for our land," a Jinsafut resident told me. "When we said no, he kept persisting. Finally, he just showed up in our field with armed men, a bulldozer, and a piece of paper that said the land was his."

On March 25, 1983, Zar was shot in the arm and axed in the neck in a field near his home by an Arab who later told Israeli police that Zar had stolen his land. Zar managed to drive to a gas station, where he wrote his assailant's name on a piece of paper before collapsing. In an interview on Israeli TV after Zar was arrested for his role in the Makhteret, he said, "I'm a victim of Arab terrorism."

On the morning of June 2, 1980, one month after the murder of the six yeshiva students and at the close of the traditional thirty-day period of Jewish mourning, Zar drove his comrades to the fashionable Rashidiya suburb of Nablus, the largest town on the West Bank and a center of Palestinian nationalism. The settlers parked in the shadows of a large Arab stone house. Carrying a bomb attached to a magnet, Nathanson and Rappaport scaled the wall surrounding the house. Then Rappaport crawled under a pale blue Opel parked in the driveway and affixed the bomb to a steel plate just above the clutch.

Shortly after 8:00 A.M., Nablus mayor Bassam Shaka, one of the PLO's most outspoken supporters in the occupied territories, stepped into his car, turned on the ignition, and depressed the clutch. The car exploded in a fireball, blowing Shaka's legs off.

Shaka was not the only target that morning. For several weeks, Yitzhak Novik, a soft-spoken chemist from the West Bank settlement of Ofra, had watched the homes of Ramallah mayor Karim Khalif and el-Bireh mayor Ibrahim Tawil. Novik discovered that Khalif left his house in a pink 1978 Cadillac each morning at seven-thirty, while Tawil, who got up later, left for work around eight-thirty. Novik's problem was that if he set a bomb to explode in Khalif's car at seven-thirty, it might forewarn Tawil. "So we made contact with an army officer and told him our plans," Novik told me. "His job was to keep Israeli soldiers away from Tawil's car."

On the night of June 1, 1980, Novik slept at his brother's house in Jerusalem. He rose at 3:00 A.M. and drove to Ofra to pick up his two accomplices. They drove to Ramallah and on to el-Bireh.

It took just a few minutes to rig the bombs. Afterward, Novik dropped off his friends in Jerusalem and returned to Ofra using side roads. "I knew it was important to stay off the main roads to avoid army roadblocks," Novik told me. But as he drove out of an Arab village near Ofra, he was stopped by an army patrol. An Israeli officer wrote down Novik's name and license number, but, Novik says, never asked why a Jew was traveling down a lonely Arab back road in the middle of the night.

At eight that morning, moments after Shaka was maimed, Ramallah mayor Karim Khalif lost a foot when a bomb exploded in his Cadillac. Despite Novik's efforts, el-Bireh mayor Ibrahim Tawil was warned by an Israeli Army officer and escaped injury; a grenade rigged to Tawil's garage door blinded an Israeli Druze bomb-disposal expert.

Novik, an Orthodox Jew from Canada who was sentenced to three years in prison, still defends the bombings. "After the murders [of the yeshiva students in Hebron]," he told me, "I felt that something had to be done. The roads on the West Bank were becoming increasingly dangerous. Jewish buses and cars were attacked daily by Arabs throwing stones, grenades, and Molotov cocktails. The government's policy toward the Arabs was lax. We held lots of protest demonstrations demanding tighter security, but nothing helped. We felt we had no one to turn to."

The Makhteret's first terrorist operation stunned Israel. Not only had the terrorists maimed two West Bank mayors, but earlier that day they also had placed a booby-trapped fragmentation grenade on Hebron's soccer field and in a mosque, injuring a dozen Arabs, including several schoolchildren.

Two days after the West Bank bombings, YESHA, the Regional Council of Judea and Samaria, held its monthly meeting with Brigadier General Ben Eliezer, commander of the West Bank. According to two settlers who were at the meeting, Eliezer expressed satisfaction with the attacks on the mayors, allegedly saying that he was only sorry that the would-be assassins had done "half a job."

"Everyone around the table was happy," recalled council member Pinchus Wallerstein of Ofra. "We didn't know who did the bombing. Some said it was the CIA or the PLO. No one said anything about it possibly being Jews. We were all smiling."

At least one person at the gathering, however, had prior knowledge of the car bombings. Natan Nathanson had been part of the team that planted the bomb in Shaka's car. Nathanson left the meeting, friends say, feeling the underground had the tacit support of the Israeli military and government at the highest levels. He interpreted Eliezer's remarks as a signal that the underground had done something for the "glory and security of the people of Israel," says Yisrael Medad, a settlement leader and friend of Nathanson's.

Within hours of the bombings, Prime Minister Menachem Begin chaired a stormy meeting with the chief of the Shin Bet (Israel's FBI), Avraham

Achituv. As early as 1978, according to interviews with Knesset members and sources close to the investigation, Achituv had warned Begin there was evidence that Gush Emunim was planning to conduct terrorist attacks on leading West Bank Arabs. Begin had denied Achituv's request to tap phones, intercept mail, and infiltrate certain West Bank settlements. Now, Achituv screamed, Gush Emunim had an organized, close-knit terrorist underground that would be extremely difficult to penetrate. "I'll get the blame," said Achituv, who reportedly resigned in 1981 because of Begin's stonewalling.

It would have been politically difficult for Begin to jail a Jew for attempting to kill Shaka and Khalef, who were generally despised by most Israelis.* Moreover, the prime minister was reluctant to confront Gush Emunim because it had so vigorously carried out his policy of establishing Jewish settlements in the occupied territories—often on illegally expropriated Arab land. Begin favored Gush Emunim with lavish budgets. Gush leaders, including several men who were later convicted of terrorism, were familiar faces in the Knesset dining room and met frequently with Begin in his office. Rabbi Levinger had a standing invitation to visit Begin whenever he liked.

Nevertheless, just six months after the bombings, Shin Bet knew the names of many people in the underground, though it lacked enough solid evidence to make arrests, according to Yossi Sarid, a Knesset member from the left-of-center Meretz party, and an expert on Israeli intelligence. "The Shin Bet was afraid to arrest the underground in 1980, because they enjoyed political support from influential political and military officials," Sarid said. "Therefore, Shin Bet had to have an airtight case, and the only way to do that was to catch them red-handed."

Liberal Israelis were appalled by the wave of violence that was sweeping the West Bank. As early as 1980, a group of fourteen jurists from universities in Jerusalem and Tel Aviv petitioned the attorney general to investigate charges that Jewish extremists were roaming the occupied territories committing acts of anti-Arab violence with impunity. Israeli deputy attorney

*The mayors had been key members of the National Guidance Committee, which was formed by Palestinians to coordinate the public struggle against the Camp David Accords and the occupation. In November 1979, the government had attempted to deport Shaka after he allegedly told the coordinator of activities in the occupied territories, Major General Danni Mat, that he sympathized with the March 1978 slaughter of twenty-nine Israeli civilians in a bus on the Coastal Road by PLO terrorists. A Military Appeals Board found that Shaka's statement did not indicate support for the massacre. The deportation order was subsequently rescinded.

general Yehudit Karp was chosen to head a secret blue-ribbon commission to investigate the allegations. After more than a year of work, the commission submitted its report, which revealed that Israeli police and military officials were acquiescing in vigilante attacks against West Bank Arabs. In 1983, Karp resigned from the commission, charging that Begin was suppressing the report because it was a political liability. Describing law enforcement in the occupied territories as "lackadaisical" and "ineffective," Karp asked, "How is it possible that they [the government] take measures against each Arab stone thrower, yet fail to bring to justice settlers who open fire on Arabs?"

On July 7, 1983, in broad daylight, Arab terrorists repeatedly stabbed Aharon Gross, a Jewish seminary student in Hebron, dumping his mutilated body in a bloody heap just outside the Casbah. Miriam Levinger, a registered nurse, was summoned to help the dying victim. But thinking he was an Arab, she walked away, leaving the young Jew to die. Nineteen days later, members of the Makhteret, including the Levingers' son-in-law, burst into the courtyard of the Islamic College in Hebron during a noon lunch break, tossing a grenade and spraying machine-gun fire. Three Palestinian students were killed and thirty-three injured. "Whoever did this," declared Rabbi Levinger, "has sanctified God's name in public."

The cold-blooded execution deeply divided both the Gush Emunim settlers' movement and the underground, and this helped Shin Bet penetrate the terrorist network. Around the same time, Begin resigned from office, and Yitzhak Shamir, a former commander of the Stern Gang who had gone on to become a high official in Mossad (Israel's CIA), became prime minister. Shamir let Shin Bet investigate the underground. Unlike Begin, who was apparently indifferent to what was happening on the West Bank, Shamir feared that the lawlessness would eventually spill over into Israel itself.

Several months after the attack on the Islamic College, Shin Bet got a major break, according to Haggai Segal, a member of the Makhteret who wrote about his experience in a book called *Dear Brothers*. During the routine polygraphing of a prospective recruit—a young Orthodox Jew who had served in an elite combat unit—the youth was asked if he had ever participated in a vigilante attack against Arabs. He said no, but the polygraph said he was lying. In fact, the underground had twice tried to recruit him. The Shin Bet agent asked him to write what he was hiding on a slip of paper. If that was the only criminal activity he was involved in, the agent said, he would get the job. The agents promised he could keep the note and would not have to reveal its contents. He not only wrote the names of two Makhteret members, but he also identified one as a participant in the mayors' bombing and the other as the mastermind of the Dome of the Rock plot, which had recently been taken out of mothballs. After answering the remaining questions to the apparent satisfaction of his Shin Bet interrogators, he was allowed to leave with the incriminating note tucked in his pocket. Later that day, he ripped it up and threw it away. But the Shin Bet retrieved it.

The underground attempted its most sensational act on Thursday, April 26, 1984, when three members, including Levinger's son-in-law, attached explosive charges to five buses parked beside the homes of their Arab drivers in East Jerusalem. One of the buses, which belonged to the Arab-owned Klandia Bus Company, had been chartered by a German tour group. The explosives were set to go off at 4:30 P.M. on Friday, when few Jewish cars would be on the road because of the approaching Sabbath. After planting the bombs, the Jewish terrorists drove to the Wailing Wall for morning prayer. Early that morning, agents of Shin Bet who had infiltrated the Makhteret dismantled the bombs and arrested more than three dozen settlers. After four years, the underground finally had been caught red-handed.

In the days that followed the arrests, the Hebrew press ran sensational front-page stories about the events leading up to the terrorists' capture. At first, a court order banned the publication of their names. When the order was rescinded, the Israeli public was shocked to learn that the terrorists were not only leading members of Gush Emunim, but also top army officers, an air-force pilot, senior officials administering the occupied territories, and the friends and relatives of Knesset members. Yehuda Etzion's father, for one, had been the adviser on settlements to Ariel Sharon when he was minister of commerce and industry in the Israeli Cabinet.

Ira Rappaport was in New York at the time of the arrests, as an emissary of the Eretz Yisrael Movement, an arm of Gush Emunim that recruits potential settlers from the diaspora. He immediately stepped down and took a twenty-thousand-dollar-a-year job to head the Jewish Community Services Coalition of Far Rockaway, Queens—a city-financed social-welfare agency. But after his connection to the underground was exposed by *The New York Times* in 1985, he went into hiding. "He's a very gentle person, a silken Jew," Rappaport's lifelong friend Rabbi Avraham Weiss of the

Hebrew Institute of Riverdale said at the time. "I pray my children grow up to love Israel as much as Ira does."

In a signed confession, Menachem Livni told Shin Bet that seven prominent rabbis, including Levinger, were actively involved in the underground and had "blessed" the attacks on the mayors. Levinger was arrested soon after Livni's confession. According to Dan Be'eri, an underground member, Levinger agonized over whether he should also confess as a show of solidarity with his jailed comrades. But the other underground members persuaded Levinger to maintain his innocence, fearing his admission would cripple the settlement movement. Levinger was released from jail after ten days. "Shin Bet didn't push him too hard, and we influenced him not to speak," Be'eri, a French-born proselyte who is now the director of several Orthodox girls' schools in Israel, told me. "I have the feeling that the government didn't really want to try him. It would have been a huge scandal to put the leader of the settlement movement on trial."

Be'eri, who had been arrested for his role in the underground's aborted plot to blow up Jerusalem's Dome of the Rock Mosque, said Levinger had known about the plan, but he did not think the timing was right. "Levinger said that he would not try to prevent the group from carrying out such an operation," Be'eri has said, "although he personally believed the nation had to be prepared in advance for such a thing."

After recovering from the shock of the arrests, Gush Emunim sympathizers set up a legal-defense fund—primarily with American Jewish donations collected by Rabbi Weiss, who raised more than $100,000. (About $75,000 of that sum was donated by Charlie Fox, an elderly Jew from Florida who had been mobster Meyer Lansky's bagman.*) A fund-raiser at the tony Beth Jacob Congregation in Beverly Hills for the families of the underground netted "very large sums of money," said Rabbi Maurice Lamm, who made the appeal from his pulpit. Lamm told me he sent the money to Rabbi Levinger in Kiryat Arba.

In a July 1984 *New York Times* column, Flora Lewis compared Lamm to Ayatollah Khomeini, for the rabbi's support of Jewish terrorism. "These men . . . are not typical terrorists," Lamm replied in a letter to the *Times*. "They are not Khomeini-like fanatics. They are not thugs, hired guns, frenzied teen-agers, zealots who think they are setting the world aright with heaven-based ideals. I know them. They are believers, but not God-push-

*Both Lansky and Fox were major financial supporters of Rabbi Meir Kahane.

ers; they are struggling to protect wives at home and children on school buses. They will not move out of their 'own' land . . . They are decent and for the most part reasonable men."

Right-wing politicians and Orthodox rabbis in Israel also rallied to the underground's defense, charging that the government was responsible for the settlers' acts because it failed to provide adequate security in the territories. Professor Yuval Neeman, the father of Israel's nuclear-weapons program and then minister of science in the Israeli Cabinet, indirectly justified the car bombings. "The attacks on the mayors," he said during an interview on Israeli radio, "actually paralyzed—without killing anyone— the chief inciters in Judea and Samaria."

During the trial, attorneys for the Gush terrorists came up with a second politically explosive defense: that Shin Bet had known the identities of the individuals in the underground soon after the attack on the mayors and had prior knowledge of the attack on the Islamic College, but failed to arrest anyone because, according to chief defense attorney Dan Avi Yitzhak, "Top political and military authorities urged the underground to take actions that a democratic state cannot." The Israeli Supreme Court spent nine months weighing these charges. Chief Judge Aharon Barak, who reviewed sixty-seven volumes of classified Shin Bet documents, ruled that the defense attorney's allegations were unfounded.

But the truth about the level of government involvement in the Gush Emunim underground will probably never be known. Knesset member Yossi Sarid claims dozens of people in the settlements and the government had some information about the underground's existence. "I'm not saying these people had full knowledge about the underground; I'm saying that a number of people had clues which might have been very helpful to the Shin Bet and could have prevented the attack on the Islamic College."

In July 1985, a three-panel court in Jerusalem convicted eighteen members of the underground,* handing out prison terms ranging from four months to life—adding, however, that the convicted men should be praised for their pioneering ethos and war records. The following day, Shamir began to press for clemency. Speaking to graduates of the Betar youth movement in Jerusalem, Shamir said the members of the underground were "excellent people who made a mistake."

---

*In all, twenty-five Jewish settlers and members of the military were eventually convicted for participating in the Makhteret.

One of the most ardent supporters of clemency was Rabbi Eliezer Waldman, then a member of the Knesset in the ultranationalist Tehiya party. Livni had alleged that Waldman was a member of the underground. Waldman was subsequently arrested and questioned, but he was never charged. "They [members of the Makhteret] are devoted citizens who must be released from prison so that they can continue to build the country," the New York–born Waldman told me one day in his Knesset office. "They have expressed sorrow and have promised it won't happen again. It will weaken the government if they are held in jail. It will arouse the bitterness of a large proportion of the population who thinks the government is responsible for the breakdown of security that led to the settlers' acts. Clemency is necessary to bring about national reconciliation. The [Israeli] left must understand that, especially after the government pardoned eleven hundred Arab terrorists.* You can't have one justice for Arabs and another for Jews. What these boys did was in reaction to, and in deterrence to, Arab terrorism."

Today, after years of intense lobbying, the entire underground has been released from jail. (Ira Rappaport voluntarily returned to Israel in 1987 and pleaded guilty to causing "serious bodily harm." He received a five-month sentence. "Any proud Jew would support the attack on the mayors," Rappaport told me in his split-level Shiloh home in October 1990.) On December 26, 1990, Menachem Livni, Shaul Nir, and Uzi Sharbaf, Levinger's son-in-law, were freed, their life sentences having been reduced by President Chaim Herzog, who said he was convinced they had expressed "unequivocal regret for their actions and renounced the path they took." Dozens of West Bank settlers danced and chanted outside the prison near Tel Aviv as the three men were released. Gush Emunim spokesmen Noam Arnon praised them for their love of Israel, adding, "They are heroes because they decided to sacrifice themselves, their future, their families, for the security of Israel." Menachem Livni told Israel Radio that he was not sorry for what he had done. "The use of the word 'regret' in this case is childish," he said as he was embraced by jubilant family and friends. Across the street from the prison, a small group of Israeli liberals held a quiet counterdemonstration. "This is a message of contempt for human life, of making a difference between one type of life and another, and it violates the

---

*In 1985, more than eleven hundred Palestinian security prisoners were released in exchange for six Israeli soldiers captured by Palestinian forces during the 1982 Lebanon war.

basic tenet of equality before the law," said Yitzhak Zamir, a former Israeli attorney general.

"There is no doubt that Levinger was the master of the underground," *Ha'aretz*'s veteran Arab-affairs correspondent Danny Rubinstein told me. "All the people in the underground were his followers. Five or six of the Makhteret were with him in the Park Hotel. One of them is his son-in-law, and three of them were his next-door neighbors." (Despite the confessions of Livni, Be'eri, and others, attorney David Rotem calls charges that Levinger was part of the underground "rubbish.")

In 1982, Rabbi Levinger helped to set up the Hebron Fund, a charitable, tax-exempt New York foundation that raises money to buy real estate in the city of the patriarchs. I attended the fund's third annual dinner, held in May 1990 in honor of Rabbi Levinger and his wife, Miriam, at the Sheraton Meadowlands Hotel in East Rutherford, New Jersey, across from Giants Stadium. Rabbi Levinger couldn't attend the gala in his honor—he was in an Israeli prison for killing an Arab shoe-store owner.

The dinner took place on the same day a young Israeli apparently went berserk and massacred seven Palestinian laborers from Gaza. Not a word was said about the slaughter by any of the speakers, who condemned liberal Jews, the American press, and James Baker, who had just called on Shamir to give up his dream of "Greater Israel." Ariel Sharon, who had been advertised as the featured speaker, sent a telegram apologizing for not being able to come. It was imperative, he said, that he stay in Israel and help the prime minister form a new government:

"We have been successful in preventing the Labor party from forming a coalition which would have been supported by members of the Knesset who follow the directives of Yasir Arafat. We will be able to form a strong Jewish government which will be able to withstand the pressures that were leading us down the road to suicidal policies . . . I congratulate Rabbi and Mrs. Levinger, my dear personal friends, true heroes of our generation."

Former assistant secretary of defense Richard Perle was the substitute guest speaker. He gave a passionate denunciation of PLO terrorism. Several weeks later, during a phone conversation, I asked Perle why he had been willing to speak at the Hebron Fund dinner, for during the Reagan administration he had been a strong advocate of a policy of combating "international terrorism." It seemed ironic that in a speech to a group that hailed Rabbi Levinger as a national hero, he advocated breaking off talks with the

PLO until it gives up terrorism. (On June 20, 1989, President Bush suspended talks with the PLO for failing to condemn forcefully the aborted May 30 terrorist attack on Israel by Iraqi-backed seaborne Palestinian commandos.)

Perle told me that he didn't support Rabbi Levinger and had never heard of the Hebron Fund before he was invited to address its fund-raising dinner. "They presented themselves as representatives of the Jewish community of Hebron," he said. Although he was aware of the controversy over Levinger, Perle said that he didn't know that some of the principal Jewish leaders of the Hebron settlement had been members of an anti-Arab terrorist underground. I told him that the former leader of Hebron's Jewish enclave and past director of the Hebron Fund, Menachem Livni, had received a life sentence for masterminding the underground (although he received clemency).

"There is something to be said for a country that puts its terrorists in jail and gives them life rather than turning them into national heroes," Perle replied rather lamely. "Whatever one thinks of the settlements from its foreign-policy aspects, Israel does not countenance acts of terrorism by its own citizens. Whatever the irony of my speaking [at the Hebron Fund dinner], there is a fundamental distinction between states that support terrorism and states that fight it."

Perle admitted that the anti-Arab hostility he sensed from some of the people at the dinner had made him "uncomfortable"; and he worried that because of the passions unleashed by the *intifada,* this might not be an auspicious time to expand the Jewish enclave in Hebron. "My hope is that in the course of an eventual settlement some understanding will be reached by which Jews will be permitted to live in places that are particularly sacred and holy to them, just as Arabs will be permitted to live in such places."

During the cocktail hour that preceded the dinner ceremonies, Dov Hikind, the New York State assemblyman from the Forty-eighth District, which includes Borough Park, a mostly Orthodox Jewish neighborhood, took me around to meet some of the guests. Hikind had been a leader of Rabbi Meir Kahane's Jewish Defense League in America. During its heyday in the late 1960s and early 1970s, the JDL waged a sometimes deadly bombing and shooting campaign against Soviet embassies and offices in the United States and Europe to publicize the plight of Soviet Jews. The JDL's actions prodded the American Jewish establishment to put Soviet Jewry at the top of its agenda. This eventually led to the passing of the Jackson-

Vanick Amendment, which withheld "most favored nation" status from socialist countries that restricted Jewish emigration. The bill's principal architect was Henry "Scoop" Jackson's Senate aide—Richard Perle.

Hikind briefly introduced me to Rabbi Yechiel Leiter, the thirty-two-year-old Scranton-born leader of the Jewish enclave of Hebron. Like Hikind, Leiter had also been a member of the JDL. Handsome, cheerful, and energetic, Leiter was greeting supporters and posing for photographers. "We can in the next two years turn the center of Hebron into a Jewish city," he said.

As we talked, corporate raider Marc Belzberg came by, as did Sam Rappaport, a Philadelphia real estate developer and the largest Israel Bond holder in America, along with several members of the extremely wealthy Reichmann family of Canada. The three Reichmann brothers, owners of Olympia and York Developments Ltd., one of the largest privately held real estate companies in the world, with properties that include the World Financial Center in Manhattan, have a net worth of more than $7 billion, according to *Forbes* magazine. "I want you to see that people, even with our views, are dignified, civilized people," Hikind said. The black-tie event raised nearly $300,000.

The five hundred or so guests then assembled in the main ballroom of the Sheraton Meadowlands for a five-course kosher dinner and speeches. I was seated at a table with Matthew Feldman, a New Jersey state senator, and Samuel Bisgay, a member of the central committee of the Republican party of Orange County, California, who coproduced the thirty-minute documentary film *In the Gardens of Abraham: the Story of Hebron,* videocassettes of which were later distributed at the dinner. The film is used by the Hebron Fund to solicit donations. "I was looking for a cause," said Bisgay.

"*Hatikva*" [Hope] and "The Star-Spangled Banner" were piped over the public-address system, and then a Torah scroll, a gift to Hebron's settlers, was carried into the hall by several dozen men dressed in tuxedos who then danced around it. "Remember the pogroms, the massacres, the Holocaust," Senator Feldman whispered in my ear as I watched the men dancing around the Torah. "Land for peace can't work."

Nathan Miller, of Fairlawn, New Jersey, dedicated the Torah from the rostrum: "We must return and restore the holy Jewish city of our patriarchs. We must rebuild Hebron and return to our roots—every Jew must thank *Hashem* [God] and pray this is the beginning of redemption. May the Torah unite all of *Eretz Yisrael* and remind us of our sacred paths and goals. May we witness the Messiah in our time."

Then a rabbi in a dark business suit and a yarmulke blessed the Torah, declaring, "May it be used to redeem all of Hebron into Jewish hands."

Following the rabbi's invocation, the master of ceremonies, a radio talk-show host in New Jersey, compared Hebron's settlers to the *chalutzim* (pioneers) who built Israel "out of rock and sand. We are here tonight," he said, "to stand side by side with our people of Hebron to swear our support to them in every way possible."

Then it was Miriam Levinger's turn to speak. When I had tried to interview her in Israel, she had acidly replied that she wasn't in the mood to talk to a Jew from "the *galut,*" a derisive term for the diaspora. But she was clearly eager to talk to this well-heeled diaspora audience.

After describing what a moving experience it is to walk through the same hills where King David wrote the Psalms, she compared her childhood in New York with her children's in Hebron. "I grew up in the East Bronx, and I was a very frightened Jewish child," she said. "I remember running away. And I see my children—the way they walk around Hebron, forty or fifty [Jewish] families in a city of seventy thousand Arabs, and not so very friendly Arabs at that—and they walk around as if they own the market . . . They are not afraid, and they have no traumas, and if they are asked, 'What are you doing here?' they say, 'We are reclaiming Hebron.' And God promised us that one day we would do this!" she said as the audience roared its approval.

"I'm sure my husband is very sorry he couldn't be with you tonight," Miriam said with a smile, prompting laughter. "He has his religious books, and I'm sure he will be occupied for the next five months. I spoke to my mother-in-law, and I think she's a bit pleased because she told me now he's going to eat regularly and go to sleep on time."

Rabbi Levinger's eating and sleeping habits had improved as a result of a wild drive through downtown Hebron on September 30, 1988. "I, my two sons, one daughter, and my granddaughter were in the car," Levinger told a reporter. "They [a group of young Palestinians] threw hundreds of stones at us. My daughter is ten years old, and my granddaughter three. All we did was to protect ourselves."

Levinger claims he fired his pistol in the air from his Fiat window to scare away the stone throwers. But according to numerous witnesses, Levinger parked his car far from harm's way and then walked determinedly toward the demonstrators, firing his pistol indiscriminately. Ibrahim Bali, an Arab textile salesman, was buying new shoes for his daughter when he heard the shooting. He was standing outside a shop when a bullet tore through his shoulder. A bullet also ripped into the chest of Khayed Salah, who was about to close the metal shutters of his shoe store. The Israeli Army company commander who witnessed the shooting said that after the rabbi fired his weapon, he walked down the road screaming "You're dogs" at Arab vendors, kicking over vegetable crates and flower containers. The officer said he grabbed Levinger's trembling hand and told him not to move. Levinger snarled back, "Leftist! Arab lover!"

Khayed Salah's older brother, Khaled, is the well-to-do owner of a shoe factory. He lives in an exclusive Palestinian suburb of modern stone apartment complexes and modest homes on a steep slope just outside Hebron, far from the crowded street where the shooting occurred. "I was working in the factory when somebody ran in and told me my brother had been shot," Khaled, a neat, trim man wearing a gray cardigan and slacks, began. "I was shocked. I went to our shop, but he had already been taken to a hospital in Jerusalem, where he died." On the day of the funeral, said Khaled, thousands of Palestinians converged on the central mosque, carrying his brother's body, wrapped in a PLO flag and surrounded by palm fronds. Suddenly, a helicopter appeared overhead and dropped tear gas. Then Israeli soldiers seized the body and dispersed the Palestinians with batons and rifle butts. "They held the body for forty-eight hours," Khaled recalled bitterly. "They said we could have it back if we held a private funeral with no more than twenty mourners, none of whom could be men between the ages of fifteen and forty."

Although settlers have killed at least forty-two Arabs during the *intifada,* only four other cases have been prosecuted. Seven months after Salah's murder, Levinger was indicted on manslaughter charges. He claimed he was being persecuted by "[Israeli] leftists who want to destroy the settlements." His colleagues mounted a vigorous public-relations campaign, lobbying Knesset members and picketing the courthouse. Nearly five months into the trial, however, Levinger plea-bargained the charge down to criminally negligent homicide. On the day he entered prison, he was carried through the alleyways of Hebron's cramped Casbah on the shoulders of his supporters, many brandishing assault rifles and singing the anthem of the West Bank settlement movement, *"Am Yisrael Chai"*

("The Jewish People Live"). He was sentenced to serve five months in prison but was released after just ten weeks.

I asked David Rotem why he advised the rabbi to accept a plea bargain. "Because Rabbi Levinger is a very difficult client," conceded Rotem, who added that he feared Levinger would lose control in court if the trial continued. "Not that he would have shot somebody," Rotem explained, "but that he would have started his defense from the days of Abraham and gone on until the coming of the Messiah.

"Frankly, however, I was amazed [that he accepted the plea] because virtually everyone wants to be found not guilty. But Levinger told me, 'Look, somebody was killed. I don't know whether this man was actually one of the people throwing stones.' Then he told me a story from the Talmud about an argument between God and Moses." Although Moses wandered in the Sinai wilderness with the children of Israel for forty years, Levinger told Rotem that God would not let him enter the Promised Land, because he had killed an Egyptian. "You know, if Moses had to pay because he killed an Egyptian without permission from God," Levinger told Rotem, "maybe I have to pay too."

Still, Levinger never expressed remorse to the Salah family. In fact, he even declared during the trial that, though he hadn't killed anyone, he wished that he'd had "the honor of killing an Arab." The remark was widely quoted in the Israeli press. Khaled says the short prison term Levinger received for killing his brother just compounds his family's grief. "When I see Levinger in the street today with a pistol and a rifle, what shall I do? There is a saying in Arabic, 'If your enemy is the judge, to whom are you going to complain?' "

Perhaps to Dan Meridor, who was Likud's minister of justice at the time of the Salah shooting. Though a self-described hawk and staunch advocate of "Greater Israel," Meridor prosecuted cases brought by West Bank Arabs against Jews in record numbers—at considerable risk to his political career. "I don't accept that you have to break the law in order to be a good Zionist," he told me in a rare interview about settler violence. "There is no contradiction between my hawkish attitudes [on the occupied territories] and my basic belief in human rights and civil rights and justice and law and morality." In February 1991, Meridor said, right-wing extremists smeared graffiti on the front door of his Jerusalem apartment, calling him a "bleeding heart" and a "leftist." "And when I indicted Levinger, I got some threatening phone calls," he said. One man called Meridor a "Kapo"—the name given to Jews who helped the Nazis run the concentration camps.

Then, shortly before the Passover holiday in April 1991, posters began to appear in Jerusalem with a photo of Meridor next to a photo of left-wing Knesset member Yossi Sarid, the bête noire of the Israeli right. "They're very similar, almost identical," the poster said. "The judicial persecution conducted by the justice minister against the Jewish residents of Judea, Samaria, and Gaza—and especially against Rabbi Levinger—is Sarid's idea scrupulously carried out by Meridor."

Meridor is the standard-bearer of the liberal wing of the Likud party. He has aspirations to become prime minister. The attacks on his "nationalist" credentials have seriously hurt his prospects. Still, Meridor said, he admires Levinger for opening up the West Bank to Jewish settlement. Meridor recalled proudly that he even played a small role in Levinger's first conquest. In 1968, while a second-year law student at the Hebrew University, he organized a group of about fifty students to stand guard at the Park Hotel during the Passover holiday break from classes.

Though Levinger's popularity among the religious settlers remains strong, some movement leaders are beginning to distance themselves from him in the wake of his highly publicized legal difficulties and his nasty dispute with Meridor. "I'd give Levinger money not to be our spokesman," said Rabbi Benny Elon, a prominent settler from Beit El whose father is a moderately conservative judge on Israel's Supreme Court. Others, however, remain steadfast. "In every revolutionary movement, you have to have someone obtuse, stubborn, very single-minded, and Levinger is that person," says settlement leader Yisrael Medad. "When we need to see the broad ideological picture, we call on Levinger, who is the anchor, who gives us our sense of direction."

Yet when Levinger ran for the Knesset in 1992, he received a mere thirty-seven hundred votes, failing miserably to win a single seat and incurring the wrath of established politicians on the right, who complained that the rabbi's campaign commercial on Israeli TV drove undecided, middle-of-the-road voters to Labor. In the commercial, Levinger, his back to the camera, fired a pistol fiercely at a paper target. Then he swirled around toward the camera, raised his gun, and growled, "Only force will end the *intifada*!"

Many Israelis fear that Levinger's vision could lead the country to disaster. They are convinced he or one of his followers would commit a fantastically violent act if it could upend a prospective Israeli withdrawal from the occupied territories. "If the peace talks progress, I have no doubt that a new [settler] underground will emerge," said Hebrew University's Avishai Margalit. "And the way to destroy a peace agreement is very clear: blow up the Dome of the Rock Mosque. Then the whole world will be against us."

In the past, Rabbi Levinger has called on his followers to join him in mass suicide if the government evacuates the territories, echoing the mad ravings of Jim Jones at Jonestown. It nearly happened at Yamit, a thriving secular town of palm trees and cafés that was built by the Labor government on the shores of the Sinai. After Camp David, in 1979, the Israelis agreed to return the desert to Egypt. Thousands of religious settlers from the West Bank descended on the city to draw a line in the sand. "Not one inch," they declared. "Today Yamit, tomorrow Hebron!" Kahane's people erected fortified bunkers, swearing to resist to the last man and woman. In a Sabbath sermon, Rabbi Levinger evoked the Jewish wars against the Romans and called for martyrdom. That night in Yamit, Gush Emunim's rabbis consulted with Israel's two chief rabbis. "All that was made public was that the rabbis ruled against martyrdom," wrote underground member Haggai Segal. "Rabbi Levinger . . . tore his clothes in mourning. Many believe that without the *Halachic* prohibition, he would have gone through with his intention."

Then in April 1991—on the eve of one of Secretary of State James Baker's visits to Jerusalem after the Gulf War to press the Israelis on a territorial compromise—Levinger declared that the only way he would leave the West Bank was in a pine box. "From this house, the army will never take me out alive," said one of Levinger's supporters in Hebron. It was a warm winter afternoon, and Jewish laborers in T-shirts were laying a sidewalk for the small enclave of Tel Rumeida, where seven families live in a trailer camp perched on a bluff above downtown Hebron. "I was in Yamit, and what happened there won't happen again," Levinger's supporter said, as a baby slept gently draped across his shoulder.

But would Levinger really give the order to fight the Israeli Army and shed Jewish blood? I asked. "Rabbi Levinger is like an egg," he replied, caressing his child. "The more you cook it, the harder it becomes."

So worried are some of these settlers about an Israeli withdrawal that they have formed a new terrorist underground. But this time, their targets are brother Jews who have advocated negotiating with the PLO. They are called the Sicarii, after a sect of Jewish Zealots who murdered Romans and "Hellenist" Jews during the Second Temple period with short daggers that they hid in their robes. The Sicarii have claimed credit for firebombing the apartments and cars of a number of prominent left-wing figures, including Yair Tsaban, leader of the left-wing Mapam party, and Dan Margalit, a prominent journalist.

Self-destructive messianism is not new to Jewish history. Masada immediately comes to mind. Masada is the ancient mountaintop fortress in the Judean Desert near Hebron where Jewish rebels held off a superior Roman force for almost three years. On the second day of Passover in A.D. 73, Roman Legionnaires stormed Masada and found the Jewish defenders— 960 men, women, and children—dead. They had committed suicide rather than endure Roman captivity. The victorious Romans denuded the countryside. The surviving Jews were scattered across the empire. Even the name of Judea was changed—to Palestine. Ironically, many of his fellow countrymen opposed Masada's rebel chief and a leader of the Sicarii, Eleazar ben Jair. They believed he was agitating not for political freedom but to express his esoteric religious beliefs. His fanaticism and that of the other Zealot groups throughout Judea put an end to the Jewish state for two thousand years—the worst tragedy in Jewish history until the Holocaust. For many centuries afterward, the rabbis declared that the task of bringing about statehood was better left to the Messiah and prohibited any mass movement of Jews back to the Holy Land.

To some Israelis, Rabbi Levinger is the direct descendant of ben Jair. Like a modern-day Zealot, Levinger insists that mysticism is a healthy part of Jewish experience. "Zionism is mysticism," he said. "Zionism will wither away if you cut it from its mystical-messianic roots. Zionism is a movement that does not think in rational terms—in terms of practical politics, international relations, world opinion, demography, social dynamics—but in terms of divine commandments. What matters only is God's promise to Abraham as recorded in the Book of Genesis!"

CHAPTER 2

Imagine

Aliza Herbst has a recurrent, heart-pounding nightmare. It begins with thousands of kaffiyeh-clad Arabs standing on the hills surrounding her West Bank settlement of Ofra, screaming "*Allah akbar*" ("God is Great") and "*Itbach el-Yahud*" ("Slaughter the Jews"). Their silhouettes illuminated by the light of the moon, they storm the lightly guarded settlement, brandishing copies of the Koran and AK-47s. In the dream, Herbst, thirty-nine, gathers her five children into her bedroom, where she keeps an Uzi and boxes of cartridges. "I take out twenty-five Arabs before they get me," she said, reflecting a mixture of stone-cold bravado and hysteria. "The Arabs are not courageous, but they can be whipped up so easily. Women [in Ofra] are afraid of being home alone and facing an Arab invasion!"

The fear that Palestinian Arabs would trade the stones and knives of the *intifada* for automatic weapons spread across the settlements like a sudden desert storm during the first days of the Gulf War. Settlers like Herbst were sure that PLO terror cells were waiting for instructions from Baghdad to ignite a bloody insurrection. When, on the second night of the war, a terrorist car bomb exploded prematurely on a deserted road in North Jerusalem near a West Bank settlement, some settlers believed the war for the territories had begun.

To face what they perceived to be a mounting threat, settlements intensified security in coordination with the Israeli Army. Regional home-guard units, which are made up of settlers, were put on a state of heightened alert.

In Ofra, settlers were instructed to start training with large-caliber, armor-piercing machine guns. Settlement leaders privately said that they had to prepare for the possibility, no matter how remote, that Iraq would invade Israel through Jordan. Their caution was underscored by the memory of Syrian tanks overrunning several settlements on the Golan Heights during the opening days of the 1973 Yom Kippur War.

Aliza Herbst was living in America when the Yom Kippur War broke out. She had grown up in San Antonio, Texas, where her father was a Conservative rabbi. When she decided to leave home after high school to try her luck as a musician, her father told her "not to bother to come back." She came of age singing in a blues band in Haight-Ashbury, San Francisco, before she embraced Orthodox Judaism and moved to the gently sloping hills of Samaria.

When I met Herbst she was a special-projects coordinator in charge of eight Gush Emunim settlements in the central Samarian region. Her job encompassed everything from helping new settlers obtain bank mortgages to resolving personal disputes. She drove more than four thousand kilometers a month and always had a loaded Uzi within easy reach under her front seat. "I carry an Uzi like a farmer carries a hoe, or like a woman in New York carries mace in her purse," she said. "My mother called once and said, 'Look at all the knifings. How can you live there?' And I said, 'What about the south side of San Antonio?' My father laughed and said, 'We get the point.' "

Herbst's pluck attracted the attention of Rabbi Levinger, who hand-picked her for the job in 1983. The two are now so close that he presided over her daughter's bat mitzvah the day after he was released from Eyal Prison, where he had served time for killing the Arab shoe-store owner. "It was a great sermon," she said with a brassy smile. "He had ten weeks to prepare."

About 15 percent of the settlers are originally from North America, and many are prominent in their communities. While Herbst's counterculture past and slight Texas drawl make her exceptional, her views on Arabs and the future of the territories are mainstream Gush Emunim.

For Herbst, religion, politics, and history are intertwined. She said she moved to the West Bank because it is the core area of the biblical land of Israel, which was promised by God to the Jewish people in perpetuity. But Herbst said she also moved to the West Bank (she uses its biblical names, Judea and Samaria, and shoots a nasty glance at reporters who say "the occupied territories") because of the lessons she said she learned from the civil-rights movement in America. "We are fighting for Jewish civil rights," she said proudly. "We should be able to live wherever we want in our homeland." The Arabs, she said, can stay and "be well"—if they behave.

I first met Herbst a few months before the Gulf War at her office in West Jerusalem, where she worked for Amana, the settlement arm of Gush Emunim. The office was in a shabby suburban tract house in a neighborhood built on Palestinian land Israel confiscated after the Six-Day War. She agreed to take me on a tour of her settlements the next day.

We arranged to meet at the American Colony Hotel in Arab East Jerusalem, a place the Israeli right reviles. The hotel was formerly an opulent Turkish manor house with elegant high-ceilinged rooms and lush gardens; its catacomblike bar was once a horse stable. Nowadays, the hotel is a mecca for foreign correspondents and the dapper, expensively wardrobed Palestinians who work for them as "resource people." Many are, in fact, political operatives for one of the various PLO factions. Besides subtly promoting their political agenda, they make a good living serving as Western journalists' "eyes and ears" in the territories. A few have earned so much money at it that fellow Palestinians have dubbed them the "*intifada* rich."

Settlers are certain that the only reason reporters would stay at the American Colony is that they are sympathetic to the Palestinian cause. At the very least, settlers believe, journalists imbibe the hotel's pro-Palestinian atmosphere, which creates an anti-Israel bias in their reporting. A settler once told me in all seriousness that the PLO pipes subliminal propaganda messages over a hidden transmitter into the rooms at night.

Herbst won't even set foot in the American Colony. Despite the massive police presence in East Jerusalem, Israelis seldom venture there. Stabbings of Israeli soldiers and police are commonplace. Cars bearing yellow Israeli license plates left unprotected in front of the East Jerusalem courthouse on Saladin Street are routinely torched by bands of Palestinian youths who smash in the windows and toss gas-soaked rags inside. Many of my Jewish friends in West Jerusalem wouldn't drive anywhere near the American Colony. Though Israeli politicians call Jerusalem a "unified" city, people who live there say it is divided by what they call a "line of fear," roughly the old border that separated East and West Jerusalem prior to the Six-Day War.

Per Herbst's instructions, we met at the hotel's front gate. She was unlike any Orthodox settler whom I had ever met before. Procol Harum's "A Whiter Shade of Pale"—an ode to psychedelic drug use—blared from the tape deck of her battered white Peugeot. She had a tangle of thick, curly black hair and wore a silver "love" ring, a Mickey Mouse watch, and a short black skirt with fishnet stockings. According to religious law, strictly observant Orthodox Jewish women are required to cover their arms and legs as well as wear a head covering. Herbst's getup was a virtual sacrilege. "Gush Emunim sent rabbis to talk to me about the way I dress," she admitted. "But in the end they accepted it, though I am considered sort of strange. I mean, I teach aerobics at Ofra, and I work out a lot. But they sort of grudgingly admire me. I'm on the road a lot, and I work at nights, and it's a hard job, and not very many people are willing to do it. But no doubt they'd prefer not to have a woman walking around the way that I dress."

As we drove along Nablus Road through a luxurious Arab suburb of enormous stone mansions—many crowned with TV antennas shaped like miniature Eiffel Towers—Herbst told me to keep my window rolled up tight but not to buckle my seat belt, as is required by Israeli law. Her car windows were made of a thick clear plastic that is supposed to deflect most rocks and bullets. Molotov cocktails, however, can explode on the roof of a car and engulf it in flames in a matter of seconds, making it safer to be free of any constraints, she said. Shatterproof windows cost up to twenty-five hundred dollars per car. The Israeli government picks up the tab.

Herbst and her husband have been stoned dozens of times by Arabs while driving on the West Bank. About a month before we met, a rock was hurled at her car with such velocity that it crashed through the protective windshield and slammed into her shoulder. She was still receiving physical therapy for the bruising wound. A few months before that incident, her husband, Gershon, was stopped outside of Ramallah by a roadblock of boulders and burning tires. He stepped out of his van and ordered a group of Arab women standing near a house on the opposite side of the road to clear the debris at gunpoint. According to one of the women, he threatened to kill them. She later filed assault charges against him in a Jerusalem court. (David Rotem is Gershon's attorney.) Aliza claimed that settlers have learned from experience not to clear roadblocks themselves because they can be pelted by stones, or the roadblock can be booby-trapped. The danger of driving in the territories hit home again when on the first night of Hanukkah in December 1991, Zvi Klein, a forty-two-year-old settler from Ofra, was shot in the head and killed as he drove along Nablus Road near el-Bireh with his teenage daughter.

We briefly stopped at Ofarim, a barren hill with a handful of families living in prefabricated trailers. The community, which is planned to straddle several hillsides, was a few years away from development. It was being designed for lower-income secular Jews who can't afford housing inside Israel's crowded urban centers.

Then we drove to Cohov Ya'acov, which in Hebrew means Star of Jacob. It was founded in 1974 by religious Jews from North Africa. Twenty-seven families lived there, mostly in cramped, beat-up prefabs, waiting for new homes to be built. Fifty-two single-family homes were going up along the lip of a towering hill with a magical view of a forested hillside. Bulldozers were kicking up a dust storm. Although the settlement was just twenty minutes away from Jerusalem by car, it seemed remote and isolated. There were no other settlements nearby, and only two Egged buses stopped in Cohov Ya'acov each day. Their only neighbors were Arab villagers, whose land the settlement had expropriated. As we slogged through the mud at a construction site, Aliza complained that everything it takes to put together a settlement is extremely expensive. It costs the government $250,000 a year, she said, just to maintain twenty families in caravans. A new four-kilometer access road into the hilltop settlement is expected to cost more than $500,000.

The settlers I met were greatly concerned about construction delays and cost overruns. I didn't hear anyone talk about the coming of the Messiah or the finer points of Talmudic law; instead, women wondered why the marble for their bathrooms hadn't been delivered on time.

It had rained the night before, and Penina Dolinsky's tiny trailer was surrounded by a watery slough. Inside, it was filled with a large Sony color TV, sleek leather furniture, and children's toys. A tower of dirty pots sat in the sink of a kitchen that was not much bigger than an airplane galley. It was Friday afternoon, the Sabbath was fast approaching, and Penina—an overweight, nervous woman in a flowered scarf and long, formless dress—started to panic. "It's not my day," she said with a short laugh. "There is no water, and that's why the dishes are piled high and I don't even have a phone to call Mother." In spite of the state of emergency, delicious home-baked brownies, cookies, and candy were heaped on a small coffee table, and we talked, drank coffee, and ate, while bulldozers rumbled outside her window.

"I have a problem with the contractor," she complained to Aliza, who listened calmly. "I don't want gray marble in the bathroom, but that's what he delivered. I ordered blue. But he's very nasty, and I'm afraid of him. I am afraid if I complain, he'll damage my house."

"What's in your contract?" Aliza asked.

"Aliza, you know there is no such thing as a contract with a contractor in Israel."

Penina's father-in-law is Morton Dolinsky, a gregarious former PR man from New York, who moved to Israel in 1969 and briefly headed the Israeli Government Press Office under Menachem Begin. A flurry of negative news stories greeted Dolinsky's appointment when the Israeli press learned that he had cofounded the Jewish Defense League in New York with the late Rabbi Meir Kahane. Dolinsky had met Kahane in Betar, the paramilitary Jewish youth movement founded by Jabotinsky. During the struggle for Jewish independence in Palestine, American Betarim smuggled weapons to the Irgun, then fighting the British and the Arabs.

Dolinsky and Kahane hadn't always been friends. A member of Betar's executive board, Dolinsky had Kahane expelled from the group when it was discovered he was stealing money from the organization. As Dolinsky tells it, late one Saturday night in 1950, as Kahane walked out of a party in Brooklyn, he was yanked off the street, blindfolded, bound, gagged, and dumped into the backseat of a Plymouth filled with five of his former friends from Betar. They drove Kahane over the George Washington Bridge and threatened to dangle him over the river by his heels. Then they drove him to Dolinsky's home in Washington Heights in upper Manhattan where the terrified Kahane was tied to a kitchen chair and tried as a thief. "He had nothing to say in his own defense," Dolinsky remembered. "We told him the Torah authorized us to give him forty lashes," said Israel Herman, one of the Betarniks who presided over Kahane's kangaroo court. But instead, the boys gave Kahane a dime for the subway and told him to go home.

Kahane and Dolinsky met again in 1967 in Laurelton, Queens. Blacks were beginning to move into the quiet, tree-lined, predominately Jewish, working-class neighborhood. "Laurelton homeowners didn't want blacks in!" Dolinsky said emphatically. "We knew what would happen to property values." The prophetic tradition of Judaism teaches Jews to fight social injustice; but as far as Kahane and Dolinsky were concerned, it was Jews who were being mistreated by blacks who were moving into their neighborhoods, taking over their schools, and turning their streets into battle zones of drugs and crime. It was Jewish civil rights, they asserted, that needed to be defended. They created the Jewish Defense League in 1968 to combat these problems as well as to prod the Jewish establishment into fighting for Jewish rights as unself-consciously as militant black leaders were fighting for Black Power. Soon squads of armed JDL members were patrolling New York's slums to protect Jews too old or too poor to move to the suburbs. Within a year of its founding, the JDL had evolved into a militant right-wing Zionist organization that used terrorist violence against its perceived enemies, most notably Arab-Americans and Russian diplomats. Dozens of its members, mostly lower-middle-class Jews from New York's ethnic neighborhoods, fled to Israel, often one step ahead of federal indictments. Many settled on West Bank settlements like Cohov Ya'acov.

Penina and her husband, Benny, a small, thin man with a high-pitched voice, who works in a biblical garden near Ben-Gurion Airport, had very little contact in Israel with the late rabbi, though he had taught Benny Torah in America. But Kahane's assassination in New York in November 1990, apparently at the hands of an Arab gunman, reinforced their view that Arabs hate Jews and will never be reconciled to a strong Jewish presence in Judea and Samaria. Penina's main fear—other than that of her Israeli contractor—is of her Arab neighbors. This fear, fueled by the *intifada,* has driven some settlers to join anti-Arab vigilante groups for reasons not dissimilar to those that had prompted Kahane and Morton Dolinsky to form the JDL. Penina told me, however, that her anxiety about living in an isolated settlement surrounded by hostile Arabs has been conquered by her all-consuming "love of Israel." "We visited here one Shabbat about five months ago, and it was very nice," she said sweetly. "We decided we wanted to live here. Our ideology is to build Israel. Judea and Samaria are part of Israel. The logical part of ideology is to build."

I called Aliza again the night the Gulf War began. She readily agreed to take me on another tour. The Israeli military had closed the occupied territories to journalists, but settlers were free to roam wherever they liked. Under a leaden January sky, we drove through East Jerusalem north along Nablus Road, into downtown Ramallah, once an Arab resort city and now a shabby, graffiti-scarred center of the *intifada.* The shops of the downtown stores were shuttered, and the doors and windows of every Palestinian home we passed were tightly closed. The IDF had orders to shoot to kill Palestinians who left their homes for any reason. On the second day of the war, Israeli soldiers shot dead a twenty-four-year-old Nablus woman who was on her balcony breast-feeding her baby.

We stopped at Pesagot, a sprawling religious settlement near Ramallah, where the Mateh Binyamin Regional Council has its headquarters. The council has thirty settlements under its auspices. Its chairman, Pinchus Wallerstein, was a small, balding man who wore a brightly colored knitted *kipa* on his head, the emblem of the religious-nationalist settler. Wallerstein was standing trial for killing an Arab youth from Beittin. The case had dragged on for more than three years. "I was trapped by twenty to thirty Arabs who had stones," Wallerstein once told me in the Knesset dining room, where he spends much of his time lobbying for the settlement movement. "Maybe stones are not guns, but stones are very dangerous. They surrounded my car. Maybe they wanted to kill me. This is a war, and we must behave as if we are in a war."

Wallerstein's case illustrates the dual system of justice that prevails on the West Bank. While he had been set free on bail by a civil court, Arabs, who are under the jurisdiction of military authorities and military courts, can spend months in jail under the Emergency Regulation Act without being formally charged with a crime. Meron Benvenisti, the former deputy mayor of Jerusalem and an expert on the occupation, pointed out in his report *The West Bank and Gaza Atlas* that Arabs have been given eight- and ten-year terms for throwing gasoline bombs at military and civilian vehicles, and they are likely to spend one year in jail for throwing stones. (Shortly after the Gulf War, Wallerstein pleaded guilty to negligent homicide and was sentenced to four months of public service, one year of probation, and a thirty-five-hundred-dollar fine.*)

Wallerstein and Herbst led me into the basement of his office building, where the council had its "war situation room." There, two middle-aged settlers in drab green military fatigues sat in front of banks of telephones that connected them to the IDF, the civil defense, other settlements, and armed guards patrolling the West Bank in all-terrain vehicles.

During the night of the first Scud missile attack, the war room received hundreds of phone calls from frantic settlers. "What do you do with the gas masks after you take them off?" one settler wanted to know. "Is it still

---

*As another point of comparison, Israeli peace activist Abie Nathan served nearly six months in prison for a 1990 meeting with Yasir Arafat, in defiance of a law that bars Israelis from talking to PLO members.

safe to eat fresh vegetables?" asked another. Many of the callers were referred to psychologists and counselors who were available on a twenty-four-hour basis.

So far, Wallerstein said, the Palestinians in his area had been quiet.

"Do you expect problems?" I asked.

"I'm not a prophet," Wallerstein replied. "But I'm sure the biggest losers in all this are the Palestinians. They chose the wrong side, and neither we nor the West will forgive them."

I asked Wallerstein if he favored expelling Palestinians from the territories. According to a newspaper poll I had just read, nearly 40 percent of Israeli Jews favored "transfer" (though only 5 percent of those who supported the idea thought it was feasible).

"Transfer is wishful thinking," Wallerstein said. "But if they disturb us during the war, the army will take very harsh measures, and that might lead to transfer."

The war did not slow down the feverish pace of settlement activity. Wallerstein insisted that their movement would emerge from the crisis in the Gulf even stronger than it was before Saddam Hussein invaded Kuwait. He pointed out that their population (not including new Jewish neighborhoods in East Jerusalem) had grown by 40 percent, from 75,000 to more than 100,000, during the three-year-long *intifada*. Confident that the Likud would remain in power for many years, he predicted that their population would double by the year 2000, and that neither the Israeli left, which he said had been totally discredited for having championed the PLO as a suitable negotiating partner, nor the United States, which calls the settlements an obstacle to peace, will be able to mount an effective campaign to stop them. It is unthinkable, one settler told me, that Israelis would trade land for peace with the people who embraced the Iraqi dictator. "There is no difference between Saddam Hussein and a big PLO terrorist, except PLO terrorists have proved to be more lethal than Scud missiles," he said.

One good omen, Wallerstein said, was that hundreds of Israelis fled the heavily populated coastal plain to seek refuge with them during the war. Many settlements are nestled among Arab towns and villages, which made them unlikely targets for Scuds. Apparently, many Israelis preferred to take their chances with angry West Bank Palestinians rather than tangle with Iraqi missiles. "My neighbor's mother-in-law wouldn't come to visit Ofra once during the *intifada,* but she wants to come now," Aliza said.

Wallerstein allowed me to sit in on a meeting with settlers from Cohov Ya'acov, who wanted to restrict their settlement to religious Jews. The government had decreed that the community should be open to secular Jews, and Wallerstein sided with the government, fearing that if they did not settle quickly with anyone willing to live there, empty land would revert back to local Palestinians. Civil suits brought by Arab villagers challenging the legality of land expropriation had already cost Cohov Ya'acov 1,000 *dunams,* or 250 acres. The meeting ended with both sides saying they would reconsider their positions, although Herbst later told me that Wallerstein had no intention of giving in.

As dusk approached, we drove to Herbst's small three-bedroom home in Ofra, a Gush Emunim settlement of some twelve hundred people located between Ramallah and Jericho, about a half-hour drive from downtown Jerusalem. Set up illegally in May 1975 on grounds where a partially completed Jordanian Army camp once stood, Ofra was located outside the area sanctioned for Jewish settlement by the Allon Plan. Allon himself adamantly opposed the settlement. But Gush Emunim, which wanted to extend Jewish sovereignty across the entire West Bank, lobbied Defense Minister Shimon Peres to allow a group of settlers to stay at the site. They proposed disguising themselves as a military work brigade to avoid a hostile reaction from the American government, which then, as now, officially opposed new settlements in the occupied territories. As he did at Sebastia with Levinger, Peres backed the settlers in order to undercut his arch rival in the Labor party, Yitzhak Rabin, then prime minister. Peres permitted the settler "brigade" to build wire fences, install lighting, and guard its perimeters. He later let their families join them. Ecstatic Gush Emunim members printed cards announcing the "re-creation" of Ofra, which was mentioned in the Old Testament as one of the settlements established by the invading Israelites. Ofra's modern-day pioneers believed they were reliving the biblical drama, having returned to holy soil once inhabited by the tribe of Benjamin.

Ofra was one of three settlements legalized by the government the day after Prime Minister Menachem Begin returned to Israel from his first meeting with President Jimmy Carter in July 1977. The prime minister refused Carter's request to halt further Jewish settlement on the West Bank. The legalization of the three settlements severely strained relations between the two leaders.

Ofra's fields, expropriated from two nearby Arab villages, were stony and expensive to clear, but underneath the stones was some of the most fertile soil in the region. Today Ofra has cherry, plum, and peach orchards as well as a chicken coop, a silk-screen factory, and a computer-software company. The majority of the residents, however, commute to Jerusalem to work.

This was not my first visit to Ofra. Shortly after Anwar Sadat's epochal visit to Jerusalem in November 1977, I spent several days as a guest in Gush Emunim activist Yonatan Blass's Ofra home. Yonatan, then a twenty-seven-year-old overweight, balding Talmudic scholar from Boston, and his wife, Sherill, a Barnard College graduate from Dover, Delaware, were the first couple to settle in Ofra. Yonatan told me he had come to Israel for spiritual reasons.

"An internal process led me here," he said. "It was a general extension of religious Zionism. I didn't come to Israel seeking a political refuge, because I already had that in America.

"It was very difficult the first year. We were living in an old Jordanian Army barrack. There was no floor and no toilet; there were holes in the walls. We had no heat or electricity. My wife, my son, and I lived in one room the size of a small bedroom, which measured ten square meters. The room next door was occupied by a family of four. We endured these hardships because I believe that settling in Judea is a *mitzvah* [good deed]. It's one of the Torah's two hundred forty-eight positive commandments for every Jew to settle the land."

I asked Yonatan if it was also a *mitzvah* for the settlement to hire local Arab labor.

"There was an argument among us at first over that question," he replied. "On the one hand, we had to prove that we were building up the land ourselves. On the other, we were living with Arabs. We needed someone to remove the rocks from our fields and empty our sewers. We could have gone to Jerusalem to obtain these services, but we decided to pay the local Arabs to do it. The farming is done only by Jews. But we do buy our food from an Arab wholesaler."

He told me that Gush Emunim settlements in Judea and Samaria facilitate harmony between Arab and Jew. "Having Jews living among Arabs helps relations. It's a positive contribution toward peace."

That was the standard line one heard from Gush Emunim at the time. It was partly wishful thinking and partly a fairy tale for the gullible among the press. Since the *intifada,* nobody in Ofra talks about Arabs playing a positive role in anything. Gush Emunim dropped all pretense of communal harmony during Camp David when Prime Minister Begin declared that he was willing to grant Palestinians in the territories some form of autonomy. That's when the Makhteret began to covertly formulate its deadly plans to sabotage the Camp David Accords. At the same time, settlement leaders openly warned Begin that civil war would erupt if autonomy translated into anything more than Palestinians collecting their own garbage.

Shortly after I visited Yonatan, I sat in the Ofra home of Gush activist Yisrael Harel as he and his cohorts planned a series of violent demonstrations throughout Israel and the West Bank to protest Sadat's peace initiative. Later that day, Harel, then an influential forty-six-year-old journalist, held a meeting with the political secretary of the American embassy. In defiance of the Begin government, Harel threatened, "There will be a civil war if the government goes ahead with its autonomy plan."

The militancy of Harel and his fellow settlers created a hothouse for the growth of Jewish terrorism. It is hardly a coincidence, then, that four key members of the Makhteret were from Ofra. They were, Yisrael Harel later said, "the pioneers, the activists." The best known and least repentant among them is Yehuda Etzion, the Makhteret's chief ideologue and the driving force behind the plot to blow up the Dome of the Rock Mosque. A tall, muscular man with a fiery red beard and piercing blue eyes, Etzion is the symbol of Gush Emunim gone haywire.

Born in Israel in 1951, Etzion grew up in a fervently religious Zionist home. His father, Avraham Mintz, fought in the Irgun with Begin. Mintz later helped found the West Bank settlement of Elon Moreh.

In many respects, Etzion was a perfect example of the post–Six-Day War generation of religious Zionist youth who struggled to shatter the Israeli stereotype that had depicted observant Jews as weak and parasitic, concerned solely with securing government handouts to fund their yeshivas. A product of B'nai Akiva and a paratrooper in the army, Etzion (he Hebraicized his surname) was one of Rabbi Levinger's young commandos at Sebastia before he led a *garin*, or seed group, to settle Ofra. When Etzion was arrested for his key role in the underground, his wife told *Nekuda* ("Point"), the monthly magazine of the settlers published in Ofra by Yisrael Harel, "He lives on another plane, having a constant sense of supreme mission and broad thinking that is solely directed by the national interest. I know it is hard to believe, but this is the truth. This is the man I live with all the time. This is a person who constantly feels he has a role in the course of redemption and who asks himself every day, 'What am I doing for the sake of redemption?' "

If Ofra's official representatives had their way, visitors would never know about the Makhteret. In 1987, I led a group of Americans on a tour of Israel and the occupied territories on behalf of *The Nation* magazine. We spent a day in Ofra, and our guide was Sherill Blass, the Barnard graduate who had been one of Ofra's pioneers. Our group sat in a mock-Roman amphitheater under a seamless blue summer sky as Sherill, who by then called herself Shifra, told us that Ofra was founded, in part, on the principles of Walden Pond, and that Gush Emunim was a movement that had borrowed from the teachings of Emerson and Thoreau. Indeed, Gush Emunim was, according to Shifra, a kind of Orthodox back-to-nature movement. Pert and bright, she was an excellent, and perhaps to some a convincing, speaker. With her flowered scarf and long, flowing white dress, she could have passed for a hippie on a commune in the American Southwest. I remember wondering how many American Jewish fund-raising groups she had tried to sell this fiction to. When I reminded Shifra that I had been a guest in her home more than a decade before and that any educated Isreali knew that Gush Emunim had borrowed about as much from Emerson as it had from Saint Francis of Assisi, she sputtered on in an embarrassed attempt to salvage her talk. When I inquired about the underground, she said that they were outcasts, and that the affair was mostly an exaggeration of the Western media, which had a strong anti-Israel animus.

In fact, the Makhteret was as controversial in Ofra as it was in Israel. A poll conducted in Ofra by Israeli sociologist Janet Aviad in 1987 found that 62 percent of the respondents supported the Makhteret's attack on the Palestinian mayors; 13 percent favored the shooting attack on Hebron's Islamic College; 11 percent agreed with the plot to destroy the Dome of the Rock Mosque; and 9 percent approved of the plan to blow up the Arab buses. Etzion himself opposed the bus attack, calling it an act of "indiscriminate terrorism."

One of the underground's most articulate critics within Gush Emunim was Rabbi Yoel Ben-Nun, a rabbi from Ofra who had been Etzion's teacher and among his closest friends. Shortly before the Makhteret attacked the Palestinian mayors, Etzion and Ben-Nun coauthored a remarkable treatise called *Guidelines and Models for the Sovereign State of Israel*, which outlined how Israel could operate as a state with laws and an educational system based entirely on the Torah. Although they agreed on the grand design, they argued bitterly about how to achieve a theocratic state. Ben-Nun, who admired the achievements of secular Zionism, asserted that the public would have to be patiently educated to accept the true Torah path. Etzion countered that the secular government would have to fall before the kingdom of Israel could be advanced.

After Etzion's arrest, Ben-Nun excoriated the underground in *Nekuda,* angrily comparing it to a messianic Jewish cult that arose in the Middle Ages, causing a calamitous upheaval. "The underground," he wrote, "is a new Sabbateanism born of despair. . . . Those who would hasten the End are delaying it. Let us dissociate ourselves from them at once!"

Released from prison in 1989, Etzion writes frequently for *Nekuda,* which has helped to legitmate his views, lectures widely about transforming Israel into a Halachicly pure state, and pines for the Third Temple. And as a faithful guardian of the Temple Mount, he has become a cultlike hero to a new generation of religious youth. Posters of Etzion are displayed prominently in dozens of yeshiva dormitories as well as in hundreds of West Bank settlers' homes. They often hang next to a color poster of the Third Temple superimposed over the Dome of the Rock. Etzion brought this picture to court on the day of his sentencing, telling reporters that "purifying the Temple Mount" should be Israel's overriding goal. "How do you think the great sages would have felt about giving back the Temple Mount to the Muslims after it was conquered by Israel?" he asked.

The awakening of the nationalist spirit of Judaism, which led Yehuda Etzion to Ofra, also coursed through America's Jewish community, where it found Aliza Herbst. Her rite of passage may have been more roundabout than Etzion's, but the spirit would bring them to the same place on the West Bank—and possess them with the same force.

But in the summer of '69, the intoxicating spirit of music summoned Aliza to the Haight—home to flower children and Black Panthers, be-ins at Golden Gate Park, and the psychedelic sounds of the Jefferson Airplane, Big Brother and the Holding Company, and the Grateful Dead. The Haight was about as far away from the Samarian highlands as one could possibly get. A trip in the Haight meant the exploration of inner space—not one's religious heritage.

Aliza lived on the 1500 block of Haight Street at the edge of the Fillmore

District—a notorious black ghetto. "There was a stoop in the front of the house," she remembered. "I used to sit on the stoop and lock the iron gate and just watch things going on in the neighborhood. You'd see things like pimps with girls that looked nice and healthy and young. And you'd see them again in a week, and the same girl was all drugged-out and dirty and skinny, and I guess that's what my parents had in mind when I left home—that that's what was going to happen to me."

Herbst was lead singer in a blues band. For seven years, they played the Fillmore and the Family Dog as a warm-up act and performed at lounges in Nevada casinos. "My friends in Amana still don't believe I was a blues singer," Herbst said. She made as much as fifteen hundred dollars a week and saved enough to buy a secluded mountain property in Boulder Canyon, Colorado, next to a large spread owned by David Crosby of the popular rock group Crosby, Stills and Nash. "He didn't let us build an access road" across his property, she said. "He said he didn't want us to visit him. Who would want to?"

In tune with the era, her group had a vaguely left-wing political bent. Aliza herself, however, wasn't an activist. "I was against the Vietnam War, but I didn't really know why. Music really takes over your life if you're working at it. We'd practice four or five hours a day and then play a gig at night and oftentimes play an after-hours bar and then go home to sleep. I really didn't have much time for anything else."

In 1973, Herbst left the hectic world of rock and roll and enrolled in the Graduate School of Social Work at the University of Wisconsin at Madison, where she met her future husband, Gershon, a budding young scientist. "When I started dating Aliza, I didn't know she was Jewish," Gershon later told me. "It wasn't a reason to go out."

Gershon had grown up in a typically Conservative Jewish home on Long Island. He attended Hebrew school several days a week in the afternoon and was bar-mitzvahed at the age of thirteen. His parents kept a kosher home (though they regularly ate nonkosher food in restaurants). Judaism was less important than baseball and football. Gershon received a Ph.D. in aquatic biology from Boston University. An environmental activist, he founded the New England Ecology Federation and helped to organize the first Earth Day in 1970.

About a month after the two started dating, Gershon said, "It was Passover, I was in Madison by myself, and I said to Aliza, 'Hey, let's do a Seder.' It was very romantic, and it made me realize that I needed a Jewish

framework in my life." Soon after, Gershon began to study with the only
Lubavitcher Hasidic rabbi living in Madison.

Most Hasidic sects shun any contact with other Jews, let alone Christian
society. But the Lubavitcher Hasidim based in Crown Heights, Brooklyn,
are missionaries. In New York, young Lubavitchers navigate crowded city
streets in Winnebagos called Mitzvah Tanks, blaring raucous Hasidic folk-
songs. Dressed in the customary formless dark coats and wide-brim hats,
they stop passersby on street corners and ask if they are Jewish, and if so,
would they like to learn how to put on *tefillin* or to join them for Sabbath
prayers? The intrepid are even invited to attend a Friday night *tisch,* where
thousands of Hasidim pack a huge synagogue on Ocean Parkway to hear
the grand rebbe Menachem Schneerson expound on the Torah—then
anxiously stand in line to receive his personal blessing or advice on such
matters as whom to marry.

The Lubavitchers, who stress that the joy of knowing God through
mystical devotion is more important than the dry, legalistic study of the
Torah, believe that the Messiah won't come until more Jews have returned
to the faith. And while they assert that only the Messiah can rule the Holy
Land—and so, strictly speaking, are not Zionists—they are hawkish supporters of the state of Israel. Since 1973, the Lubavitcher rebbe has called
for the annexation of the occupied territories, insisting that the Torah
absolutely forbids surrendering so much as one inch of the Holy Land to
"idolators."

Gershon told me that his studies with the Hasidic rabbi not only
strengthened his Jewish identity, but also influenced his decision to eventually make *aliyah.* "I realized in college that one person couldn't save the
world, but one person could help save the Jewish world," Gershon said.
Aliza told me that she was fed up with life in America long before she met
Gershon. There were too many social problems and too few solutions, she
said. "I wondered if I should devote my life to social change in America.
In the end, I wasn't prepared to do it." She briefly thought about going
to India with the Peace Corps. "But a friend of mine who had been there
in the Peace Corps told me, 'Go anywhere but India; they have all sorts of
strange worms and parasites. Things get into your system that you never
get rid of.' "

Aliza and Gershon trekked to Israel in 1979 with a three-year-old
daughter and one-year-old twins. "We had all sorts of potential and advanced degrees and had confidence and faith in our lives," Aliza remem-

bered. The Egyptian-Israeli Peace Treaty had just been signed, and militant settlers were planning ways to scuttle it. They had no intention of granting Palestinians autonomy or withdrawing from the territories. But Aliza didn't know about any of that. She didn't follow Israeli politics, had never heard of Gush Emunim or of its volatile leader, Rabbi Moshe Levinger. She had visited Israel once during high school for seven weeks and liked it. But at home in Texas, "We were passive Zionists," she said. "We never talked about Israel," although her father had been born in Jerusalem to Orthodox parents.

Gershon got a job with the Israeli version of the Environmental Protection Agency. Aliza had her fourth child. "One day," she said. "I was looking for things to do. It was really nice weather, and I wanted to take the baby out, and I saw a newspaper advertisement for day trips to Judea and Samaria. It seemed like a nice way to spend the day. I hadn't even really heard of the places we were going to. It was just more of a lark than anything else. It was a bus tour of four or five settlements. There was a man and a woman who spoke on the bus. I don't even remember where all we went, except that one of the settlements was Ofra. I was really surprised how nice it seemed. It was out in the country, the people were nice, a lot of them spoke English, and there were social services like schools and things."

Impressed, the Herbsts started to seriously consider moving to a West Bank settlement. After two years in Israel, they were still living in a rent-free, government-sponsored absorption center for new immigrants near Jerusalem. "The little I knew then about Gush Emunim and the settlements, I figured the settlers were all superfanatics, like guys with long *zitses* hanging down to their knees and an Uzi on their shoulder and dancing around a boiling pot of something, singing and dancing. I thought they were probably like crazy people. And the people that I met in Ofra were really normal. They really believed in what they were doing, but they weren't any crazier than anybody else in this country, which is not saying a lot, but there you have it."

The Herbsts moved to Ofra in 1981. Like all candidates for membership in a Gush Emunim settlement, they had to be approved by an acceptance committee. Then they had to pass a five-hour written test and an interview with a psychologist. They were asked about their politics, their religious views, and their sex lives. The examination is supposed to weed out candidates who can't cope in a close-knit, ideologically charged, intensely religious environment. After all that, they were placed on probation for a year.

Aliza got to know Rabbi Levinger during the winter of 1984, while he was conducting a highly publicized hunger strike in front of Deheishe refugee camp near Bethlehem. The sprawling camp of some five thousand Palestinians straddles the main road connecting Jerusalem to Hebron. Cars with distinctive yellow Israeli plates were often showered with stones as they passed by. The army had erected a fifteen-foot-high hurricane fence around the camp and blocked all but one entrance with oil drums, but Levinger wanted the camp dismantled and the refugees moved—preferably to Jordan.

Aliza had cousins who lived in Kiryat Arba, and on the way back from visiting them, she would sometimes stop off at Levinger's tent in front of the refugee camp with her children. "My kids admired him a lot for his stubbornness and persistence," she said. "They developed a personal relationship with him, and they consider him to be their rabbi." Levinger subsequently hired Aliza to work at Amana. At the time, she was in charge of an absorption center in the West Bank settlement of Kedumin. "He wasn't exactly sure where I'd fit in, but he felt that with time, I'd find my place there. And since then, he's sort of kept track of how I'm doing in Israel. He's a very warm person. Most people have a hard time believing that."

On the drive from Pesagot to Ofra, the countryside looked green and peaceful. Olive trees, some hundreds of years old, climbed the steep, fertile hills in neat rows. Palestinian peasants harvest the trees by shaking them and catching the olives in blankets, which they bundle off to market. Aliza and I didn't talk about the Scuds or the *intifada,* but rather about whether I'd like to watch tapes of *Saturday Night Live* that she had rented from a video store in Jerusalem.

After dinner, Pinchus Wallerstein dropped by with his wife to chat, but an air-raid siren began to wail, and they bolted for the door. We moved into Aliza and Gershon's bedroom, together with their children. I sat on the bed wearing a gas mask and playing Go Fish with the children until the all-clear was sounded. Then Wallerstein called to see if the American writer was all right. Later Gershon and I stayed up late watching pictures on TV of the Scuds' destruction. "It's not nice," he repeated over and over again as we watched television. But like most Israelis, he said he understood the advantages of not retaliating. Though settlers are not known for their self-restraint, most of them knew that in this case restraint had won Israel worldwide goodwill, which it would need to draw on once the war concluded and the U.S. government renewed its pressure on Shamir to relinquish all or part of the occupied territories.

We had bagels and coffee for breakfast seated around a brown-lacquered picnic table in the kitchen. The kids had already eaten. "We don't think we will be here for the rest of our life," said Gershon, munching on a toasted bagel, "but there is no reason to leave. There is no dope here, and it's more wholesome than America. You've seen my kids. They are square. They go to B'nai Akiva, and they wear white shirts. It's hokey, but real. I thought it would be this way here."

Before leaving Ofra in the morning, I dropped in on an elementary school class, which was being held in a hardened concrete bomb shelter with heavy metal blast-proof doors. The children sat in their winter coats in front of a small electric heater. The teacher quoted from Rav Zvi Yehuda Kook, the late spiritual leader of Gush Emunim. " 'Have love in your hearts for your people and your country,' " the teacher said. " 'Believe in God and believe in the Land of Israel. It is our land, the land of David. We have come back to our Holy Land.' "

It is difficult to write about people whose politics one abhors yet who in other respects are fundamentally decent. The Herbsts are hardworking pioneers who have sacrificed yuppie careers in America to build their version of an idealistic Zionist society. They are not unlike the early Zionist pioneers in their work ethic, their love of the land—and their moral blind spot when it comes to Arabs. In their view, they are merely completing the task that the early *chalutzim* began—building and settling the land. Palestinians are simply "resident aliens," who if they choose to remain may do so, but without political rights. For settlers, it is that black-and-white. They have no qualms about ruling over another people.

"I don't feel I'm oppressing them," Aliza said as we drove back to Jerusalem in a heavy downpour. "I'm living in Ofra fighting for the self-determination of the Jewish people. If you want to understand us, you have to put your biases aside. The Palestinians—I call them Arabs—are not fighting for civil rights. They are fighting to destroy us. Try to be sensitive to our civil rights as a people. As a person, I should be able to live wherever I want as long as I don't oppress anyone. I know it's difficult to understand. It sounds loopy. But until we got here, the Arabs never had it so good. We built them hospitals, roads, modern irrigation techniques. We've been trying to create an environment of coexistence.

"We want to build something positive and do away with racism and sexism. I chose a meaningful life; a rural, nonviolent life with a commitment to human rights just like I had in San Francisco. And just as I felt in San Francisco that I had to protect myself from police brutality and the very poor in the Fillmore District, I have to protect myself and my children from Arab terror.

"We are defending the ramparts of Western civilization against militant Islam as we build settlements in our homeland," said Aliza without a trace of irony. Maybe now, she said, because of the Gulf War, the world will see how really ugly Palestinians and Muslims are, and that the settlers are fighting the good fight. "I know it's a simplistic view," she said, "but I guess, in a respect, I have an 'Imagine'/John Lennon outlook on life."

CHAPTER 3

A Tale of Two Cities

Several months after the *intifada* erupted, residents of the Arab village of Bidya on the West Bank assassinated their *mukhtar,* or headman, whom they had accused of being an Israeli collaborator. The *mukhtar,* Mustafa Salim Abu Bakr, was a well-known land speculator who villagers claim defrauded them out of hundreds of *dunams* of land, sometimes by tricking them into signing over to him the deeds to their property. Like many West Bank *mukhtars,* Abu Bakr had been appointed by the Israeli Civil Administration to run the village and to act as a middleman between the villagers and the authorities. He was supplied with Uzi machine guns and a beeper that connected him to the nearby Jewish settlement of Ariel, which sent squads of armed settlers to Bidya whenever he called for protection. Abu Bakr gave the Uzis to a small band of followers, who used them to intimidate the villagers and collect "taxes" from them. The villagers twice appealed to the Israeli Civil Administration to remove Abu Bakr. In November 1986, the house of the villager who led the opposition against the *mukhtar* was riddled with machine-gun fire.

Abu Bakr himself survived six assassination attempts, including one in early 1988 in which several villagers rammed his car with a Plymouth as he pulled out of his driveway one morning. The *mukhtar* was unhurt. But his nineteen-year-old pregnant daughter had been sitting in the backseat and was crushed to death by the steel-gray Plymouth—a car the villagers had selected for its size and weight. A few months later, on March 5, 1988, young people in the village threw firebombs at Abu Bakr's house. Israeli soldiers and Jewish settlers quickly intervened; they arrested several young men who had allegedly taken part in the killing of his daughter, put the village under curfew, demolished three houses, and uprooted more than two hundred olive trees.

The military government finally gave in to the villagers' request and on May 15, 1988, dismissed Abu Bakr. But before the order could take effect, Abu Bakr sold Bidya's water-pumping and electrical equipment. He also pocketed more than thirty-three thousand dollars that villagers had given him to pay for their electric bills, causing the Israeli electric company to shut off the current in the village for several months. Then, in September 1988, Abu Bakr was shot to death by two masked men as he was driving in front of Bidya's high school. The gunmen set fire to his corpse as villagers looked on; some even danced around the body. "It was our biggest achievement of the *intifada,*" said Amir Abu Bakr, the director of Bidya's high school, which, along with all other West Bank schools, had been shut down by the Israelis in reprisal for stone throwing and other activities.

More than 520 Arabs suspected of collaborating with Israel have been killed by Palestinian militants since the beginning of the *intifada.* Palestinian sources told me that PLO officials in Tunis approved most orders to kill suspected collaborators after underground trials had been conducted by local Palestinian activists. The killings—often carried out by masked youths wielding axes—got so out of hand that Arafat himself publicly appealed for the bloodletting to end.

Soon after the shooting, in which the *mukhtar*'s eight-year-old son was seriously wounded, Bidya was surrounded by 150 soldiers and settlers from Ariel. The entrances to the village were blocked with earthen barricades, and all the men between the ages of fourteen and forty were herded into the mosque for questioning. Seven villagers, including the sheikh of the village mosque, were subsequently arrested in connection with the assassination. Five houses belonging to the suspects were blown up by the army, and another house was sealed, leaving forty-five people homeless. Bidya was placed under curfew for four days. Israeli soldiers forced villagers to remove from their roofs stones and bottles that could have been used as weapons, to paint over nationalist graffiti, and to take down Palestinian flags from trees and telephone poles.

I drove to Bidya in March 1989 with Osama Odeh, a thirty-three-year-old chemical engineer from Ramallah whose family has had a house there, he told me, for 125 years. Bidya is a dusty, nondescript farming village of some six thousand people near the Nablus–Tel Aviv Highway, which is heavily used by Israeli settlers. Passing Israeli cars and trucks have frequently been attacked with stones and firebombs by the people of Bidya, and several settlers have been injured. In reprisal, Bidya has been raided by the army and groups of settlers. In January 1989, soldiers entered Bidya at 3:00 A.M., rounded up the men, and forced them to sit in a freezing drizzle in the high school courtyard while an Israeli official confiscated the identification papers of residents who had not paid Israeli taxes. The authorities have raised the taxes Palestinians must pay in the occupied territories to cover the costs of putting down the *intifada,* and many Palestinians have stopped paying them as an act of resistance. Confiscation of identity papers is a serious matter. If a Palestinian is found to be without papers when stopped for questioning, he or she is subject to immediate arrest and imprisonment.

Shortly before our visit, Osama's three-story stone house, which was vacant at the time, was broken into by Israeli soldiers, who, according to villagers, were looking for an illegal printing press. The cast-iron front door was blown off its hinges by an explosive charge. Furniture, mirrors, and windows were smashed, and food scattered. Someone mixed salt in the coffee. A glass frame holding a medical diploma belonging to Osama's uncle, a doctor in Germany, lay shattered in the study, along with a microscope and other expensive medical equipment. Hundreds of books were pulled from their shelves and lay in heaps in the library. They included *A Short History of the Saracens,* published in 1924; a Kansas State College bulletin from 1947–48; and a leather-bound copy of *The Knights of the Round Table.* "It's very sad they did such things to books," Osama said.

Osama made arrangements to hire some workmen from the village to clean up and repair the damage. Then we walked along an unpaved street to the house of his cousin, the educator Amir Abu Bakr. We were joined by several other men, including Muhammad Odeh, Osama's twenty-seven-year-old cousin, who had spent five years in prison for throwing a Molotov cocktail at an Israeli Army jeep. More than three hundred of Bidya's young men, I was told, have been imprisoned since the beginning of the *intifada.* The men were reluctant to talk about the *intifada* because they said they feared reprisals. They spoke with satisfaction about the *mukhtar*'s murder, and the new town council they recently set up, in defiance of the military, to run village affairs.

Like most other West Bank Arab villages, Bidya included members of various PLO factions and Marxist groups, as well as Hamas—an Islamic fundamentalist underground movement created in the spring of 1988 as an offshoot of the Muslim Brotherhood. But as in most other rural villages on the West Bank, Yasir Arafat's mainstream Fatah has overwhelming support in Bidya. There was also a small but influential group of Communists that both Israeli and Palestinian sources told me has had a central part in planning much of the local resistance to the occupation.* The Islamic fundamentalists are especially strong in Gaza, where they were originally encouraged by the Israeli authorities as a counterforce to the PLO. Hamas has denounced Arafat for recognizing Israel; its communiqués sometimes quote from the *Protocols of the Elders of Zion*. The *intifada* itself has been coordinated by underground committees made up of all the Palestinian factions except for Hamas. Secular Palestinian nationalists I spoke to believe Israel is supporting Hamas in order to divide the Palestinian community, although they had no evidence that this was so.

At the time, the villagers in Bidya were sharply debating whether Arafat had gone too far in recognizing the Jewish state. But while they had little enthusiasm for coexistence, many of Bidya's men worked in Israel and wanted to continue to do so. "It's mutually convenient," said Muhammad Odeh. If there was one thing the men agreed on, however, it was their hatred of Ariel, the large Jewish settlement that looms over the village. Ariel sits on land that was either confiscated by the army for what it claimed were security reasons, or willingly sold by nearby villagers, or, according to some villagers, acquired by fraud by Arab middlemen such as Mustafa Abu Bakr.

Ariel has established a vigilante militia that has often attacked Bidya. Increasingly during the *intifada,* groups of settlers from Ariel—sometimes as many as three hundred—have pulled villagers from their houses and cars and beat them; they have smashed their windows and burned their olive trees. In one of several attacks, Ariel's militia swarmed into Bidya in February 1989, firing rifles and stoning Arab cars after a Jew from the neighboring settlement of Alfei Menashe was found burned to death in his van on a West Bank highway. Army investigators later determined that the settler's gas line had leaked and exploded. The settlers forced one Arab

*According to an *Al Fajr* poll of Palestinian residents of the West Bank and the Gaza Strip taken in 1986, 93.5 percent of the respondents said the "PLO is the sole and legitimate representative of the Palestinian people." Seventy-one percent of the respondents preferred Arafat as their leader, and 78.4 percent agreed with the statement "Acts of violence are justified in the pursuit of the Palestinian cause."

vehicle carrying two men and a pregnant woman off the road. Hauling the men from the car, the settlers proceeded to beat them savagely. One settler told me such attacks wouldn't be necessary if the army weren't so easy on the Arabs. "I can't say what we'd do if someone from Ariel was killed by an Arab," said Yezekiel Amber, one of the founders of Ariel's militia. After the attack, settlers left behind a flyer in Arabic, warning that violence is a "two-edged sword," and if the residents of Bidya continued to throw stones and firebombs at Jews, both the villagers and their property would be "destroyed."

After Osama and I left his cousin's house, he dropped me off at the entrance to Ariel—a gleaming town of about ten thousand people who live in tree-shaded villas and row after row of low-rise apartment blocks set into the Samarian hillside. I had been invited to watch the making of a promotional film that Ariel's mayor planned to show on a fund-raising tour of America. To hear the citizens of Ariel tell their story to the camera, one would never guess that an Arab rebellion threatened their presence on the West Bank, or that Ariel had a well-armed militia, or that the militia's leader was said to be Ariel's mayor.

As klieg lights glowed, a young Jewish couple in their late thirties from Portland, Oregon, seated in their neatly furnished apartment, told an off-camera interviewer why they moved to Ariel: "The first time we came here," said Naomi, an African-American teacher of English who has converted to Judaism, "there was nothing here but Arabs and rocks. I thought we had lost our way."

"Now, five years later, we are a city of eight thousand residents, with stores, parks, a good school system," said Naomi's husband, Dan, a soft-spoken computer engineer.

"It's such a wonderful feeling to see a town grow up around you," Naomi continued. "I remember the day when my neighbor got a telephone. I opened a bottle of wine, and we danced on the table . . . It's important to make *aliyah*, but in Ariel it really counts. My three-year-old was born in the city, and my eight-year-old can go anywhere in town even at night without me having to worry. It's like one big family. . . . People say I sound like a salesman, but I love it here. I couldn't live anyplace else."

"It's home," said Dan. "It's almost impossible to put into words."

The crew had been filming in Ariel since early morning. The film would be used to show potential donors and settlers in America, who have been troubled about the *intifada*, that Ariel has much in common with a well-to-do American suburb. "We want cable TV, a good transportation system—all that good American suburban stuff," Dina Shalit, the forty-year-old Canadian-born assistant to the mayor, told me. "People move to Ariel for the same reasons Americans move to the suburbs."

On the surface, Ariel certainly seems a place many Israelis—not to mention many Americans—might find attractive. It has the look and feel of an American Sunbelt suburb in the midst of a boom. In the mall in the heart of town, shops sell everything from falafels for $1.50 to expensive clothes. A large outdoor swimming pool attracts suntanned secular settlers in skimpy bikinis. (At nearby Bidya, indoor plumbing is a luxury.) A five-star tourist hotel, complete with potted palms and an artifical waterfall in the lobby, is Ariel's gaudiest monument to its faith in its future. A high-tech park is rising at a noisy construction site on Ariel's outskirts; another industrial park on the edge of the city already employs two thousand people. City planners say they are aiming for a hundred thousand residents who will be housed along 7.5 miles of bulldozed ridges.

Only rows of young olive trees set in brightly colored oil drums keep Ariel from growing even larger. These fields, planted by Arab farmers, ring the Jewish city. Under Jordanian law, which still applies in principle on the West Bank, although not always in practice, if Arab land is cultivated, it is proof of Arab ownership, and it is therefore not to be expropriated. "Look how they block us," Ariel's forty-six-year-old mayor, Ron Nachman, said as he led me on a tour of what he called Israel's "city of tomorrow."

Nachman is not one of the bearded, machine-gun-toting mystics who inhabit some of the religious settlements in the Gaza Strip and the West Bank. A fourth-generation Sabra, born near Tel Aviv, he is a clean-cut young promoter with a fast-talking used-car salesman's manner, who describes Ariel as Israel's "yuppie" community. He said he was a representative of white-collar Israelis who began to move to the occupied territories in the early 1980s not for religious reasons but because it was possible to live well there cheaply. They mainly wanted apartments or houses that were larger and cost less than what they could find in Tel Aviv or Jerusalem, and they benefited from government-subsidized mortgages and tax breaks.

These so-called yuppies now outnumber the intensely religious, ideological settlers affiliated with the right-wing messianic movement Gush Emunim by at least four to one. The nonreligious settlers, however, are just as hawkish. For example, about 80 percent of Ariel's settlers voted for the Likud or for parties to its right in the 1992 Knesset election. Though before the uprising neither the suburban settlers nor members of Gush Emunim had good relations with the local Arabs, the suburbanites tried to maintain at least the appearance of coexistence. Nachman used to boast about Ariel's neighborly relations with the Palestinians. He would, he told me, drive to a nearby Arab village to get a shave from an Arab barber. But that was before the *intifada*—and before Nachman's friend Mustafa Abu Bakr was gunned down in front of Bidya's high school. While I was with him, Nachman looked at Bidya from his balcony and said, "Every house will be destroyed if they don't watch it!"

Liberal Knesset members and army officers had accused Nachman of helping to lead the settlers' militia that has attacked Bidya and other Palestinian communities. When I asked Nachman about this, he did not answer directly. He said there would have been no *intifada* in the first place if the Israeli left and the U.S. government hadn't encouraged the Palestinians with talk of self-determination. "The recognition of the PLO by the U.S. was like putting oil on the fire," Nachman said. "Instead of starting a peace process, it will lead to war!"

Even before the Labor party's surprise victory in 1992, Nachman told me he felt surrounded by threatening, even apocalyptic, developments: the *intifada* itself, followed by the Middle East peace talks and American pressure on Israel to end its settlement drive. At the same time, as several settlement leaders told me, they sensed that opposition to their enterprise was rising in Israel itself. No matter how many times Israeli prime minister Yitzhak Shamir vowed that he wouldn't surrender one inch of *Eretz Yisrael*, many settlers feared he would sell them out. They constantly talked of Menachem Begin's decision in April 1982 to surrender the Sinai with its five thousand settlers. Many settlers told me they were afraid that Shamir's idea of limited autonomy for local Palestinians, though obviously unacceptable to the PLO, would lead to a Palestinian state and then to Israel's destruction. It is the settlers' version of the domino theory—first Ariel will fall, followed by Haifa and Tel Aviv. It is a hysterical polemic designed to close off rational discussion about political compromise with Israel's Arab adversaries.

To prevent any softening of the Likud's position on settlements, movement leaders had organized protest demonstrations. In the winter of 1989, Ron Nachman joined Rabbi Levinger and other leaders from Gush Emunim in an around-the-clock vigil in front of Shamir's house to protest the lack of security in the territories. In March 1989, tens of thousands of supporters of the settlements took part in a rally in Tel Aviv. "This demonstration is to tell the world that *Eretz Yisrael* is Jewish," Rabbi Levinger told me as he looked over the vast crowd.

The settlers' constant complaining infuriated Shamir. "The settlers are driving us crazy," an official in the Prime Minister's Office told me. "We are with them, but they are being needlessly noisy and provocative. Their behavior will make Bush think everyone in Israel is a crackpot extremist." Shamir had from time to time shown himself impatient with the settlers' demands for unconditional support. At a religious ceremony at a West Bank settlement, Shamir was challenged by Eliyakim Haetzni, an eloquent but volatile settlement leader from Kiryat Arba and then a Tehiya member of the Knesset, who criticized Shamir for his failure to promote new settlements and for failing to crush the *intifada*. "You go to hell, prophet of doom," Shamir shouted; he then slammed a wine bottle down on the table and walked away.

The settlers' attacks on Shamir were not merely verbal. Shamir's motorcade was besieged by one thousand armed mourners when he came to Ariel to pay his respects to a settler killed by Palestinian shepherds in 1989. As the settlers jeered, Shamir said, "God will avenge Frederick Rosenfeld's blood spilled in such a vicious way. He fell victim to the hand of cruel murderers lacking any semblance of humanity, whose greatest desire is the spilling of Jewish blood. This small land belongs exclusively to the Jewish people. It is our land by right and by justice!" After the speech, settlers rushed Shamir as he tried to return to his car, punching and kicking his security guards. The settlers then stormed Bidya, shooting and stoning the residents. Later that day, Israeli police arrested a settler who fired an Uzi submachine gun into a crowd of Palestinian workers waiting for a ride at a busy Tel Aviv highway junction, seriously wounding two persons.

Ariel's Wild West image is personified by the indefatigable Nachman, who favors cowboy boots and a rattlesnake-skin belt with RON stitched across the back in big black letters. He got the western outfit from a rich Jewish wildcatter in Texas during an eighteen-city, thirty-five-day fund-raising tour of America in 1989. The tour netted Ariel more than $1.5 million.

In 1987, Nachman set up the Ariel Development Fund, which has raised more than $5 million. One major contributor is Albert Reichmann, the Canadian billionaire who is head of Olympia & York, one of the largest real estate development firms in the world. Reichmann donated money toward building an Orthodox synagogue in Ariel. Nachman has also raised considerable sums from Michael Milken's family. In 1989, Lowell, the brother of convicted junk-bond baron Michael, attended a ceremony in Ariel, where he was presented with the town's "Man of the Year" award. The Milken Family Foundation has financed the building of elementary and secondary schools in Ariel.

Nachman has had less luck raising money from mainstream Jewish organizations in America. In 1987, he asked Peggy Tishman, then president of the New York chapter of the United Jewish Appeal–Federation of Jewish Philanthropies, if she would fund projects in Ariel. A charitable, not-for-profit foundation, the UJA raises hundreds of millions of dollars annually for Israel. Some of the money is later discreetly channeled to settlement activity through the UJA's sister organizations in Israel. Tishman explained in a letter to Nachman that the UJA was afraid to fund projects overtly across the Green Line, Israel's pre-1967 border, because either the State Department or the IRS might retaliate against the UJA, given the U.S. government's hostility to settlements. "It is for this reason," she wrote, "that I have to be careful about my gifts in Israel. I am in a very visible position and that is why I have to be extremely careful. You know that I have tremendous respect for you and what you have done in Ariel. I think it's wonderful, and I can only encourage you verbally. At the present time, I have to adopt an arms-length approach."

In 1988 Nachman helped American Jewish activists linked to Gush Emunim and the American chapter of the Tehiya party to bring a class-action suit against the Jewish National Fund in a New York court for consumer fraud, claiming that it had refused to allocate funds across the Green Line despite fund-raising letters and advertisements to the contrary. The JNF is a charitable New York–based foundation that was set up in 1901 to raise money for land acquisition in Palestine. Currently, the JNF raises money from American Jews for land-reclamation projects primarily within the Green Line. In a letter to right-wing Jewish radicals in America, Nachman wrote, "We who live 'beyond the Green Line' are becoming increasingly angry at being demoted to the status of second-class Jews in the eyes of the major Jewish fundraising organizations. For years, world Jewry has been battling against the Arab boycott of Israel. We have waged consumer wars against major companies who have yielded to Arab pressure and refused to deal with Israel. Now, the Jews of Judea, Samaria . . . and Golan are confronted with a Jewish boycott against us. We will not con-

tinue to accept this passively." The lawsuit, which has cost the JNF hundreds of thousands of dollars in lawyers' fees, was still under litigation as
of the spring of 1992.

Ariel is a paradigm of the settlement movement—with its expropriation
of vast tracts of Palestinian land, its creation of an anti-Arab vigilante force,
its courting of top leaders in the American Jewish community and the
intimidation of those not favorable to its settlement activity.

Ariel was established in February 1978 on five hundred *dunams* of partly
cultivated Palestinian land confiscated by the Israeli Army for "security
reasons." The following year, the land was turned over to a group of forty
families who moved into caravans perched on a rocky outcrop near Bidya.
Most of the men were scientists and engineers employed at Israel Aircraft
Industries outside Tel Aviv. They paid for their homes with no-interest
bank loans collateralized by the state treasury. Likud planners designated
Ariel to become the largest Jewish town in Samaria, with as many as one
hundred thousand residents by the year 2010.

The initial plans for Ariel had been prepared in 1974 by Moshe Dayan,
who argued that a settlement was necessary there to protect the road
leading to the Labor party's small agricultural settlements in the Jordan
Valley. Founded as a secular community, Ariel allows its citizens to drive
on the Sabbath and barbecue in their backyards. Until the late 1980s, the
town had only one synagogue. Though Ariel's development did not begin
until the Likud took power, many of the early pioneers were Labor party
members. The Histadrut, the giant trade union and holding company
affiliated with the Labor party, was well represented there. Solel Boneh, the
Histadrut's multinational construction company, built much of the housing, the Histadrut's Bank Hapoalim opened a branch in the mall, and the
Co-op Supermarket chain, another Histadrut enterprise, started the town's
first grocery.

Ariel expanded rapidly as the Likud's settlement drive took off. When
Likud took power, only five thousand Jews lived on the West Bank. But
between 1977 and 1984, successive Likud governments invested more than
$1 billion in building nearly sixty new settlements, increasing the number
of Jewish settlers to more than thirty-eight thousand.

Israel's foothold on the West Bank increased dramatically just before the
1981 elections, when the Likud engineered a massive land grab, expropriating more than thirty-six thousand *dunams,* according to a statement issued

in April 1981 by the Prime Minister's Office. (Palestinians claim the total was twice that amount.) Of this, Ariel received six thousand *dunams*. Sharon, then minister of agriculture, and Matityahu Drobles, the cochairman of the settlement division of the World Zionist Organization, which since Mandate times has been responsible for building new settlements, worked closely together trying to establish enough "facts on the ground" to permanently forestall the possibility of Palestinian autonomy. The Labor party, running on a land-for-peace platform, was expected to win the 1981 elections. "It will now become necessary," Drobles wrote, "to conduct a race against time. During this period everything will be mainly determined by the facts we establish in these territories . . . This is therefore the best time for launching an extensive and comprehensive settlement momentum, particularly on the Judea and Samaria hilltops." Part of Likud's plan was to deny Palestinians residential building permits in an attempt to stem their expansion on land they had resided on from time immemorial and squeeze them into crowded cities.

In June 1981, Begin won by a wider margin than in 1977. Six months later, the Israeli government formally annexed the Golan Heights and installed Menachem Milson, a professor of Arabic Literature at the Hebrew University, to head the newly created civilian administration in the occupied territories. Milson had written a much talked-about article in *Commentary* magazine, explaining how Israel could dissolve PLO power in the territories by creating an "alternative leadership" loyal to Israel. Once in office, Milson deposed the democratically elected mayors Shaka, Khalaf, and Tawil (targets, the year before, of the Makhteret) and closed two Palestinian newspapers and Bir Zeit University, a center of Palestinian nationalism. He also encouraged the development of the Village Leagues, a coalition of mostly corrupt *mukhtars* who were armed by the Israeli military and collaborated with the government in ruling the West Bank. The Village Leagues quickly degenerated into a Lebanon-style militia, terrorizing West Bank Palestinians and extorting money for such things as permits to travel to Jordan—effectively alienating them even further from Israeli rule. Milson, an Orientalist who had spent a lifetime studying the "Arab mind," was supposed to bring a measure of intellectual respectability to Israeli rule. Instead, his policies provoked a mini-*intifada,* resulting in scores of dead and injured Palestinians in the inevitable military crackdown. Milson and Sharon, who was appointed defense minister in 1981, had hoped that Jordan would support the Village Leagues. But King Hussein announced that Palestinians who joined them were committing a capital offense punishable by death. Several members of the Village Leagues were assassinated by PLO hit squads.

At the same time that Milson was employing his heavy hand, the Likud was expropriating hundreds of thousands of *dunams* of Palestinian land. When the occupation began, only 0.5 percent of the West Bank was in Jewish hands. By 1984, Israel controlled more than 40 percent of the land, much of it acquired under a number of spurious pretexts. The most nefarious method employed by the Likud, from the Palestinian perspective, was to confiscate vast tracts of land that had been owned by the Jordanian government (much of which was cultivated by Palestinian farmers) or that Israel claimed was unregistered. Under Ottoman, British, and Jordanian rule, many Arab villagers did not bother to register their landholdings in an attempt to escape taxation and the draft. They were simply following an old Arab adage that counseled it was best to have as little to do with governments as possible. Thus, many Palestinian landholdings were unrecorded, and after Israel occupied the West Bank in 1967, it prohibited further registration. The Likud obligated Arabs to prove legal title to their land, even if it had been been passed down through the generations. In order to do so, poor, often illiterate peasants had to hire expensive Israeli attorneys, pay for aerial land surveys, and sometimes send emissaries to Istanbul or Amman to track down extant land documents. It was a daunting and often impossible task.

Before the Likud came to power, the Israeli government had prohibited Jews from buying Arab-owned land on the West Bank. But this changed too under Sharon and Milson. Israeli land brokers and their Arab associates began to drive about the territories looking for parcels that could be obtained and later sold for steep profits to land-hungry settlements. One of the biggest land dealers was Sharon's protégé Rafi Eytan, the Mossad spy who would later head Lekem, a secret intelligence unit in the Prime Minister's Office that ran Jonathan Jay Pollard, the U.S. naval intelligence officer. Pollard, an American Jew, received a life sentence for passing classified documents to Israel. Eytan's business partner in the land deals was Avraham Mintz, an adviser on settlements to Sharon and the father of Yehuda Etzion of the Makhteret.

The Israeli press published a great many exposés of West Bank land fraud, in which elderly and illiterate Palestinians signed away their land without being fully aware of what they were doing. Tens of thousands of *dunams* of land were obtained from Arabs through the services of Arab land brokers like Bidya's Mustafa Abu Bakr.

Indeed, a 1983 report by the Israeli state comptroller said that much of the thirty-one thousand acres of West Bank land bought by Jews had been fraudently obtained. On August 23, 1985, a *Ha'aretz* editorial strongly criticized unscrupulous Israeli land brokers for conducting business on the West Bank as if it were "the Wild West." "The swindlers must be dealt with in a most forceful manner." On December 1, 1985, Avraham Gindi, a prosperous Israeli building contractor, was arrested for using Arab middlemen to obtain forged Arab land deeds. On December 13, minutes before he was to be charged in a Tel Aviv district court for fraud, Gindi bolted from his guards and attempted to commit suicide by jumping out of the court building's sixth-story window. Several months later Gindi committed suicide by setting himself on fire.

The corruption spread to the Likud party itself. On April 11, 1989, Michal Dekel, the prime minister's adviser on the Jewish settlements, was indicted for using his post as deputy agriculture minister under Ariel Sharon in 1984 to help contractors get licenses to build on the West Bank in return for contributions for Likud's 1984 Knesset campaign. The indictment alleged that one meeting to solicit bribes took place in Yitzhak Shamir's office while Shamir was present, although he was not indicted. "He [Shamir] said if Likud continues to be in the government, we will help you, but in order to continue to be in the government, we need help," Shmuel Einav, a land dealer who arranged the meeting that was attended by twenty land dealers, told *Newsday.* "Shamir didn't say money, but that's what I understood." The meeting raised $150,000 in donations to the Likud, according to the indictment. Einav was subsequently convicted of bribery and fraud. *The New York Times* reported on August 20, 1985, that Shamir had ordered the police not to look too deeply into West Bank land-fraud cases, saying, according to the *Times* reporter, that "a certain amount of sleight of hand" was needed to obtain land from the Arabs. "Redeeming land in the Land of Israel often necessitated crafty and tricky devices," Shamir said in a speech at about the same time.

With characteristic chutzpah, Likud was soon sending its pitchmen to Manhattan to promote West Bank land sales to well-heeled American Jews. At one daylong conference in 1983, sponsored by the tax-exempt Americans for a Safe Israel, three hundred prominent Jews gathered at the Sheraton Convention Center, where they were given maps and brochures describing how easy it was to buy a piece of the West Bank (non-Jews were not eligible), according to *The Washington Post*. Warning that "prices are rising rapidly," the brochure compared its bargains on the West Bank, where it was offering land at $3,800 a *dunam*, to pricey land near Jerusalem that was going for more than $80,000 a *dunam*. Featured speakers included Ehud Olmert, a prominent Likud member of the Knesset, and Ira Rappaport, the Makhteret member who bombed Nablus's mayor Bassam Shaka's car in 1980.

AFSI is probably best known in the American Jewish community for publishing McCarthyite smears against liberal Jewish organizations and non-Jewish groups, such as the American Friends Service Committee, which it accused of working with the PLO against Israel. AFSI even petitioned the Federal Communications Commission to revoke NBC Television's license, claiming its coverage of the Lebanon war was so anti-Israel that it violated the fairness doctrine. The petition was dismissed. In 1983, AFSI brought an Israeli delegation to the United States to campaign against the Reagan peace plan, which was a halfhearted attempt to prod Begin to negotiate what he was ideologically opposed to negotiating, the West Bank and the Gaza Strip for peace with the Arabs. Among the delegates was Yigal Kutail, who was employed by Rabbi Levinger to solicit funds for the Jewish community of Hebron.

AFSI was founded in 1976 by Shmuel Katz,* the South African–born propaganda chief for the Irgun who became foreign-press adviser to Begin when the former Irgun commander became Israel's prime minister. In 1977, Begin brought Katz to Washington to lecture Jimmy Carter on Jabotinsky's vision. After Begin spoke to an audience that included the U.S. president and his secretary of state, Cyrus Vance, Katz took over, arguing that most Arabs in Palestine had arrived in the last hundred years in the

---

*The JDL was instrumental in distributing Katz's classic Revisionist polemic, *Battleground: Facts and Fantasy in Palestine*. The crudely written tract's main contention is that the Arabs of Palestine are recent immigrants from other Arab countries and so do not deserve self-determination. "The physical reacquisition of the land from the handful of existing [Arab] inhabitants presented no moral problem of choice for the Zionists," wrote Katz. The JDL purchased five thousand copies of the book, at a steep discount, directly from Katz, who had bought thirty thousand copies from the publisher, Bantam Books. Katz wrote to JDL cofounder Bertram Zweibon that the entire first edition was "covered in advance by the Israel-British Bank in Tel Aviv," which loaned the money against the guarantee of a well-to-do right-wing Jewish businessman. Thousands of copies of *Battleground* were subsequently distributed by Israeli embassies, and pro-Israel lobby groups such as AIPAC. Zweibon contacted various libraries to make sure that they purchased the book. "*Battleground* is a fact-laden book constructed in such a manner as to afford the reader thereof with the intellectual ability to combat Arab propaganda in the United States and in particular on the college campus," Zweibon wrote to the American Jewish Committee's head librarian in February 1973. "It contains an analysis of the problem in an historical perspective which puts lie to much of the Arab myth."

wake of the Zionist enterprise and therefore were not entitled to national rights. "It was almost certain," said Katz, "that that was the reason why so many Arabs had fled so easily in the 1948 war. Farmers rooted in their soil did not behave that way."

When Moshe Dayan, then Israel's foreign minister, read a cabled report of Katz's remarks, he was appalled. "I did not even try to guess what the Americans must have thought when they heard them," he wrote in his memoir *Breakthrough*. Dayan understood the Palestinians' deep historical attachment to the land. In April 1956, at the funeral of a close friend who was murdered by Palestinian terrorists while working in the fields of Kibbutz Nahal Oz near the Gaza Strip, Dayan said, "How can we complain about the [Arab refugees'] fierce hatred of us? For eight years they have been sitting in the refugee camps of Gaza while right in front of their eyes we are turning the land and villages in which they and their forefathers dwelled into our patrimony. . . . We are the generation of settlement, and without cannons and steel helmets we won't be able to plant a tree or a house."*

In 1983 Gush Emunim planners working closely with the Begin government decided that in view of the dwindling supply of religious settlers, the only way to "Judaize" the West Bank was to offer huge public subsidies and attractive housing to lure secular Jews from inside the Green Line. By the following year, government subsidies to West Bank settlements were nearly four times higher than per capita aid to Jewish residents of the Upper Galilee, according to a study by Meron Benvenisti, then director of the West Bank Data Project. The Likud government planned to construct its new settlements close to Arab population centers, so that even if relatively few Jews moved beyond the Green Line, the concentrations of Jewish settlements around Arab towns would "neutralize" them politically. The Likud's larger aim was to build enough settlements inside the territories to

---

*Given AFSI's extremist views, it is not surprising that its members are about equally divided in their support for Likud, Tehiya, and the racist Kach party founded by the late Meir Kahane. AFSI's legal counsel, Bertram Zweibon, was cofounder of the JDL. What is more surprising is that AFSI has been so adept at camouflaging its extremism, enabling it to solicit support from respectable elements in the American Jewish community by preying on fears that Israel is not secure. After the Lebanon war, for example, AFSI helped to establish a short-lived, New York–based, tax-exempt front group called P.E.A.C.E.—the Prevention of the Emergence of Another Arab Country in *Eretz Yisrael*. The group's mission was to propagate the notion that Jordan is the Palestinian homeland and to legitimize Israel's de facto annexation of the occupied territories. Among the organization's founding members were Ariel Sharon and his close friend Manhattan district attorney Robert Morgenthau, according to its letterhead and fund-raising letters.

form an interest group capable of blocking any hope of territorial compromise. Begin's attempt to build a political constituency on the West Bank was similar to what Labor had done with its communal settlements in the pre-state era.

The increase of new settlements slowed down in 1984, when Labor joined Likud in a broad national-unity coalition government. Between 1984 and 1986, the government spent $150 million on the settlements annually, $100 million less than at its peak in 1983. Only eight new settlements were built during the first coalition government, although existing settlements were "thickened" with thousands more people. In 1989, Shimon Peres, then treasury minister, blocked funds for eight new settlements that were agreed upon in the coalition deal between Labor and Likud in December 1988. So the start-up costs for a new settlement that went up on a rocky hilltop near Bir Zeit University in March 1989 were paid for with funds raised by the settlers themselves, as well as from the budget of the local regional council.

The coalition government fell in May 1990 over the issue of whether Israel should participate in the Baker peace plan, which called on Israel to hold municipal elections in the occupied territories, including East Jerusalem. Though Shamir had publicly declared his willingness to discuss the idea with Palestinians in his own 1989 four-point peace plan, he opposed the involvement of Arabs from East Jerusalem—arguing that it had already been formally annexed to Israel.

The Likud managed to form a new government by joining with several small religious parties and three parties of the ultranationalist right. One, the Moledet or Homeland party, which then had 2 seats in the 120-seat Knesset, is headed by Rahevam Ze'evi, a retired major general and former Labor party member, who seeks to transfer the Palestinians across the Jordan River. "He is Kahane in a general's uniform," said Nachum Barnea, a popular Israeli newspaper columnist. A man of imperial tastes, Ze'evi kept two full-grown pet African lions tethered outside his office when he was military commander of the West Bank in the early 1970s. After his election to the Knesset in 1988, Ze'evi tried to cajole Shamir into naming him Israel's police commissioner, but stories in the Hebrew press linking him to organized crime scuttled the appointment. Just before the Gulf War, Shamir made Ze'evi, who is inexplicably nicknamed "Gandhi," a Cabinet minister without portfolio. "Gandhi" created a diplomatic flap when he called President Bush "a liar and an anti-Semite" after Bush blocked Israel's request for a $10 billion loan guarantee to settle Soviet Jews.

In the summer of 1991, while Secretary of State James Baker was nudging Israel into peace talks with its Arab neighbors, the Shamir government initiated a land grab reminiscent of the great land grab of 1981. In the two months after the Gulf War, the government expropriated at least seventy thousand *dunams* of Palestinian land, much of it under cultivation. In the case of Artas, a Palestinian village near Bethlehem, the confiscation of fifteen hundred *dunams* virtually wiped out its agriculture. Israeli spokesmen claimed the land was legally confiscated because the Arabs could not prove they owned it. Many more thousands of *dunams* were expropriated after the Gulf War by the Israeli Army for "security reasons." In all, between January 1988 and June 1991, more than 504,120 *dunams* were confiscated on the West Bank, according to Palestinian and Israeli human-rights groups.

According to government documents obtained by Peace Now, former housing minister Sharon planned to build thirteen thousand new homes on the West Bank in 1992, increasing the Jewish population in the area by 50 percent, at a cost of more than $1 billion. The Housing Ministry offered to pay contractors a five-thousand-dollar bonus if they completed the work in less than eight weeks. More than 75 percent of the ministry's 1992 budget was earmarked for the occupied territories, where only 2.5 percent of the Jewish population lives.

Sharon also greatly increased subsidies to Jewish settlers. In 1991, a family buying a home in the West Bank could take out a $71,000 mortgage, all but $17,500 of it interest-free. The interest on the remaining sum would be 4.5 percent. After five years, $10,000 of the mortgage becomes a gift. "When you look at the mortgages, a young couple that doesn't move into the territories is an idiot," said left-wing legislator Dede Zucker. "It is clear that young couples and new immigrants without money will move into the territories because they have no other choice." The government also provides free sewage, water, and electrical lines for private homes in the territories, at a savings to a new settler of at least $15,000. If this was not inducement enough, starting in November 1990, Sharon began giving away free housing plots to Jewish settlers, who previously had to buy land from an Israeli government agency, the Land and Development Authority. The program was secret until it was exposed by the Labor party–affiliated newspaper *Davar* in July 1991. In April 1992, an official report by the State Comptroller accused the Housing Ministry of mismanagement, waste, and corruption. Sharon himself was heavily criticized in the report, which called for a criminal investigation into the activities of several Housing Ministry employees. Fallout from the Housing Ministry scandal contributed to the Likud's electoral defeat in June 1992.

The rapid rate of land expropriation, coupled with the bitterness over the failure of the *intifada* to end the occupation, has strengthened the position of Palestinian radicals who advocate terrorism. Nineteen Israelis have been killed in the territories by Palestinians since the outbreak of the *intifada,* seven of them since the eve of peace talks. The settlers complain that the army is not doing enough to quiet the Arabs and say they are justified in taking the law into their own hands. Several settlers I talked to acknowledged that they deliberately attacked Arabs, hoping to provoke a violent response that would bring in the army. In September 1989, eight settlers from Ariel were questioned by Israeli police on suspicion of firebombing Israeli property and stoning settlers to stir up anti-Arab sentiment. Israel Radio, quoting Israel's northern district police spokesman Gideon Arbel, reported that the settlers, pretending to be marauding Arabs, had attacked their fellow Israeli settlers and hurled a firebomb at an Israeli-owned car as a pretext to launch "counterattacks" against Arab villages. Ron Nachman called the allegations "a bit of a fantasy. I just can't believe it."

Yet many settlers told me that the worse they can make life for the Arabs, the easier it will be to drive them across the Jordan River. Haggai Segal, a slenderly built Gush Emunim settler from Ofra who spent three years in prison for his part in the car-bomb attacks on two West Bank mayors, said, "You can't make a big roundup and put them on buses, but you must make conditions bad for the Arabs—and if they continue the war [*intifada*], you must make them leave. I drove by the American consulate in East Jerusalem yesterday and saw a long line of Arabs waiting to get visas. The situation is very hard for them now, and it must get harder."

Expelling Israel's Arabs was hardly ever openly discussed in Israel until the *intifada*. Kahane may have broken the taboo in the early 1970s, but the *intifada* gave the concept urgency. Now prominent politicians on the "respectable right," from Likud to Gandhi's Homeland party, are recommending transfer as a solution to Greater Israel's "demographic" problem. Rafael Eitan, the hardline head of the Tzomet party and the army's chief of staff during the Lebanon war (who once referred to West Bank Arabs as "drugged cockroaches in a bottle") told *The Jerusalem Post* in 1988 that "if war breaks out and they make trouble, then we'll simply have to deport a million people." When the war in the Gulf began, the PLO ordered the residents of the occupied territories to stay at home so Eitan would not have a chance to carry out his threat.

The sentiment for transfer is strong in Ariel, where even Ron Nachman concedes that the Palestinians' "stone revolution" has shattered the "good life" publicized in the city's glossy brochures and promotional films. Besieged by the *intifada,* and increasingly isolated from their friends and families in Tel Aviv who are afraid to visit them, many residents I spoke to fear that Israel will eventually abandon them in a peace accord—unless the *intifada* is soon crushed. Indeed, for the 140-odd Jewish settlements scattered across the occupied territories, there was a new, depressing reality. Overnight, it seemed, the Palestinians had been transformed from an easily intimidated people into determined fighters—and skilled diplomats and peace negotiators. "The settlers are now facing a proud, self-confident people," said Knesset member Dede Zucker. "The rules of the game have changed."

As a result of these fears, Ariel set up its well-armed milita, which is linked to groups operating in five nearby settlements. The settlers are called to arms by an announcer who breaks into closed-circuit cable television programming broadcast from Ariel. Some Israelis, such as Zucker, have charged that an embryonic right-wing army is taking shape that could violently challenge the government if it tries to negotiate the fate of the occupied territories.

One settlers' militia thought to be operating out of Kiryat Arba has even published a guerrilla-warfare manual on combating the *intifada.* Calling on settlers to "impose justice themselves," the seven-page guide recommends that settlers shoot Palestinian stone throwers from an open car window so that spent cartridges fall inside the vehicle, making it more difficult to trace the gun. Settlers are also advised to use bullets that spread on impact so ballistic experts cannot easily identify the shell. If arrested, one should "behave like a prisoner of war: name, father's name, identity card—and that is all!" The booklet, entitled *Active Defense,* ends by severely criticizing the army's "defeatist" conduct "in confronting the daily eroding situation in Judea and Samaria."

Another militia based in Kiryat Arba, called Committee for the Safety of the Roads, has organized a number of dead-of-night armed raids on local

Arabs. "They [the Arabs] are not afraid of the soldiers, but they are afraid of us," said Shmuel Ben-Ishai, a committee cofounder. Ben-Ishai is under investigation in ten criminal cases in Israel. In 1989, settlers affiliated with the committee started using German shepherd attack dogs against Palestinian stone throwers. Dogs "are more effective than shooting," said settlement spokesman Aharon Domb.

A new militia arose on the eve of Middle East peace talks in October 1991 in a blatant attempt to derail them. Using terrorist attacks on settlers as a pretext, it staged armed raids into Arab villages, breaking windows of cars and homes and cutting down olive trees. Villagers said the settlers also cursed them and distributed leaflets vowing further reprisals. "We hope the [peace] talks will break off as soon as possible without success," said Gush Emunim official Benny Katzover, who defended the settlers' actions. "We want to exert pressure on our government." Israeli newspapers quoted police and army officers as saying privately they believed the settlers were being intentionally provocative because they were convinced the right-wing Shamir government backed them.

Members of the various militias, which carry Israeli Army weapons, have rarely been punished for illegal attacks because West Bank army commanders seek "quiet with the settlers at any price," said Zucker, who has written complaints about their behavior to the Attorney General's Office, recommending prosecution. Zucker told me that while under Israeli law it is legal for settlers to carry weapons and open fire if their lives are in danger, it is illegal for Israeli civilians to stage punitive raids against Arab villages, no matter what the provocation. As for stopping the militias, Zucker said, "The army can't cope with the *intifada;* it can hardly cope with the settlers."

Two of the founders of Ariel's militia, called Kullanu ("all of us"), are Samuel Rafaeli, a thirty-nine-year-old electronics engineer, and Yezekiel Amber, a forty-two-year-old engineer who left Iraq in 1950 as a child. They agreed to talk to me, along with Dina Shalit, the assistant to Ariel's mayor, about the frustrations that led them to create the militia and what they would do if the government evacuated the territories.

RAFAELI: "The Arabs behave like they are already in their own country. It's not just the rocks and petrol bombs. For example, they throw trash all over the road."

AMBER: "They don't care about traffic rules anymore. They've started driving their cars with six, seven, eight people in the front seat."

FRIEDMAN: "Who cares?"

SHALIT: "We care. It's not their country."

AMBER: "They are not following the rules."

RAFAELI: "It's an act of rebellion. Once you start letting them get away with this stuff—once you start retreating—you never stop . . . Everyone knows that most of the people in Bidya are peaceful. There is only a small gang from Hamas and a few Arabs from the PLO that are forcing the others to throw stones. We are fighting gangs that are hiding behind women and children. We know who the instigators are. Exile them. Throw out the troublemakers from every village on the West Bank. Just round them up and throw them away. You don't have to kill them. Just exile them and their families and blow up their houses. It will be quiet again—in two weeks."

FRIEDMAN: "What would you do if the government withdrew from the West Bank?"

RAFAELI: "On a clear day, after a rain, I can see the coastline from my home. I can't believe the Israeli government will give up this place. It would be the end of Israel. Anyway, it never belonged to the Arabs in the first place."

SHALIT: "I would take my kids to the airport and return to Canada. I would never stay in this country, because I would feel betrayed. I came to Ariel with the encouragement of the government—to a legal settlement—with a government mortgage. If the government of Israel can do that to me in Ariel, they can do that to me wherever I move in Israel."

AMBER: "If they give Ariel back, Tel Aviv will be in danger. That's how I see it. I have an obligation to my family. I cannot let them live on the coastline under Arab guns. I would leave Israel too."

As I traveled through the occupied territories talking to settlers, I was struck by their insistence that they are the weaker party in the conflict—the Palestinians, they say, have on their side the Israeli left, most of the Hebrew and foreign press, the U.S. government, and world public opinion, while they are being threatened by the shower of stones thrown at their cars. Their civil rights are being violated, they say. And in my talks with hundreds of settlers, I found that with very few exceptions they exhibited either complete indifference to the brutality employed by the army in combating the *intifada*—or complete denial of it.

"The Arabs are not being persecuted," said Rabbi Meyer Berglas, a Canadian-born founder of the Neve Aliza settlement near Nablus and dean of the Israel Institute of Technology for Women in Jerusalem. "They are not being occupied in the sense that anything evil or bad is happening to them. There is nothing whatever that is happening that is immoral. We are not in any way denying Arab rights. We are not in any way interfering with their lives. We are not in any way persecuting them [or] hurting them." On the contrary, the rabbi said, the *intifada* is a PLO-led war aimed at Israel's destruction—and the overriding Jewish moral imperative is to respond in self-defense: "There's a basic moral value, which I think is even a universal value, that if someone is coming to threaten your life, you have a right to defend yourself. You have an obligation to defend yourself. According to Hebrew law, it is forbidden to commit suicide."

I heard repeated comparisons between Palestinian stone throwers and black rioters in America. "Why don't you withdraw from Liberty City in Miami?" said Harold, a mechanic from Queens who lives in Neve Aliza. "Why don't you let them run wild and break into stores?"

Jacob Narodetsky, a mechanical engineer at Israel Aircraft Industry who moved to Israel from the Ukraine twenty years ago and who founded Bet Areye in 1980, told me that granting West Bank Arabs political rights would ultimately harm them: "The black revolt against European rule in Africa brought tragedy to the blacks. They went back in history one hundred years. The same thing would happen to the Arabs here if we gave them self-rule. It's a mistake to give people who are not politically mature the tools of democracy so they can misuse them."

Most settlers have had almost no direct contact with the Arabs who live near them on the West Bank. Yet this doesn't stop them from talking about the Arab psyche. Libby Reichman, a former New Yorker with a master of social work degree from Columbia University who lives in Efrat, a well-to-do Orthodox but not Gush Emunim settlement near Bethlehem, told me in 1989 that West Bank Arabs are much better off than Arabs elsewhere. She also said that Arabs are "inherently" brutal, that most Arab men are incapable of expressing love to their children, and that most Arabs don't care for books and education. But she told me she has never visited an Arab village in Israel or the West Bank—let alone had a conversation with a college-educated Palestinian. Virtually her only encounters with West Bank Arabs were in talking occasionally to Efrat's maintenance workers and her household help.

Libby's brother, a writer of children's books, and her sister also live in West Bank settlements. Her mother, Hadassah Marcus, is a leader of Gush Emunim in America who helped organize the suit against the JNF with her friend Ron Nachman. Libby, who told me she had twice been stoned while driving past Deheishe refugee camp with her children, said, "The *intifada* could have been destroyed if the army went in and killed everybody. It would have ended a long time ago. But that is not the Jewish way. The reason that the *intifada* stays in the headlines and the reason it goes on day after day is because Israel doesn't respond like most countries in the world would in a similar situation. . . . What hurts me, and is lost on the press, is that the reason the *intifada* goes on is because there has been such a gentle response. . . .

"If the PLO let the Arabs live in peace and stopped stirring them up with the idea that this is their country, I think they could . . . really enjoy being part of this country. I lived in America as a minority, and I was very happy. Christmas was going on outside, and it wasn't my holiday—but that was okay. I think that a minority in a country can be happy."*

A German shepherd growled menacingly as Dina Shalit and I walked up a steep cobblestone path toward the front door of the Bernsteins' sprawling home in Ariel shortly before the outbreak of the Gulf War. Fortunately, the dog was chained to a post behind a shrub. "It barks when it smells an Arab," said Mrs. Bernstein, a slatternly middle-aged woman who is the head nurse in an intensive-care unit in a Petah Tikva hospital. "The dog hates Arabs. They give off a smell. It's genetic."

"But I'm Jewish," I protested.

"Are you a leftist?" Mr. Bernstein, a tall, thin man, twittered.

"Robert sides with Peace Now," said Dina. "But he's a serious writer, and we think it would be nice if he got to know Ariel."

"Peace Now supports the PLO," said Mrs. Bernstein, perturbed that I was not of her political persuasion. "Maybe that's why the dog went crazy. Listen, you can't turn your back on an Arab. Do you know why Arabs

---

*Libby Reichman was so displeased with the way I portrayed her in a 1989 *New York Review of Books* article about the settlers that she wrote to the Israeli weekly newspaper *Kol Ha'ir,* which reviewed the article, to complain that I perversely distorted her remarks. "To act as a host to Friedman was just like sitting on the mouth of a volcano," huffed Reichman, who had invited me to her Efrat home one Shabbat. "After Friedman left on Saturday night, I was wondering how could a person who is so interested in violent subjects digest such a restful and refreshing Shabbos." Later, Reichman complained about me in a letter to the Israeli Government Press Office, in an attempt to dissuade the government from issuing me a press card.

don't have friends? Because they will stab anyone—even their own mother—in the back. They will tear your heart out the first chance they get!"

To illustrate the point, the Bernsteins told me about the brutal murder of Ariel resident Frederick Rosenfeld, a forty-eight-year-old settler from Washington, D.C. It was at Rosenfeld's funeral that irate settlers attacked Prime Minister Shamir's motorcade. Rosenfeld, a divorcé, had been walking alone in the hills near Ariel one afternoon in 1989, when he was approached by three Arab shepherds from the nearby village of Salfit. The Arabs, in their early twenties, chatted amiably with Rosenfeld, then shared a picnic lunch. Afterward, the Palestinians asked if he would photograph them with the camera he had brought along on his hike. The Arabs smiled for the camera; one grinning Arab wore a blue T-shirt with the word "peace" printed on it. Minutes after the picture was taken, they stabbed Rosenfeld in the back with a hunting knife, then fled, thinking he was dead. Rosenfeld had the presence of mind to take the film from the camera and hide it in his pants before he bled to death, the knife still embedded in his back. Remembering the camera, the Arabs returned and smashed it on a rock. Then they stole Rosenfeld's pistol and a pair of binoculars. The body was discovered at 8:00 P.M. that evening by an Arab villager, who alerted the army. Israeli police found the film and used it to identify, and subsequently convict, Rosenfeld's attackers. "You see why you can't turn your back on an Arab?" Mr. Bernstein said at the end of the story.

The Bernstein family made *aliyah* in 1969 from the United States. An aeronautical engineer at Israel Aircraft Industries, Mr. Bernstein works in the electronic-warfare department, where he is an antenna expert. The couple have four children; two were born in Israel. One, a fifteen-year-old high school student named Aliza, eyed me suspiciously. "All the kids my age are supporters of Kahane or Moledet," she proclaimed, hoping, I thought, to provoke me. "Tehiya is too moderate for kids my age. We are very hotheaded."

Her brother, a muscle-bound high school student, told me that he was considered the liberal of his class. "I want Arabs out," he said, "but I'm not crazy. Kahane says kill the Arabs. That's crazy."

Other than Arabs, Mrs. Bernstein's main obsession is eight Jewish families in Ariel who are members of Jews for Jesus, a religious cult that believes Jesus is the true Messiah of the Jewish people. After they started proselytizing elementary school students, Mrs. Bernstein organized a committee to pressure them to leave Ariel. The committee tried to get local merchants to refuse their business. But the Jews for Jesus people turned to the Israeli Justice Ministry, which threatened to prosecute members of the committee for discriminatory behavior. "There were hotheads who wanted to get violent against them," Mrs. Bernstein offered, "but we turned them down."

I was supposed to spend the night as the Bernsteins' houseguest, but they made me ill at ease. After dinner, Dina took me to her house to spend the night. "I'm sorry I brought you there," Dina said as she drove down a wide, nearly deserted street lined with large villas with lushly landscaped yards. I thought she was referring to the Bernsteins' ugly remarks. It wasn't that, Dina said. She didn't want me to know that in Israel's so-called "city of tomorrow," there was a problem with cults. "The Jews for Jesus people are Americans," Dina said. "They are very friendly and well bred. We didn't know they were Jews for Jesus until they started to proselytize. We ostracized them, hoping they would leave, but it didn't work. We even offered to buy them out."

Dina's large three-story home was, to put it charitably, disheveled. Her husband, Mendy, was sprawled out in front of the TV on a thickly upholstered reclining chair, watching the news, and sucking on a bottle of cold Maccabee beer. Dressed in a T-shirt and jeans, he sputtered obscenities every time an Arab appeared on the tube. Mendy had moved to Israel from Canada in 1983 at the age of thirty-three. He never served in the IDF and now works for Moked Gilad, the largest private security company on the West Bank. In 1989, the company won a lucrative government contract to protect *mukhtars* who collaborated with the occupation authorities. One of their clients was Mustafa Abu Bakr, Bidya's corrupt *mukhtar*.

In an exposé of Moked Gilad that appeared in the Israeli daily newspaper *Yediot Achronot*, reporters Yigal Sarna and Anat Tal-Shir told the following story: "One afternoon in the winter of 1989," the article began, "six men from the Moked Gilad security company, carrying walkie-talkies, pistols, and submachine guns, came in two cars to a . . . construction site in Ariel. They came to carry out a 'sentence' against construction worker Ma'azua Mareita, who was fourteen-years-old.

"They brought a [Jewish] girl with them. She pointed at the youth, who was standing in front of a muddy pit, and said, 'He's the one who tried to hug and kiss me.' The men aimed their weapons at the other [Arab] workers and said that anyone who moved would get a bullet. Ma'azua was pushed inside one of the cars, and the little convoy drove off.

"They drove quickly in the direction of the deserted Ariel science park with its huge empty structures. There, next to one of the buildings, far from any witnesses, they pulled out Ma'azua, who had been beaten on the way. When he fell to the concrete floor, they resumed beating him. They kicked his head, his abdomen, his groin, and his limbs, and they cursed him. One of the men was the girl's father, a kibbutznik who was working as a security man for Moked Gilad. 'Dry blows,' said their commander, Roni Gilad, meaning punches and kicks in the abdomen that don't leave marks.

"Then the commander ordered his men to stop the beating. He pulled out his pistol and ordered the youth to stand against the wall. Gilad aimed the pistol at the youth's head and pressed the metal barrel against his temple. Ma'azua wailed and trembled. Gilad squeezed the trigger. There was a hollow click. The pistol wasn't loaded.

"When the 'execution' was over, they wiped the blood off the youth's face, loaded him into one of the cars, and delivered him to the Ariel police like a crumpled package."*

Dina's husband wouldn't talk about his work with Moked Gilad. Dina said he is the company's director of sales. Other settlers I met told me he sometimes works as an armed guard.

Dina and I stayed up late talking *tachlis*—the Yiddish word for getting to the heart of the matter. We are close in age, enjoy each other's sense of humor, and, in another time or place, might have become friends. What most stands between us is her theory of Zionism. "Zionism *is* racism," she said, echoing the infamous UN resolution condemning Israel as an apartheid state, which was rescinded in December 1991. "Zionism means an exclusively Jewish state. If you think Palestinians should have a state here, do you also think America should be returned to the Indians? You slaughtered them—so who are you to tell us how to conduct our affairs? If blacks became a majority, would you turn over America to them? Would you still believe in one man, one vote?"

---

*Shortly after Roni Gilad's arrest in connection with the beating, Israeli's attorney general concluded there was not enough evidence to prosecute him, and dismissed the case. Knesset member Dede Zucker publicly complained that the dismissal amounted to negligence, arguing that, as so often happens when Palestinians file charges against settlers, the police investigation was lax. Gilad refused the author's request for an interview.

No matter how often I visited the settlements, I told Dina, I was always amazed at how illiberal those Jews who came from the Western democracies to live in the territories were. Raised in societies that place a premium on civil rights and the rule of law, they come to Israel and behave like beer-guzzling rednecks. Kullanu and Moked Gilad were no different, I said, from the Ku Klux Klan. And in his cowboy getup, Ron Nachman was like the J. R. Ewing of Judea and Samaria. I recalled that Nachman had been severely criticized, even by Likud party leaders, when in June 1989 he proposed that Arab workers entering Ariel be forced to wear colored tags identifying them as "alien workers." Nachman backed down after Israeli critics compared the tags to the yellow Stars of David that Jews were forced to wear in Nazi Germany.

Unlike Ariel's unreflective mayor, some settlers in Ariel look in the mirror and see the ugly Israeli. One is Yael Steinfeld, a pert forty-year-old mother who is working on a master's degree in social work at Tel Aviv University. Raised by staunch Labor party parents, she used to argue with her father about her move to the territories until they agreed not to talk about politics anymore. "My parents said we were nuts to live among the Arabs," said Yael, who was born with a withered right arm, a result of her mother taking thalidomide when she was pregnant. "We had a big apartment in Petah Tikva, but we wanted to be *chalutzim,* pioneers." Yael lives in a beautifully furnished home built by local Arab laborers. It has a large, modern kitchen, a spiral staircase in the living room, and a picture window that looks out onto a pristine valley. Her husband, who was born in Poland and moved to Israel in 1957, is a well-paid engineer at IAI.

"When I came here in the first *garin* in 1979, everyone told me go and build a new city and help Israel grow and be strong—not strong in the sense that we would oppress the Arabs, just to help Israel to be a big, strong country," said Yael. "Now everyone looks at me and thinks I am a bad girl. My friends at the university don't say it to my face, but I feel it—and sometimes I want to leave here. Before the *intifada,* Israelis thought it was interesting that I lived in Ariel. Today, I look at a person's face and wonder if I should tell them where I live.

"I am doing a project in graduate school with four other girls. We're supposed to take turns working at each other's homes. They won't come here. It's a horrible thing. Some won't come here because they are afraid. Some won't come out of principle. They make me feel like a bad girl. And

I don't think I'm worse than anyone else in the class. I think I'm a very good person, and I don't like it when they make me feel bad. I don't think I'm doing anything bad to anyone really.

"You asked me before what I would say to an Arab if he told me, 'Go away, it's my land.' When the Six-Day War began, I was eighteen years old. We never dreamed we would have such an incredible victory. Many of my friends had just gone to the army, and they died. It was a terrible trauma. I had just finished high school. You just start to live, and some of your friends die. We felt, and I still feel, that we didn't ask for this land—we didn't fight because we wanted to make a bigger Israel. We fought because the Arabs made us. And now you just can't come and say, What are you doing here?

"We didn't come and settle here immediately after the war because the government thought they would have to give this land back for peace. But time passed. Nothing happened. The Arab governments didn't ask for peace.

"So I would tell the Arab that I didn't ask for this land. I was forced to take it. And secondly, I would say, although I feel it is my land, I'm ready to give up parts of it. Under the right circumstances, I would be willing to leave. I wouldn't leave because I want to. I'd do it because I don't think there is another solution. I won't fight for it. You've probably heard people say they'll take rifles and fight the army. No. I won't fight for it. I do want peace. But I want a real peace that guarantees Israel's security. If Israel withdraws, I won't sit in Ariel. I'm an Israeli citizen, not a Palestinian."

Osama Odeh, my Palestinian acquaintance from Bidya, was late. We were supposed to meet at the office of his cousin, a dentist, in downtown Ramallah. We had planned to spend the day together in Bidya, nearly two years after my first visit. I sat in a small anteroom with peeling green walls adorned by a painting of an old Arab man, hobbled by the weight of a burlap sack slung over his shoulder as he entered the main portal of Jerusalem's Old Walled City. As I waited, Dr. Ramawi, Osama's cousin, introduced me to a patient, Feryel Salam. A short woman, she was covered from head to toe by a long ash-gray gown and scarf. Her face was horribly scarred, and she was missing several fingers on her right hand. Her left eye was made of glass.

In 1977, a colleague of Feryel's was killed instantly when a terrorist bomb he was making prematurely exploded. Feryel, who was standing on the man's porch, was knocked unconscious by the force of the blast. Besides the grievous injuries to her face, both of her legs and arms were broken. When she regained consciousness seven days later, Israeli soldiers were standing guard over her hospital bed. One soldier placed a pocket mirror in front of her and, with a cruel laugh, ordered her to look at her face.

"I knew my friend was making a bomb," Feryel told me, "but I told Shin Bet I didn't. The Shin Bet agent said he was alive and had confessed. I was sure he was dead. I said nothing. I received an eight-year prison sentence. Otherwise, it would have been twenty to twenty-five years."

After she was released from prison, she traveled to Paris, where plastic surgeons repaired her face. The surgery was paid for by the Franco-Palestinian Medical Association. During her stay in France, she studied at the Sorbonne and received a master's degree in geography. As we spoke, Osama and his sister, a matronly looking high school teacher at a nearby refugee camp, joined us. "Feryel was my geography teacher," said Osama's sister, as the two women embraced. "I'm so proud of her!"

Osama himself had just got out of jail. He owns a small electroplating factory in Ramallah and a large olive-oil processing plant in Bidya. In January 1991, he received a letter from the Israeli tax authorities, stating that he owed twenty-five thousand shekels, or nearly thirteen thousand dollars, in back taxes. He drove to military headquarters on the West Bank, bringing with him his business records and documentation of various sorts. "They wouldn't even look at the books," Osama said. He was immediately handcuffed and driven to a tent prison compound outside Ramallah, where he spent four days before he was transferred to a large prison in Jeneid near Nablus on the West Bank. "There was no appeal process," said Osama, who was permitted to leave after he paid twenty thousand shekels.

As Osama and I drove along the Trans-Samarian Highway, past terraced ridges, quaint Arab villages, and huge refugee camps, he told me that the Israeli Army had just lifted a state of siege at Bidya. A twenty-four-hour-a-day curfew had been clamped over the village, and several hundred Israeli soldiers had encamped in town after Bidya's youth went on a rampage, showering setters' vehicles with stones and Molotov cocktails.

Bidya, as I was to learn, had a long history of violence and rebellion—and Osama's family had always played a key role in it. Originally Bedouin from Taif, Saudi Arabia, the Odeh clan migrated to Palestine some five hundred years ago. One branch settled in Gaza, another in Bidya, where it became the predominant clan. Known for their prowess in martial arts, many clansmen fought in the Ottoman Turkish Army against the Russians in the Crimean War. One very old man in Bidya, known as Hosni the Trumpeter, is said by villagers to be a veteran of that war.

In 1936, when Palestinian Arabs began a three-year revolt against the British, Bidya became a staging base for *fedayeen* or Palestinian guerrillas. The British Army was far more brutal putting down the revolt than the Israeli Army has been during the *intifada*. British planes strafed Arab villages, thousands of Palestinians were herded into concentration camps, and Mandatory authorities passed emergency laws that made the possession of a gun—or even ammunition—a crime punishable by death. More than ten thousand Palestinians were killed in the fighting. In the time-honored tradition of the Arab world—where the enemy of my enemy is my friend— some prominent Palestinians, including the grand mufti of Jerusalem, joined the Axis during the Second World War. "My uncle met Mussolini and was fascinated with Fascism," Osama matter-of-factly said.

The Odehs were later in the forefront of Palestinian opposition to Jordan's King Hussein—a Hashemite originally from Saudi Arabia who treated West Bank Palestinians with high-handed contempt. The Jordanian Arab Legion occupied the West Bank and East Jerusalem in 1948 during its war with Israel. The territory had been set aside by the UN for an independent Palestinian state. Only Britain and Pakistan recognized Jordan's annexation of the West Bank. "Middle-class, educated Palestinians of Jerusalem and other West Bank towns who had thought of Transjordan as a desert backwater (if they thought of it at all) and who had never seen any reason to visit Amman, now found themselves subjects of the Hashemite king," wrote Middle East scholar Michael C. Hudson. In 1951, when Hussein was a teenager, his grandfather, King Abdullah, was gunned down in front of him by an angry Palestinian at Jerusalem's al-Aqsa Mosque. In 1959, fifteen high officials of the Jordanian military, including Osama's uncle, plotted King Hussein's assassination. But the Jordanian *mukhabarut,* or secret police, discovered the scheme, and the plotters were sentenced to death. Osama's entire family was forcibly expelled from Bidya and exiled to the desert south of Aqaba, where they remained for several years before returning to Bidya. Shortly before he was to be hanged, Osama's uncle won a reprieve and left for Iraq.

In 1967, just before the outbreak of the Six-Day War, Osama's father founded Bidya's high school for boys. (Osama's grandfather had established Bidya's first elementary school in 1922.) "When the Israelis came to our village [in June 1967]," said Osama, "they made a gentlemen's agreement with my father and uncle, a lawyer. 'We know your family is very nationalistic and won't accept occupation,' they said, 'so if the *fedayeen* [Palestinian guerrillas] come to Bidya, you can feed them so long as you then tell them to go. We will give you money for your new school and build roads and sewers.' The first three or four years of Israeli rule were good. Then the relationship deteriorated because of the corruption of the Israeli-installed collaborators and, later, the growth of Ariel."

The Israeli-appointed *mukhtar*, Mustafa Abu Bakr, was the son of a black Sudanese slave. The Arab slave trade was quite active in Palestine until the British put a stop to it. Abu Bakr was said to have had an inferiority complex about his ancestry. He never attended high school, and until he went to work for the Israelis was a simple shepherd. At first, Bidya's elders did not protest Abu Bakr's appointment, believing that "it was better to know your enemy," said Osama.

Then Abu Bakr started stealing villagers' land. The crafty *mukhtar* tricked people into signing papers that they believed were applications for social welfare, or birth certificates, or appeals to military courts to be lenient with their sons, when, in fact, they were documents that transferred their land to Israeli construction companies. Once, Abdul-Rahmin al-Akra, a seventy-year-old Bidya resident, was drugged and his thumb prints were placed on a document deeding his land to Ariel. In another case, an elderly man from Bidya went to Abu Bakr to complain that a neighbor had assaulted him. Abu Bakr took the man to an Arab lawyer. The man's "affidavit" describing the attack turned out to be a contract for the sale of the man's land. Then there was Mustafa Akra of Bidya, who was shot dead by border police as he tried to prevent Israeli bulldozers from breaking ground for a Jewish housing project on his farm. The land had been fraudulently brokered by Abu Bakr. At least one dozen Palestinians have been killed in disputes arising from fraudulent land sales.

At the same time that Abu Bakr was bamboozling villagers out of their land, the economy went sour. High taxes and limited access to foreign markets systematically ruined Bidya's agriculture. More and more villagers were forced to leave farming and become day laborers in Israel. Meanwhile, Bidya's olive-oil business, its largest cash crop, has been decimated. Osama claimed that more than five thousand of Bidya's olive trees have been chopped down by the army and settlers during the first three years of the *intifada*. The region lost many more olive trees, he said, when Israeli road crews straightened out a bend in the Trans-Samarian Highway linking Tel Aviv to the Jordan Valley. Some of the lush green olive trees, called Romanies, are more than five hundred years old. "The Israelis are ruining the natural topography," said Osama. "Our beautiful hills, our fauna, the graceful old Arab homes, are being replaced by Jewish cities and rip-and-tear roads. Who knows what Ariel is dumping into the ground? We have no power to control it. People are crying about the [destruction of the] Amazon rain forest. No one mentions this. We need Greenpeace."

When we arrived at Bidya, the main entrance was blocked by a knot of heavily armed Israeli soldiers in riot gear. "A shooting took place," said a soldier, who looked no more than eighteen. "The road is closed. If you go in, we will shoot you."

We drove to a cluster of neat single-story homes just outside the village, where we called on one of Osama's cousins, a high school teacher, who met us at the front door in his pajamas. His sons, who were in pajamas too, joined us on the front porch, while burly women in peasant dresses hovered about serving sweets and coffee. Earlier that day, Osama's cousin told me, a group of about ten to fifteen masked *shebab* (youth) entered the village's four schools with megaphones. The *shebab* told the elementary school children to go home, but ordered the high school students to participate in an anti-Israeli demonstration. Israeli soldiers had raided the village twice in the past week, making many arrests and forcing people to sweep the streets and whitewash nationalist graffiti. "It was humiliating and provocative," Osama's cousin said. "So today, the *shebab* struck back."

The students gathered in the center of the village shouting anti-Israeli slogans under a huge banner that said FATAH AND HAMAS TOGETHER. Then hundreds of youth marched to the Trans-Samarian Highway. "I was on the roof," said Osama's cousin. "I saw boys and girls stone two settlers' cars." Soldiers raced to the scene and shot in the air, trying to disperse the demonstrators, he said. Then, several armed settlers got out of their cars and fanned out among the almond trees that lined the side of the road and started shooting. Akhlam Abed, a thirteen-year-old girl, was shot dead. She was Bidya's first casualty of the *intifada*. "She was stoning settlers when she was shot," admitted Osama's cousin. "If more soldiers hadn't arrived, there would be more dead."

"Are you sympathetic to the *shebab*?" I asked.

"Very sympathetic," said Osama's cousin.

"The masked youth hold the spirit of our nation in their hands," Osama interjected. "They risk their lives for us, so are accorded great respect. They are our avant-garde—leading the fight against the Israelis."

We decided it was best to return to Jerusalem before dusk, when Arab stone throwers have a hard time distinguishing between Palestinian and Israeli license plates. By the time we said our good-byes, however, it was dark. As we cruised down the Trans-Samarian Highway, which cuts through Palestine's ancient hills, dozens of bonfires lit the night sky. It was the season when Arab families stayed up the entire evening harvesting olives. Osama talked at great length about expanding his family's olive-oil business.

The reverie ended in front of an Israeli roadblock. Soldiers in flak jackets and lime-green berets glared ominously inside the car and asked to see our identity cards. We had been stopped on the road in front of Jalazone refugee camp, nestled in a picturesque valley below. Four watchtowers stood like sentinels above the camp, their spires fixed with observation decks and powerful binoculars. A small blimp silently floated overhead, a minivideocamera in its nose transmitting pictures to army headquarters. Jalazone is home to hundreds of families who fled or were expelled from Palestine during Israel's 1948 War of Independence. More than seven hundred thousand Palestinians became part of the great exodus, which they call the *nakbah,* or the catastrophe. Palestinians talk about it as Jews talk about the Holocaust. It is the grandchildren of the generation of 1948 who are waging the stone revolution. "The first act of regaining our land is regaining our dignity," said Osama. "The children are heroes." The soldiers waved us on, and Osama spoke of his desire to market his family's olive oil in America. "I'd call it Holy Land olive oil," he said, adding that the label would be green and white, the colors of the Palestinian flag.

CHAPTER 4

The Priestly Crown

No settlement activity has created so much controversy as Jewish efforts to "redeem" East Jerusalem's Old City from its Christian and Muslim inhabitants. The roots of the controversy date back to the first night of Hanukkah in December 1978, when eight young Orthodox Jews announced they had set up a yeshiva in the Muslim Quarter of East Jerusalem's Old City. They called it Ateret Cohanim, "the Priestly Crown." The yeshiva students said they came to the Old City to prepare for the last battle—the quintessential struggle between good and evil that will precede the End of Days and the Redemption of Mankind. The students said they wanted to study the ancient priestly texts in anticipation of the coming of the Messiah and the rebuilding of the Second Temple, which they believe are imminent. Although al-Aqsa Mosque and the Dome of the Rock now tower over the ruins of the Second Temple, the students contend that removing the Muslim holy place is the final step on the path to the Messianic Age.

Matityahu Dan, the powerfully built, bearded yeshiva student and army veteran who founded the Priestly Crown, is a disciple of Rav Zvi Yehuda Kook—the spiritual leader of Gush Emunim. Kook encouraged Dan to devote himself to the question of how the Third Temple should function once it was brought into being. Soon students in rumpled shirts and slacks were studying how to slaughter a red heifer, whose ashes must be mixed with incense and then used to purify the high priests before they enter the temple. Other students practiced weaving the sacred garments to be worn by the temple high priests, while chemists mixed squid and snail extracts, trying to recreate a bluish-purple dye that was used in priestly robes some two thousand years ago.

Dan had more on his mind than mastering ancient rituals, however. He believed Gush Emunim's holy crusade to settle and rebuild Judea and Samaria should be carried into East Jerusalem itself. If Judea and Samaria were the heart of the ancient Land of Israel, then Jerusalem and the Temple Mount were its soul. How, he asked, could the Messiah come to Jerusalem if Jerusalem was no longer an exclusively Jewish city, the kind of city described by the prophet Isaiah? "Dan became a regular fixture in the halls of the Knesset, lobbying for Jewish settlement in the [Muslim Quarter of the] Old City," said Yisrael Medad, a leader of the ultranationalist Tehiya party. According to Medad, Dan became closely associated with Ariel Sharon, who at the time was agriculture minister, in charge of Israel's settlement program in the occupied territories.

In the early 1980s, Dan founded the Jerusalem Reclamation Project, a division of Ateret Cohanim. Its goal was to buy the estimated eleven hundred properties in the Old City's Muslim Quarter, thus helping to turn Jerusalem (including its Muslim and Christian holy places) into an entirely Jewish city—the prelude to redemption. Many Jews had lived in the Muslim Quarter before 1936, when pogroms and political unrest drove the last Jews out. "We will not employ fanaticism to embrace [our] vision," an internal Ateret Cohanim memorandum said. "That is why it is a difficult goal to carry out—because we must move carefully and cautiously . . . every piece of property we buy cements our ties to the heart of Jerusalem. Every new [Jewish] family that moves into a redeemed house means an Arab family of larger numbers has willingly consented to move. . . ."

Ateret Cohanim initially hoped it could establish a benign Jewish presence in the Muslim Quarter—a winding labyrinth of narrow cobblestone streets crowded with outdoor meat and vegetable markets, donkeys laden with produce, and caravans of Western tourists hunting for bargains. It even set up a dental clinic for its Arab neighbors. But tensions grew as the group enlarged its property holdings among the twenty thousand Muslims in the quarter, which has the highest population density in Israel. At the same time, other yeshivas, less sensitive to Muslim sensibilities, moved into the quarter, while another group of zealots, the Temple Mount Faithful, began to agitate for the right to hold religious and political demonstrations on the Temple Mount where the Dome of the Rock now stands—a right denied to Jews by the Israeli government. One of the most disruptive yeshivas in the Muslim Quarter is Shuvu Banim, whose students pore over the teachings of nineteenth-century Hasidic mystic Nachman of Breslav, frequently climbing onto the yeshvia roof in the dead of night to sing magical incantations in full voice. By day, according to Jerusalem city officials, they have been known to brandish lead pipes to beat and intimidate their Arab neighbors. More ominously, Israeli police have uncovered numerous plots by Jewish extremists, including radical members of Gush Emunim, to blow up the Dome of the Rock.

Even students at Ateret Cohanim have occasionally clashed with local Arabs. In 1982, Ateret Cohanim students began to tunnel under the Temple Mount in search of a chamber where King Solomon is thought to have hidden many of the gold vessels used in the First Temple. Arab guards heard the digging, a riot ensued, and Israeli police later sealed the tunnel. "Of course we want to take the place of the Moslems on the Mount and clear away their mosque," Ateret Cohanim's director of public relations in Jerusalem, Menachem Bar-Shalom, wrote to Monroe Spen, an American Jewish militant from Sarasota, Florida, in March 1986. "But I don't think that violent means are a solution."

By 1987 Ateret Cohanim, according to the organization's officials, owned more than seventy properties in the Muslim Quarter, worth an estimated $10 million. Their holdings included a yeshiva that had been a synagogue before 1936, several other buildings that were converted into student dormitories, a museum, and about fifty apartment units housing some two hundred persons. Some of the property acquired by Ateret Cohanim had belonged to Jews who had at one time lived in the quarter. Ateret Cohanim officials estimate that the cost to purchase the rest of the buildings in the Muslim Quarter is $100 million, with another $100 million for renovations.

Working out of a cluttered office in the Muslim Quarter, Ateret Cohanim salesmen show prospective Jewish real estate buyers three maps. In one, East Jerusalem is empty of Jews, as it was under Jordanian rule between 1948 and 1967. A second map shows the changes that have transformed Jerusalem under Israeli rule, which began after the June 1967 Six-Day War, when the government bulldozed a Muslim neighborhood in front of the Wailing Wall* in order to create a grand open plaza for

*The Jordanian government had turned the Wailing Wall into a public latrine.

religious observance, and began to restore the Old City's Jewish Quarter, whose inhabitants had been forcibly expelled by the Jordanian Legion during Israel's War of Independence. In a third map, the Dome of the Rock has been replaced by a splendorous Jewish temple. For the first time since the Herodian period, Ateret Cohanim officials say, a wholly Jewish Jerusalem is possible if Jews outside Israel will financially support it. "I appeal to all those who are so able to give a helping hand [to Ateret Cohanim] in this sacred burden . . . and restore the light on the Torah to within the Old City of Jerusalem," Avraham Chana Shapira, the Ashkenazi chief rabbi of Israel, wrote in a 1984 fund-raising letter on behalf of Ateret Cohanim that was circulated among well-to-do observant Jews in America.

Ateret Cohanim's messianic vision directly contradicts Jerusalem mayor Teddy Kollek's policy of keeping the Old City's four quarters—Muslim, Christian, Armenian, and Jewish—culturally separate. To preserve the homogeneity of the Jewish Quarter, Israel's High Court ruled in 1981 that non-Jews could not buy property there. But there are no laws prohibiting Jews from buying property or living in Arab East Jerusalem. "We don't have apartheid in Israel," said Nachum Barnea, a columnist for the popular Israeli daily *Yediot Achronot.* "Teddy Kollek wants to keep the city ghettoized with people living in their separate religious and ethnic enclaves, but he doesn't have the power to hold the mosaic together anymore." Kollek's languid, chain-smoking aide Rafi Davara once told me that "four or five times when we heard that Ateret Cohanim was negotiating with Arab property owners in the Old City, we went in and put pressure on the Arabs *not to sell.* We can slow them down, but we can't stop them."

That became painfully evident on April 11, 1990, during the Easter Holy Week and Passover, when 150 armed Jewish settlers affiliated with Ateret Cohanim moved into the seventy-room St. John's Hospice near the Church of the Holy Sepulchre. The hospice is owned by the Greek Orthodox Church, but it had been leased since 1932 to an elusive Armenian by the name of Martyos Matossian, who rented rooms to Arab families and European pilgrims. On June 28, 1989, Matossian sublet the building for $3.5 million to a mysterious Panamanian company called SBC Ltd., which turned over the building to the settlers. The settlers renamed the site Ne'ot David, put up a Star of David, and invited Ariel Sharon for a visit.

Sharon had created a furor two years earlier when he occupied an apartment in the Muslim Quarter that had been purchased for him by Ateret Cohanim. Sharon had an enormous menorah placed on his roof and draped a huge Israeli flag over the side of the building. It now costs some $156,000 annually to provide security for the general for the few nights a month he spends in the apartment.

Yet the settlers expressed surprise that their venture into the Christian Quarter* touched off riots and condemnation in Israel and throughout the world. All the major Christian churches in Israel and the occupied territories closed on Friday, April 27, 1990, and rang funeral peals in protest. It was the first time that the Church of the Holy Sepulchre had been closed in eight hundred years. New York's John Cardinal O'Connor went so far as to denounce the takeover as an "obscene" plot to acquire Christian property in the Holy Land. Sharon attributed these protests to anti-Semitism and the PLO.

Prime Minister Yitzhak Shamir initially denied that his government had helped the settlers. But David Levy, who was then housing minister, revealed that $1.8 million had been covertly channeled by his ministry to the Himnutta Company, a subsidiary of the Jewish National Fund.† The Himnutta Company then passed the money to subsidize the purchase of the sublease to the mysterious SBC. The Greek Orthodox Church, which has considerable real estate holdings in West Jerusalem, argued that the sublet to SBC was illegal, on the grounds that the original lease agreement with Matossian prohibited subleasing. The church's claim was subsequently upheld by an Israeli court, which then ordered the settlers to vacate the property but permitted twenty security and maintenance employees to remain in the building pending further litigation. The "employees" are actually settlers from Ateret Cohanim who are living in the hospice with their families.

A key figure in the scheme to acquire St. John's Hospice was Shmuel Evyatar, a gaunt, bearded former Mossad officer with a gift for languages (he speaks five fluently), and a fascination with Christianity. Blessed with a beautiful voice, he enjoys singing Christian hymns and spirituals in Latin. According to those who know him, Evyatar joined Mossad right out of college, easily passed its brutal indoctrination and training program, and was sent to Mossad's London station as a rising star.

---

*According to Israel's Statistical Yearbook of 1988, 3,900 Christians and 700 Muslims lived in the Christian Quarter.

†The Housing Ministry has been quietly helping Ateret Cohanim purchase Arab real estate since at least 1986, according to *The Jerusalem Post*.

Sometime in the late 1970s, Evyatar was transferred to Mossad's station in Junieh, Lebanon, as an expert on Christian affairs. He arrived soon after Mossad had placed on its payroll Bashir Gemayel, the baby-faced Lebanese gangster who had a taste for shiny silk suits, attractive women, and pornography. As the head of the twenty-two-thousand-member Maronite Catholic Phalangist militia, Bashir was Mossad's Great White Hope. Mossad had calculated that with generous supplies of covert arms and money, the Christians could defeat the PLO and its Muslim allies in West Beirut and unify Lebanon under the tutelage of Israel.*

Certainly, Israel's proximity and support had been a comfort to the Christians through the darkest days of Lebanon's civil war. Traumatized by a lingering war that they felt could end with their annihilation, these Maronites nursed a fierce hatred of the Muslims, and especially Lebanon's large and unruly Palestinian population, which they blamed for triggering the conflict. Pro-Israeli slogans in French and Arabic were prominent on Christian East Beirut walls—and in the militia barracks. Evyatar constantly heard that only Israel stood between the Christians and genocide. This fear fueled sentiment among the poor and middle class for a separate Christian state, regardless of its probable economic and political isolation from the Arab world.

Convinced that the Phalange would fight alongside Israel, Mossad sent back glowing reports about the New World Order the Maronites and Jews would create after public enemy number one—the PLO, which had built a formidable armed presence in Lebanon—was destroyed. The problem was that many in the Phalange, including the movement's founder, Bashir's father, Pierre, didn't much care for Israel. Pierre had developed an affinity for Fascism on a visit to Italy and Germany in 1936. "I was immensely impressed by what I saw," he told me during an interview in 1981 at his East Beirut headquarters near the demarcation line, a netherworld of fortified bunkers and bombed-out buildings. "I saw well-organized, hardworking, disciplined youth toiling to build a dynamic, well-ordered society. I wanted to create an organization in Lebanon that could instill the same kind of civic and moral courage I saw the Italians and Germans developing in their youngsters." The Phalangist party, a paramilitary organization founded in 1936 after Pierre's return from Europe, was modeled after Hitler's Brownshirts.

*Bashir Gemayel had been on the CIA's payroll since the early 1970s, according to Bob Woodward in his book *Veil*.

The Maronites' Jesuit religious training also nurtured their anti-Semitism. The ruling Maronite Christian upper class was, almost without exception, educated at East Beirut's Jesuit Catholic University. Its rector, John Ducrie, has left his imprint on three generations of Christian leaders. This Maronite Svengali, as he was sometimes called, was violently anti-Semitic and anti-Israel, and supported the concept of a military-technocratic state that would have good relations with the Arab world. "He controlled Pierre like a puppet," said a Phalangist official who knew them both.

More than that, the Phalange craved the good life, which they paid for through their control of Lebanon's rampant vice trade, including hashish smuggling and extortionist protection "taxes." Junieh Bay, where Mossad maintained its office, thrived even during the height of the civil war, which would leave more than two hundred thousand Lebanese dead. In 1980, twenty-seven tourist complexes, then worth about $3 billion and featuring ultramodern duplexes, Olympic-sized swimming pools, and marinas, were built between Junieh Bay, twelve miles north of Beirut, and the Maronite enclave's northern border near Tripoli. Inland resorts with Las Vegas–style casinos and discos glittered from mountaintops. Violence was close, but as before the civil war, everyone looked remarkably elegant, dressed in the latest Paris fashions. Although most Maronites wanted to rid Lebanon of the Palestinians and the Syrian Army, which occupied parts of the country, they hoped Israel would do it for them—then retreat across the border.

Somehow, Mossad confused the Maronites' virulent hatred of the Palestinians, their obsequious flattery, and *joie de vivre* with camaraderie and a steadfast fighting spirit. To be fair, the Phalange told the Israelis exactly what they wanted to hear. During the early 1980s, Ariel Sharon made secret visits to Bashir's yacht on Junieh Bay, where the young warlord promised the hawkish general that he would attack PLO positions in West Beirut as soon as Israeli tanks rolled across Lebanon's southern border. Sharon took these empty promises to Begin. When PLO renegade Abu Nidal's gunmen shot and seriously wounded the Israeli ambassador to England, Shlomo Argov, late in the evening of June 3, 1982, Sharon had the excuse he needed to invade Lebanon. The PLO's destruction in Lebanon, Sharon believed, would pave the way for Israel's annexation of the occupied territories. Without the PLO to lead them, the Palestinians' opposition to Jewish control of the occupied territories would collapse.

Sharon's grandiose scheme, nurtured by Mossad's optimistic reports, proved disastrously misguided. The Phalange never fired a shot during the war. Israeli troops, who defeated the Palestinians in the war, derisively called Phalangist troops "chocolate soldiers." After the Israelis routed the PLO from Lebanon, a Phalange unit entered the Sabra and Shatila Palestinian refugee quarters in West Beirut, and turned it into a killing field, methodically murdering more than one thousand unarmed women and children. The massacre was committed in full view of Mossad and Israeli Army officers who stood on the roof of a nearby building scanning the area with powerful binoculars. Television pictures of the bloated, mutilated bodies drew hundreds of thousands of Israelis into the streets of Tel Aviv to protest their government's apparent complicity. An official Israeli commission of inquiry decreed on February 9, 1983, that Sharon bore "personal responsibility" for the atrocity. He was forced to resign as head of the Defense Ministry. Mossad was criticized by many Israelis for promoting an alliance with a gang of bloodthirsty Lebanese mobsters.

To be sure, Sharon had not initiated the covert partnership between Israel and the Phalange. It was forged in the mid-1970s by then–Prime Minister Yitzhak Rabin, who established Mossad's station in Junieh and who armed the Christian armies, bringing their troops to Israel for secret military training. Mossad observers even accompanied Christian militiamen in August 1976, when, using Israeli tanks and armored personnel carriers with IDF markings in Hebrew clearly visible, they overran Tel al-Zaatar refugee camp, a PLO stronghold in Beirut, massacring thousands of Palestinians. While Lebanon's Christian leaders implored Israel to openly enter the civil war on their side, Rabin had the good sense not to get bogged down in a mad military adventure in Lebanon. Not so Sharon.

Though Mossad misjudged the worth of an alliance with the Phalange, Evyatar's career remained on track. In 1983, he was appointed deputy head of the Mossad station in Stockholm. A few years later, he was transferred to Africa, where he remained until 1988, when he retired from the service.

Evyatar became a *baal teshuvah,* a newly observant Jew, and moved to Eli, a mountaintop West Bank settlement. In the Bible, Eli was the mentor of the prophet Samuel, who lived in Shiloh. Soon Evyatar began to meet with Ateret Cohanim's chief rabbi, Shlomo Aviner, a Parisian-born Jew with a wispy beard who was at the Levingers' historic Seder at the Park Hotel. The men had served in the Mossad together, and Aviner was still known to vanish occasionally for months on end while on covert assignment, according to several of his disciples.

Aviner is an extremely approachable man who, unlike some of his col-

leagues at Ateret Cohanim, enjoys sparring with liberal, assimilated Jews
about religion and history. In Aviner's view, Palestine was a barren and
empty wasteland until the Jews returned. "The Arabs are squatters,"
Aviner told me. "I don't know who gave them authorization to live on
Jewish land. All mankind knows this is our land. Most Arabs came here
recently. You perhaps read the book *From Time Immemorial* by Joan
Peters?* . . . And even if some Arabs have been here for two thousand
years, is there a statute of limitations that gives a thief the right to his
plunder?"

Like Evyatar, Rabbi Aviner believed that a Jewish communal presence in
St. John's Hospice, a cavernous two-story building just a few meters from
the Church of the Holy Sepulchre, could be the springboard for a more
substantial Jewish presence in the Christian Quarter. In 1987, a wealthy
American supporter of Ateret Cohanim had offered Matossian $5 million
for the building, but he turned it down, saying it was too risky to do
business with Jews.

Nevertheless, Matossian was eager to get rid of the hospice. The Greek
Orthodox Church had been trying to evict him since 1980 as an undesir-
able tenant. Several of his relatives had been convicted of operating a
heroin-smuggling ring in the Gaza Strip, and there were rumors that
Matossian himself was involved. In 1986 Matossian received an eviction
notice. The case was still on appeal when Israeli attorney Eitan Geva
phoned Matossian, saying he represented well-to-do Christian clients who
were interested in purchasing the hospice's lease from him, according to
members of the Matossian family.

In the summer of 1989, the family members say, Geva introduced
Matossian to Nabil Nicola Sahnawi, who said he was a pious Greek Catholic from Lebanon and the owner of several supermarkets in Paris and a
Panamanian company called SBC. In fact, Geva was Ateret Cohanim's
attorney. And Sahnawi was a prominent Lebanese Christian businessman
from Junieh who was allegedly recruited by Evyatar to act as a middleman.
Because both Jordan and the PLO have made it a capital crime for Palestinians to sell property to Jews, Ateret Cohanim has often employed Christian
Arab middlemen to purchase property in the Muslim Quarter in order to
disguise the Jewish identity of the buyer.

---

*Peters's book, which was heavily criticized for historical errors, argued that most Palestinian Arabs are late
nineteenth- and early twentieth-century immigrants to Palestine, who were attracted by the economic
opportunities offered by the Zionist enterprise.

The men toured the hospice, then Sahnawi walked around the corner to the Church of the Holy Sepulchre. "He was amazed at how close it was" to St. John's Hospice, said a relative of Matossian's, adding that Sahnawi prayed with fervor, kissing every icon. At the end of the visit, the Lebanese front man offered to buy the hospice's lease for $3.5 million, leaving a check for $1.5 million as a down payment. The contract was signed in Geneva a few weeks later by Sahnawi and Joseph Butros, a Lebanese who also claimed to represent SBC.

Evyatar disputes key parts of the Matossians' version of events. According to Evyatar, Matossian actually had been bargaining directly with Ateret Cohanim for several years, and it was the Armenian who insisted on using SBC as a front for the transaction. "He knew perfectly well who was behind SBC," Evyatar told me. "He negotiated with Ateret Cohanim, not with any Lebanese. Matossian asked that somebody would be a front man in order to minimize the dangers that he assumed existed."

Although the contract was signed on June 28, 1989, the settlers waited for ten months—until Holy Week—to occupy the building. When asked at a press conference why they moved in on a day that was so important to Christians, Evyatar, looking fatigued (his baby had just died of sudden infant death syndrome) said the settlers didn't know it had any special significance. It was an odd comment coming from a man who was supposed to be an expert on Christianity.

When I asked Evyatar about the timing of the move into the hospice in an interview in Jerusalem in February 1992, he said sarcastically, "First of all, after we have crucified Christ on Easter, whatever else we do is nothing in comparison. The *big crime* was already done two thousand years ago. Now what is left? If we enter a building, something will happen to Christianity?"

On the day the settlers entered the hospice, with Passover soon approaching, they began to scour the building, dumping into the cobblestone street old furniture as well as religious objects, including crosses, which they deliberately broke, and paintings of the Virgin Mary. A large Byzantine cross embedded in the stones on the front of the hospice was covered over by plywood on which the settlers painted a blue Mogen David, the Jewish star.

Officials in the Mayor's Office had heard rumors that Jewish extremists were planning to demonstrate in the Christian Quarter during Easter, but dismissed them as too outlandish to be true. While militant Jews frequently demonstrated in the Muslim Quarter, the Christian Quarter was generally considered taboo. Later that evening, however, a distraught Lutheran minister called Kollek, reporting that he could see a large group of what looked like Jewish settlers singing and dancing and waving flags outside the derelict hospice. "They are making a hell of a lot of noise," the minister complained. "Tell the police it's the eve of Easter!"

Kollek dispatched his adviser on Arab Affairs, Amir Chesin, to the hospice, where he discovered that Ateret Cohanim had bought the building's lease and that several dozen Jewish families were in the process of moving in with all their possessions. Recalling how Rabbi Levinger had used the Park Hotel as his beachhead in Hebron, Chesin hurried to a nearby police station and demanded that the settlers be thrown out. Without a court order, the police replied, nothing could be done. Shortly before midnight in a drafty West Jerusalem courtroom, the Greek Orthodox Church's Jewish attorney argued that the settlers had illegally occupied the building. But Eitan Geva, who appeared as SBC's attorney at the hastily called hearing, won a temporary stay of eviction.

The following morning was Holy Thursday—for the Greek Orthodox Church one of the most solemn days of the year. It is an occasion when thousands of poor, simple peasants from Greece and Cyprus travel to Israel to congregate in the small courtyard in front of the Church of the Holy Sepulchre for a ceremony known as "the washing of the feet." (According to Christian legend, the Wandering Jew enters the courtyard once every century to beg admission, and hears a voice that tells him to resume his endless journey.) On Holy Thursday, in a ritual symbolizing how Jesus, in an act of humility, cleansed the feet of the Twelve Disciples, the patriarch gently bathes the feet of his priests. Then, like a king in medieval times, the patriarch, dressed in a floor-length robe of gold cloth and a crown encrusted with jewels, flamboyantly dips a bouquet of roses into the bathwater and sprays it on the crowd, which ululates in ecstasy as church bells chime.

Following the ceremony, the priests form a procession that sonorously winds its way through the Christian Quarter to the church's tomblike monastery. But on this occasion, they proceeded to St. John's Hospice. There, they joined hundreds of Arab demonstrators chanting pro-PLO slogans and jostling Israeli police guarding the building while settlers peeked out the windows looking very frightened. At the height of the demonstration, a plump, black-bearded monk climbed on the shoulder of a colleague and pulled off the plaque bearing the Jewish star. An Israeli officer grabbed the cleric in a headlock, while other police fired tear gas. Panic ensued, and several clergymen, who had fainted from the gas, were trampled. The patriarch, a seventy-eight-year-old man who is diabetic and extremely obese, tripped over his robes and tumbled to the ground, breaking his heavy silver crucifix. He later falsely claimed that he had been pushed to the ground by Israeli riot police.

The St. John's Hospice affair was a disaster for Kollek, who had devoted a career to maintaining Jerusalem as a religiously pluralistic city as well as the capital of Israel. Kollek grew up in Vienna just after World War I and witnessed that city's pluralistic culture collapse with the rise of Nazism. That experience, Kollek has said, has remained with him as a warning. Though Jerusalem's Arabs have faulted Kollek for doing nothing of significance to develop their neighborhoods, they respect his tolerance and sensitivity to others.

"Teddy gives us the feeling of not just tolerating but wanting a Christian presence in Jerusalem," the Reverend Petra Heldt, who heads an intra-Christian ecumenical group in Jerusalem, has said. "I think it is important for him that the Jews not live totally isolated from non-Jews, that they have other cultures against which they can check themselves out and develop."

The Greek Orthodox Church has existed in Jerusalem since the second century. It is the most senior—and most powerful—church in the Holy Land. Because of its importance, it has acquired virtual control of the major Christian holy places such as the Holy Sepulchre and the Church of Mary (although parts of these buildings are held by the other churches). Radio reports that the Greek patriarch had been beaten by Israeli police and that Christian holy places had been desecrated were broadcast in Greece on the afternoon of the riot. The Greek government dispatched a delegation of Parliament members to Jerusalem to investigate the charges.

"After we heard that the patriarch fell and that priests were gassed, the mayor decided to visit him on the same day," recalled Naomi Teasdale, Kollek's adviser on Christian affairs. That afternoon at 4:00 P.M. a seven-person delegation from the Mayor's Office that included Teasdale and Amir Chesin entered the Christian Quarter. As the group approached a narrow road leading to the patriarch's residence, "We were attacked by huge stones thrown from the rooftops," Teasdale said. "They were brick size. We couldn't advance. We saw hooded figures, *shebab,* dancing in front of us and also throwing stones. As we had a representative of the police with us who had a walkie-talkie, we called for reinforcements, while we waited out of the range of the stones. It was very unpleasant. It was the first time that there was a riot of such scale in Jerusalem. We had it in Gaza and the West Bank, but never in Jerusalem."

Kollek started defiantly to march past the stone-throwing youngsters and into the patriarch's residence; "So we held him back," Teasdale said. Though eighty-one years old, Kollek sleeps only four hours a night and works almost all his waking hours, prompting one friend to note that he's something of a "genetic miracle." When riot police arrived, the mayor ordered them to fire tear gas, which sent the masked youths scurrying to the rooftops.

The delegation found the patriarch huddled in a small, dirty, seldom-used room off the main entrance. "He was in an awful state," Teasdale remembered. "He was incoherent." About sixty *shebab* had besieged the patriarch's reception hall, forcing him to withdraw to the anteroom. They accused him of accepting a bribe from the Jews who had occupied the hospice. The police wanted to evict the Palestinians, but the patriarch cried, "Teddy, if you arrest them, my life won't be worth living."

Until the St. John's Hospice affair, the Greek Orthodox Church had managed to remain relatively neutral during the *intifada*. The church's senior clergymen are Greek. Their five-thousand-member flock, however, is made up of predominately affluent Christian Arabs from Jerusalem and the territories whose militant nationalist sentiments are growing.* Palestinian Christians always seemed to have to prove their patriotism to their Muslim brothers; their insecurity only intensified with the rise of Islamic fundamentalism, with its acute hostility to both Judaism and Christianity. The strength of the fundamentalists was underscored when 26 percent of the Palestinians said they favored a Palestinian state based on Islamic religious law, according to a 1986 poll conducted by the East Jerusalem Arabic-language daily newspaper *Al-Fajr*. During the *intifada*, it was not unusual to see graffiti in the occupied territories warning, FIRST THE JEWS, THEN THE CHRISTIANS.

Kollek had taken extraordinary measures to keep the Greek patriarchy on Israel's side. In 1987, a few months before the outbreak of the *intifada*, the Greek patriarch was arrested crossing the Allenby Bridge into the West

---

*Approximately 95 percent of the Palestinians in the West Bank are Muslims. The figure for the Gaza Strip is 98 percent.

Bank. Israeli police found eight-and-one-half kilos of heroin concealed in the side panels of his black Mercedes. The patriarch denied that the drugs were his, and claimed that he had been set up. Israeli police believed, however, that he was part of a vast drug-smuggling ring. Aharon Sarig, the former attorney for the city of Jerusalem, told me that he and Kollek persuaded Police Commissioner Shlomo Bar-Lev not to press charges "so we'd have the goodwill of the patriarch."*

It was not the first time Kollek had helped the Greek Orthodox Church avoid a scandal. In 1986, Kollek discovered that Rafi Levy, the Jerusalem district commissioner, had tried to blackmail the Greek patriarch's assistant, Bishop Timothy, into helping him carry out a fraudulent West Bank land deal. As district commissioner, Levy had immense power. A Palestinian living in his district could not build a house, start a business, or travel outside Israel without obtaining a permit from his office. In a phone call taped by Israeli police, Levy threatened to physically harm the clergyman and to deport his family if he failed to cooperate in the land scheme. In another call, Levy threatened to expose the bishop's purported homosexuality as well as the names of his alleged sexual partners.

After Levy was arrested in 1986 for his role in masterminding fraudulent land deals, Kollek, who had seen transcripts of the police phone taps, informed the cleric that he would personally see to it that rumors about his sexual predilections would not leak to the press. Perhaps the mayor was trying to be helpful. But two Jerusalem city officials told me Kollek mentioned the tapes to encourage the man's fealty. (Levy, who was convicted on June 28, 1988, and sentenced to three and a half to six years in jail, proved the old Arab proverb that says no people are more corrupt than the residents of holy cities.)

In the weeks following Ateret Cohanim's takeover of St. John's Hospice, an obsequious Kollek repeatedly apologized to the patriarch, pleading with him not to ignore all the good works Israel had undertaken on behalf of the Christian community. "I have full understanding for your feelings of hurt and anger after the unfortunate incidents at St. John's Hospice and, particularly, after seeing senior Israeli politicians visit the settlers," Kollek wrote to the patriarch on June 5, 1990, more than two months after the takeover. "At the same time, I would like to reiterate my assurances that

*Christian clergymen have been searched entering Israel ever since Hilarion Capucci, the Greek Catholic patriarch of Jerusalem, was convicted of smuggling explosives into Israel for the PLO.

this was the act of an extremist Jewish group and not the policy of the Israeli government (and I have the word of the Prime Minister on this matter) and, certainly, not the policy of the municipality of Jerusalem. I would like also to reiterate my assurances that we are determined to safeguard the freedom of worship, freedom of access to the Holy Places and the traditional rights of the Christian communities in Jerusalem.

"The question of the legality of the lease is on the agenda of the courts and the government cannot take any action before the courts have given their verdict. However, I repeat that if the lawyer of the Patriarchate has any suggestions as to the way I can personally help you, I shall be very happy to do so.

"You know very well that since the establishment of the State of Israel, we have always enjoyed friendly relations with the Christian communities in general and with the Greek Orthodox Patriarchate in particular and, since the reunification of Jerusalem in 1967, we have given every possible assistance to them. After Jordanian restrictions on building of churches and land acquisition by Christian communities for 19 years, we have helped in building, renovating, and restoring of over 20 churches and Christian institutions since 1967, including important houses of worship of the Greek Orthodox Patriarchate. We have also renewed the infrastructure in the Christian quarter and the Via Dolorosa and helped the churches in various other ways.

"It would, of course, make it much easier for us to continue our efforts on behalf of the Christian communities if Your Beatitude would help clear up the current misunderstanding by giving public expression to the fact that there is no Israeli conspiracy to take over church property and expel Christians from Jerusalem."

Kollek said he did not know the hospice had been obtained by Ateret Cohanim with covert government help when he wrote to the patriarch. Shamir "lied" when he said the government wasn't involved in the take-over, an indignant Kollek later told me. But to some observers, the St. John's Hospice affair is evidence that Kollek's control over the city is slipping. One famous Israeli writer who lives in and has written eloquently about Jerusalem told me, "He's fading as his dream of Jerusalem, the glorious mosaic—which was always a fiction—fades with him. Kollek still believes that peace between Arabs and Jews will come even if it takes one hundred years. He is still fired by the Zionism of his youth. But Jerusalem is a miserable failure. There is no master plan for the Arab neighborhoods, which are surrounded by a spiderweb of encroaching Jewish settlements. Likud's goal is to drive them [the Arabs] out, although the Arab population of Jerusalem has doubled in the last twenty-five years. [Jewish] West Jerusalem is poor, religious, right wing; the city's next mayor will be very hard-line."

Jerusalem *is* a melancholy city; the *intifada* has added a menacing air. The Palestinian mood has only darkened as bulldozers prepare the ground for massive Jewish housing projects in former Arab areas of the city; not since Herodian times, in fact, has Jerusalem seen as much construction as it has under Kollek's administration. (A seventy-two-square-kilometer area of the West Bank was incorporated into "united" Jerusalem's boundary, along with seventy thousand Palestinians who lived there, three weeks after the June 1967 Six-Day War, when Israeli law and administration was applied to occupied Arab East Jerusalem.)

Despite Kollek's extraordinary efforts to curry favor with the Greek Orthodox Church, His Beatitude journeyed to Damascus to embrace Israel's implacable enemy Hafiz al-Assad, soon after it was reported in the Hebrew press that the Housing Ministry had underwritten the purchase of St. John's Hospice. Then, on the eve of the Gulf War, the cleric reportedly wrote a letter to Saddam Hussein in which he prayed that Allah would send the Iraqi Army to "liberate Palestine."

"For the sake of one building in the heart of the Christian Quarter coveted by fundamentalist Jews, decades of work by Kollek to forge decent relations with the Christian community in the Holy Land were ruined," said Aharon Sarig, the former attorney for the city of Jerusalem. With the benefit of hindsight, after the patriarch's letter to Saddam Hussein, Sarig said that Kollek should have allowed Bar-Lev to arrest the patriarch for heroin smuggling. "We in the city made a mistake," Sarig said, "and I'm taking the blame too. They [the Greek Orthodox Patriarchate] didn't understand [Kollek's] good faith," and held him responsible for what a few fundamentalists and fanatics had done on their own.

Kollek also casts the blame squarely on Ateret Cohanim for what he has called the worst experience of his career. While he said that he understands their sentiments, and, in principle, agrees that Jews have the right to live anywhere in the Jewish state, he called Ateret Cohanim's acquisition of real estate in Muslim and Christian neighborhoods provocative, insensitive, and politically unwise. "If you want to say that we are a sovereign and that our sovereignty will be measured by the way we treat minorities and others, and if you think for a moment that we are after all judging governments by how they treat Jews, we therefore cannot afford to treat minorities differently than we would like Jews to be treated in Argentina or Syria or in the Yemens," a spirited Kollek told me during an interview in his office on February 10, 1992, the day Ateret Cohanim moved into yet another Arab house on Via Dolorosa just inside the Lion's Gate in the Old City's Muslim Quarter.

"Ateret Cohanim doesn't appreciate that the connection of Christians as well as Muslims to Jerusalem is an extremely deep one—they would say as deep as ours," Kollek continued. "I think an objective observer would find that ours goes back longer and that we show much more concern for Jerusalem than either the Christians or the Muslims do. But subjectively their attachment is extremely great. There are some Israelis who are kidding themselves that gradually the Arabs will leave, and gradually the Christians will leave, and the Jews will be left here alone—maybe in twenty years, maybe in fifty years. This is absolutely mistaken thinking. Ateret Cohanim also has no clear view of the value or the potency of world opinion. This city is a very poor city. In order to become a little better off, it needs tourism, it needs investment, it needs immigrants. All this will not come if there is not peace and quiet in this city. So Ateret Cohanim's activities are very counterproductive from the point of view of the future of Jerusalem."

Not only Teddy Kollek but pro-Israeli Jewish leaders in the United States, concerned with counteracting negative publicity, denounced the takeover of St. John's Hospice as insensitive. "It cuts the ground from under us," said Seymour Reich, then chairman of the Conference of Presidents of Major American Jewish Organizations. Supporters of Ateret Cohanim tried to justify their move into the Christian Quarter by falsely claiming that many Jews had lived there during the nineteenth century. While it is true that Jews had lived in the Muslim Quarter in substantial numbers (and that many Muslims had lived in the Jewish Quarter) during the nineteenth century, "there were no Jews [living] in the Christian Quarter," according to Yehoshua Ben-Arieh, professor of geography and former dean of the Faculty of Humanities at the Hebrew University, in his authoritative book *Jerusalem in the Nineteenth Century*.

Many of Ateret Cohanim's officials also argued that moving into the Old City's Christian and Muslim quarters should be as natural for Jews as moving into an exclusive American suburb. "If Jews who were trying to move into an apartment building in Scarsdale or Beverly Hills were attacked by a rioting anti-Jewish mob, decent people everywhere would be outraged," said Dr. Irving Moskowitz, a Miami physician and Ateret Cohanim board member who has donated millions of dollars to its real estate projects, including the hospice. Writing in the Orthodox Jewish weekly tabloid *The Jewish Press,* published in Brooklyn, Dr. Moskowitz argued that dividing the Old City into quarters "has no historical validity," and that Jews have an "obligation to repopulate" those parts of the land of Israel that have been "made *Judenrein* by Arab pogromists."

Further, Moskowitz contended, Jews who moved into the hospice did so legally because they were "pilgrims." " 'Pilgrims' is a key legal term in the controversy," he wrote. "The lease permits 'pilgrims' to live there. The Israeli judge who initially ordered the Jews to be evicted from the hostel assumed that the lease was referring to Christian pilgrims. But is that a fair assumption? Hasn't Jewish tradition always mandated pilgrimages to Jerusalem during the Jewish Festivals? Don't Jews have as much right as Christians to come to the Holy City?"

Moskowitz was among those who in 1984 formed the American Friends of Ateret Cohanim, incorporated in New York State as a charitable, tax-exempt foundation. Before that, Ateret Cohanim had donations from America passed to it through PEF Israel Endowment Funds, Inc., a tax-exempt public charity in New York. According to the foundation's statement of purpose on file with the New York State Attorney General's Office, the American Friends of Ateret Cohanim was formed to publish and distribute material concerning "the priesthood [and] functions of the Temple" and "to acquire in any manner whatsoever and especially by grant, gift lease or purchase—land, rooms, or houses [in Arab East Jerusalem.]" Between 1989 and 1990, according to its annual IRS reports, the American Friends of Ateret Cohanim recorded more than $1 million in donations. Some of the money has come from Christian Evangelicals in America who view the Jewish return to Israel as the prelude to the Second Coming.

Ateret Cohanim officials say that most of the money the group collects in the United States goes to its subsidiary, the Jerusalem Reclamation Project, whose primary purpose is to purchase Arab property in East Jerusalem. Originally, Ateret Cohanim's officials say, they wanted to register the Jerusalem Reclamation Project in the United States as a tax-exempt foundation but were advised by their attorneys that the IRS wouldn't grant tax-exempt status to an organization that primarily deals in commercial real estate.

Among the largest contributors to Ateret Cohanim are Marc Belzberg, the thirty-six-year-old Canadian president of First City Financial Corporation, an investment bank in New York, well known on Wall Street for its large profits as a corporate raider, and Cyril Stein, chairman of the Ladbroke Group, a large British hotel, gambling, and real estate company with extensive holdings in America. Dr. Moskowitz has purchased the fifty-two-room Shepard Hotel in East Jerusalem, formerly owned by the grand mufti of Jerusalem, for "considerably more than one million dollars. I am doing everything I possibly can to help reclaim Jerusalem for the Jewish people," Moskowitz said. Rabbi Marvin Hier, executive director of the Simon Wiesenthal Center in Los Angeles, himself a supporter of Ateret Cohanim, told me, "I love the idea of beautifying the Muslim Quarter. Not a Jew in the world would object to that. The 'Who's Who' of world Jewry has put money into it." The members of the Belzberg family, who are worth more than $400 million, according to *The Wall Street Journal*, are the major financial contributors to the Simon Wiesenthal Center, and Rabbi Hier has personally given religious instruction to Marc Belzberg, a *baal teshuvah*, or a Jew who has embraced Orthodoxy.

On May 27, 1987, the American Friends of Ateret Cohanim held its first annual fund-raising dinner for the Jerusalem Reclamation Project at the Hilton Hotel in Manhattan. More than five hundred people attended, paying $180 each. Israel's UN ambassador, Benjamin Netanyahu, was the keynote speaker, as he was also to be at the 1988 dinner. "I support the idea that Jews can live anywhere in the land of Israel," he told me. New York senator Daniel Patrick Moynihan sent a congratulatory letter, published in the American Friends' 1987 dinner program, praising Ateret Cohanim for being an "inspiring" example of "Jews and Arabs living peacefully throughout the Old City of Jerusalem." When I telephoned the senator's office, David Luchins, Moynihan's aide, told me that the senator wrote the letter after his friend Israeli president Chaim Herzog "spoke highly" of Ateret Cohanim. Herzog denies making a favorable comment about Ateret Cohanim to Senator Moynihan. In 1990, Luchins said, Moynihan rejected Ateret Cohanim's request to use his name in advertisements for the dinner.

In the spring of 1989, the American Friends of Ateret Cohanim held its third annual fund-raising banquet at the Hilton Hotel in Manhattan. According to a report in *Ha'aretz*, $2.25 million was raised at the dinner, where the guests included Malcolm Hoenlein, the executive director of the Conference of Presidents of Major American Jewish Organizations, who served as the master of ceremonies; New York district attorney Robert Morgenthau; New York City Council president Andrew Stein; Marcus Katz, an Israeli arms dealer based in Mexico City who represented Israel Aircraft Industries in Latin America; and Ed Koch, then mayor of New York. The guest of honor and keynote speaker was Ariel Sharon, who was introduced at the dais by Mayor Koch as "a prince of a man." Koch told me that he attended the dinner simply because he was invited by Sharon, whom he describes as a very close friend. "I don't support [Ateret Cohanim], because of what we now know about their fanatical ideas," said Koch. "But they are not terrible people. They are zealots. I generally find zealots—in all fields—to be pleasant people."

Ateret Cohanim's fourth annual fund-raising dinner at the Hilton Hotel took place in May 1990, a month after the takeover of St. John's Hospice. The mood was defensive and subdued. Three of the four public figures whose presence had been advertised failed to show up—claiming in two cases that they had never agreed to come in the first place. Spokesmen for Democratic senator Joseph Lieberman of Connecticut and Republican representative Bill Grant of Florida said they had repeatedly declined Ateret Cohanim's invitations, yet the organization's ads announced that they were coming. Michael Lewin, Lieberman's aide, told me that he had warned Ateret Cohanim's U.S. director, Jack Friedler, that he would file a complaint with the New York State Attorney General's Office if the organization didn't stop using the senator's name and photograph in newspaper ads. Elie Wiesel, who was listed as a member of the dinner committee on the invitations, said that he had never heard from the group. "They even totally misspelled my name," Wiesel said.

Rabbi Hier of the Los Angeles Simon Wiesenthal Center told me he canceled his scheduled appearance as the benefit's master of ceremonies after he heard about Ateret Cohanim's incursion into the Christian Quarter. "The move increases Israel's isolation at a time when we have to go full out against the idea of a Palestinian West Bank Gaza Strip state," Hier explained. "This undermines us."

At the Hilton, at around 10:00 P.M., in the middle of Jeane Kirkpatrick's after-dinner speech, a pipe bomb exploded on the floor below the main ballroom. Next to the first device police found an unexploded pipe bomb, which had failed to detonate because of a defective fuse. Police officers told me that the first bomb, which was placed next to a coatroom, was supposed to attract spectators in time for the second bomb to go off. "The bombs were meant to maim or kill," an FBI agent said. Police suspected that the bombing was either directed at Ateret Cohanim, or it stemmed from a labor-union dispute.

The bombing didn't seem to faze the prosperous-looking crowd of some seven hundred people, who paid $250 a plate. Most of them, I was told, were Orthodox Jews from as far away as Florida: The men were dressed in dinner jackets and black yarmulkes, the women in evening dresses. A five-piece band played Israeli dance music. (The year before, I was told, Ed Koch and General Sharon had danced the hora together. This time people barely stirred from their seats.) Larry Reinhardt, New York City's taxi and limousine commissioner and the only Republican in the Dinkins administration, was there, as were Dr. Samuel Korman, chief of the cancer division of the Kingsbrook Jewish Medical Center and a board member of Americans for a Safe Israel, an extreme right-wing group that advocates annexing the occupied territories, and Rabbi Walter Wurtzberger, the former head of the Rabbinical Council of America. Former U.S. attorney Rudy Giuliani and his wife, Donna Hanover, a television reporter, were listed on the paid guest list, but they were not there. Giuliani had been supported by most of the right-wing Jewish community during his failed campaign for mayor.

The editor and owner of *The Jewish Press,* Rabbi Sholom Klass, appeared at the dinner with an employee who handed out complimentary copies of his paper. The front page featured a salute to Ateret Cohanim as well as an editorial highlighted by a bold blue headline calling for New York Mayor David Dinkins's resignation. Elected in 1990, Dinkins was the first African-American mayor in the history of New York. "He is clearly not up to dealing with the virtual criminal revolution that pervades New York City," said the editorial, "and is afraid to issue any orders which might be opposed by vocal members of the Black community." Unless Dinkins steps down, "a mass exodus from our crime-ridden city is a distinct prospect," the editorial concluded.

With a circulation of more than 160,000, *The Jewish Press* has considerable political clout in New York, and elsewhere. Politicians ask for its endorsement. After the 1980 presidential election, Ronald Reagan, who had been endorsed by the paper, called it one of the "most powerful" Jewish newspapers in America. For more than two decades, *The Jewish Press* published three separate columns per issue by Rabbi Meir Kahane (one was written under the pseudonym David Sinai), until his assassination in November 1990. Kahane had used the paper to launch the Jewish Defense League and, later, the anti-Arab Kach movement in Israel. His column, which frequently attacked the black community and liberal Jews, did much to pollute political discourse and heighten racial tension in New York.

Inside the banquet room, a banner with one of Rabbi Zvi Yehuda Kook's sayings was draped across the length of the stage. It said, THAT WHICH UNITES US IS FAR GREATER THAN THAT WHICH DIVIDES US.

I asked Julie Frank, who works as liaison to the Jewish community for City Council president Andrew Stein, what divides one Jew from another. "If all Jews believed in God, there wouldn't be so much divisiveness in our own community," said Frank, who grew up in what she said was a "modern Orthodox home" in Far Rockaway, Queens. "I think that as the messianic period grows closer, we have to show our support for Israel by either supporting it financially or moving there: Jews have to be there rather than criticize Israel."

Frank was seated at my table along with her companion, Dr. Ken Kellner, a psychiatrist and president of the Manhattan region of the Zionist Organization of America—a strident pro-Likud group, which, far from trying to unite the Jewish people, has launched a harsh campaign against Jewish doves. Kellner told me he came to the Ateret Cohanim dinner "because I have a number of friends who are part of this organization. I believe in what they are doing . . . I think they have a perfect right to expand the Jewish presence in Israel's eternal capital," he said gravely.

Jeane Kirkpatrick was the only national figure to attend the benefit. In her talk, she joked that when she was initially contacted by the "Jerusalem Reclamation Project," the innocuous-sounding arm of Ateret Cohanim, she thought it was part of Teddy Kollek's Jerusalem Foundation. After she learned the group's identity, Kirkpatrick said that she decided to attend despite several warnings from friends who said it was politically unwise.

Kirkpatrick went on to chide Ateret Cohanim gently for its move into the Christian Quarter: "I thought it was—what do you call it?—insensitive to move in during the middle of Holy Week," she said. "It struck me that this is not a moment when Israel needed more problems." But she then criticized Christian groups for treating the move into the hospice as if Jews had desecrated a holy shrine. "Sensitivity to Christians is one thing. Hysteria about a 'Jewish plot' is quite another."

Kirkpatrick's candor earned her only lukewarm applause, and after she finished speaking, she left to return to Washington. The next speaker, Dr. Moskowitz, the dinner's guest of honor, proceeded to denounce those who would deny Jerusalem to the Jews. "Jerusalem is the center of the Jewish people, and it will be the center of attention of the non-Jewish people," he warned. "We must work for a unified Jerusalem until the Messiah comes!"

For Ateret Cohanim and its fundamentalist supporters, the Messiah will come only after Jews return to Israel, settle the land, and live their daily lives according to the Torah. They believe that the Land of Israel was given to them by God and must be secured and defended at any cost. Therefore, for many of them, the land takes on more importance than the principle of *Pikuach nefesh*—preserving life. Rabbi Aviner has put it this way: "We must settle the whole Land of Israel, and over all of it establish our rule. In the words of [Nachmanides]: 'Do not abandon the land to any other nation.' If that is possible by peaceful means, wonderful, and if not, we are commanded to make war to accomplish it."

Unfortunately for Ateret Cohanim, most Palestinian Arabs have tenaciously clung to the land. "The Arabs of Israel have to realize they don't belong [in the Land of Israel]," said Menachem Bar-Shalom, the former head of public relations for Ateret Cohanim. "They have to go where they belong." Bar-Shalom made this remark to a reporter for the *Washington Jewish Week* at the fund-raising dinner, saying openly to a secular Jewish publication what many Ateret Cohanim officials and followers say all the time among themselves. Some Ateret Cohanim supporters that I have talked to justify the expulsion of Arabs by evoking Maimonides, the revered medieval Jewish religious scholar, who said that after the Messiah comes, only Jews will be permitted to live in Jerusalem.

Ateret Cohanim members say they want to prepare the way for the Messiah by "redeeming" the Old City stone by holy stone, until they have quietly transformed Jerusalem into what they hope will become the pride of Jews everywhere—a holy city in the service of the Third Temple. When Dr. Moskowitz says that Jerusalem will become the "center of attention" for non-Jews, he is restating the biblical prophecy that after the Messiah comes and the Temple is rebuilt, Israel will become a light unto the nations—and spiritual master of the universe.

In the winter of 1977, not long after Egyptian president Anwar Sadat journeyed to Jerusalem, I had the opportunity to talk to Rav Zvi Yehuda Kook about biblical prophecy and the Jewish people's quest for redemption. He greeted me at the door to his West Jerusalem study with a firm handshake and a broad, joyous smile. He was dressed in the traditional long black coat and black trousers; his feet were covered by soft brown-and-orange plaid slippers. His eyes were strong and commanding; his physical agility, as he bounded around the room pointing out pictures of his father and various other Talmud scholars, was remarkable for a man of eighty-seven. He said that he had just written a letter to Menachem Begin, urging him not to surrender an inch of Jewish territory. "I told the prime minister," he said, "that Judea and Samaria [are] our land, absolutely, belonging to all the Jewish people."

Like his father before him, Rav Kook believed the diaspora demoralized and sickened the Jewish spirit. As he saw it, only by returning to Israel and settling and building up the land will the Jewish people be able to recapture their holy essence—and Gush Emunim, a spiritual movement, has been divinely created to achieve this end. God, the Torah, the land, and the Jewish people are an inseparable link between a divine past and a glorious future. It is vital for the Jews to retain sovereignty over all the Promised Land; otherwise the Torah's commandments would be imperfectly fulfilled.

"Our main purpose, therefore, is to follow the Torah's commandments in the Land of Israel," he said. "By doing so, after a time, we will automatically become a light unto the nations. Those who can't see the light are wicked. Other nations will learn from us, and by so doing raise the morality of the world. Thus, once we recover from the sickness of the diaspora, we will be a light to the rest of humanity.

"Gush Emunim relates to the whole of Zionism by being the very soul of Zionism. God promised He would shine a light on Zion, and this is the real root meaning of Zionism. Gush Emunim is facilitating this."

Rav Kook realized that though God promised Judea and Samaria to the Jewish people, they are also claimed by the Arabs. But, he thought, the conflict with the Arabs—a pure, monotheistic people who he claimed are closer to God than the "idolatrous Christians"—is temporary. In any case, he said, the Israeli Army is strong enough to conquer Judaism's foes: "The power of our army and state institutions is growing. Thus, so grows our influence. Our people are experiencing a rebirth. More Jews are returning to the Torah. Through this physical and spiritual growth, we become stronger, and the world becomes more moral."

I asked Rav Kook if he thought Anwar Sadat had sincerely offered peace to Israel. "Above all, Divine Providence orders history," he replied. "Whether Sadat loves us or recognizes our power, God sends our messiahs. Herzl, Begin—maybe Sadat too has been a messenger of God. Some people think this attitude is mysticism. It's not. Seeing the hand of God in history is normal and healthy—it is not mysticism."

But even messianic groups have internal power struggles. A few days after Ateret Cohanim's 1990 fund-raising dinner at the Hilton Hotel in Manhattan, there was a shakeup inside the movement. Baruch Levine, the group's director in America, was encouraged to step down. Apparently, there was much unhappiness over the misuse of names in advertising and a drop in donations. At the same time, the millions of dollars that Ateret Cohanim paid for its sublease of St. John's Hospice had vanished along with the building's Armenian leaseholder. "He's running for his life," Mickey Peled, Ateret Cohanim's Israeli-born fund-raiser in America, told me. But according to Eitan Geva, Matossian's lawyer, the Armenian is living comfortably in Los Angeles. (Geva is also the attorney for SBC, which he told me is a hotel-management company.)

In spite of all the negative publicity, Ateret Cohanim has continued to attract high-powered friends. In 1991, New York senator Alfonse D'Amato delivered the main address at its fund-raising dinner in Manhattan. "I applaud the philosophy of the Jerusalem Reclamation Project, which holds that Jews, like everyone else, have the right to legitimately acquire lands and homes and institutions in any part of Jerusalem," he told the group to warm applause. In February 1992, Secretary of Housing Jack Kemp was the group's keynote speaker, helping to raise more than $100,000.

Still, the lingering controversy over the hospice has made it more difficult—and possibly more expensive—for Ateret Cohanim to continue to do business as usual in the Old City. At the same time, the faltering real estate market in the United States has reduced donations to Ateret Cohanim because many of its supporters are developers. Nevertheless, an Ateret Cohanim official told me that the movement is secretly negotiating for a number of additional properties in the Old City and has a large waiting list of yeshiva students and families who are ready to move into the Muslim

Quarter.* "The only thing stopping us now is money," an official for Ateret Cohanim said. "But I think that within ten years we will have made . . . Jerusalem Jewish again forever."

The struggle over real estate is at the heart of the conflict between Arabs and Jews in the Holy Land. Slowly but surely, the land in East Jerusalem (as elsewhere in the occupied territories) is moving from Arab to Jewish hands. What is happening may be in keeping with the Zionist tradition, yet it is hard to imagine a more effective way to provoke Palestinian terrorism and violence than to increase the Jewish presence in the Muslim and Christian quarters of Jerusalem's Old City, while denying Palestinians the right to self-determination.

But that is exactly what continues to happen. On December 12, 1991, in one of the most ambitious attempts yet to take over Arab areas of East Jerusalem, armed yeshiva students allied with Ateret Cohanim forcibly occupied six Arab homes in Silwan, pushing the occupants into the pounding rain in the dead of night, clutching copies of their leases and bundles of clothing. The settlers, who received covert financial support from Sharon's Housing Ministry, claim they have legal title to the homes in Silwan, as well as to twenty more. As in the St. John's Hospice affair, the settlers were allowed to remain in the homes until the courts sort out the legal issues. "This move into Silwan was deliberately provocative," said Tzali Reshef, a Peace Now leader who organized a protest march of three thousand Arabs and Jews in Silwan, a poor Arab neighborhood just outside the Old City Walls and in the shadow of the Dome of the Rock. Mayor Kollek denounced the takeover as another example of Shamir catering to "extremists, people with a fanatically shortsighted understanding of Jerusalem's true interest."

Jerusalem city lawyers subsequently ruled that the settlers in Silwan could be evicted by police for security reasons, regardless of the legality of their leases. But the city was overruled by the Israeli Cabinet, which decreed that the settlers had a right to remain, and that Kollek was responsible for providing them with police protection. The Jewish fundamentalists plan to link Silwan, the site where King David established Jerusalem, to the Old City's Jewish Quarter, according to Israeli press reports.

*On March 27, 1992, Ateret Cohanim and Israel's Housing Ministry announced plans to build a 200-unit apartment complex inside the Muslim Quarter, near Herod's Gate. Teddy Kollek told reporters that the plan "surely will not contribute to Jewish-Arab co-existence." Rabin opposes the plan.

On the night of an earlier takeover of Arab homes in Silwan, the settlers were joined by Tehiya party Knesset members Yuval Neeman and Geula Cohen, a deputy science minister who broke her ankle while being hoisted through an open window. Cohen was taken to Hadassah Hospital in West Jerusalem. The following night an Arab worker set fire to the room next to hers and was arrested. The night after that, her bodyguard found a jellylike substance in her fish dinner. It turned out to be nonlethal industrial soap. Six more Arab hospital workers were jailed. "This only proves to me that an Arab does not have to be a member of the PLO to try to harm Jews," said the sixty-five-year-old Cohen. "Everyone is doing it in their job. If he's a laborer, then he is clogging pipes. If he's a driver, he rams a hitching post. If he is a cook, he puts poison in your food."

CHAPTER 5

Temple Mount Faithful

Gershon Solomon doesn't look like a man who could trigger a blood-bath. With his thick, graying hair, black mustache, and soft brown eyes, the fifty-four-year-old Israeli looks like a gracefully aging American television soap star. Yet when word spread through the Israeli occupied West Bank in October 1990 that Solomon and his group—the Temple Mount Faithful—were going to demonstrate at the Dome of the Rock Mosque in East Jerusalem, thousands of Palestinians raced to the city to defend their holy shrine. The day would end as one of Jerusalem's bloodiest since the founding of the Jewish state.

Palestinians recalled that just the year before, in 1989, the Temple Mount Faithful had unsuccessfully sought police permission to hoist a three-ton cornerstone up the asphalt ramp that leads from the Western Wall Plaza to the Mughrabi Gate and into the Temple Mount compound—a thirty-five-acre stretch of flat, elevated ground just inside the Old City's walls where the Jewish temples of Solomon and Herod once stood, and where two Muslim mosques now mark the third-holiest place of Islam. With its exquisite blue-tile mosaics and golden dome, the larger of the two mosques, known as the Dome of the Rock, is the crown jewel of Jerusalem's skyline.

Spokesmen for the Faithful had announced that the cornerstone was to be part of the Third Temple and even unveiled architects' plans for the building at a press conference. Noticeably absent from the plans were the Muslim holy places. Solomon suggested they could be moved to Mecca.

"Muslims would never agree to a Jewish holy site in Mecca, so why should we agree to their holy site here?" he declared. Blowing rams' horns and strumming on harps, the Faithful carted the cornerstone to a nearby Arab stone quarry, where a Jewish "high priest" wearing dark sunglasses and a coarsely woven linen robe consecrated it with drops of holy water from Shiloach's Pool. An outraged Mayor Kollek described the group as "dwarfs" walking in the footsteps of a false messiah who could bring disaster on the Jewish people. Kollek added that while most Israelis paid groups like the Temple Mount Faithful no mind, the Arabs certainly do.

Arabs had good reason to be sensitive about Jewish designs on their holy places. Virtually every year since Israel's annexation of Arab East Jerusalem following the Six-Day War in 1967, Jewish extremists armed with guns and Bibles have stormed the gates of the mosque compound. Zealots like Solomon view Muslim control of the Temple Mount both as a sign of Israeli national impotence and as an obstacle on the road to redemption. The Jews' return to Israel and the building and flowering of the land, they believe, are the first stages of the Messianic Age. The Israeli right has already succeeded in settling more than one hundred thousand Jews on the West Bank—and as Ehud Sprinzak, a Hebrew University expert on Jewish extremist groups, said, "The next stage in the advancement of the future kingdom of Israel is [taking over] the Temple Mount—the holiest place in the Jewish religion."

For two millennia, the Temple Mount has been the object of conflicting Jewish, Christian, and Muslim political and religious aspirations: King Solomon built the first Jewish temple there, Jesus taught there, and Muhammad rode his horse into heaven from the Temple Mount. In A.D. 70, the Tenth Roman Legion destroyed the Second Temple, following a five-year struggle between Jewish Zealots and Rome. After a five-month siege, Titus set fire to the temple—the symbol of Jewish national sovereignty—leaving it a heap of ashes. The surviving Jews were subsequently scattered across the empire, putting an end to the Jewish state for two thousand years.

All that remained of the Second Temple after its destruction was the western retaining wall of the Temple Mount. In the seventh century, the Arabs built the Dome of the Rock Mosque on the ruins of the temple. The Western Wall, also known as the Wailing Wall, became a site of Jewish prayer and lamentation.

The Temple Mount and the adjacent Wailing Wall became a symbol of uncompromising nationalism during the clash between Arabs and Jews over the fate of Palestine. In 1929 Rabbi Moshe Segal, who had formed a religious underground allied with Menachem Begin's Irgun, led a rally past stunned British troops on Tishah-b'Ab (the day that commemorates the destruction of the First and Second Temples) to the Wall. There, the demonstrators violated the laws of the British Mandate by singing the Zionist anthem *"Hatikva."* The Palestinians, who feared they would be swept aside by the rising Zionist tide, slaughtered Jews in pogroms that swept the country. Armed Jewish groups retaliated, killing about an equal number of Arabs. The Wailing Wall riots introduced an element of religious fanaticism previously unknown in the conflict between the two communities.

Israel's triumph in the Six-Day War rekindled Jewish messianic aspirations. While all religious Jews pray for the restoration of the temple, there is sharp disagreement over when and how it will happen. Most Orthodox rabbis maintain that the Temple Mount is so holy that Jews are prohibited from even setting foot there until the Messiah appears and the temple is rebuilt through divine intervention. But a growing number of rabbis in Israel, led by former Ashkenazi chief rabbi Shlomo Goren, insist that Jews can pray on the Temple Mount—an act that combined with other "good deeds" will encourage the coming of the Messiah.

During the Six-Day War, Goren, who was then chief rabbi of the Israeli Army, accompanied Jewish troops as they stormed past Islamic guards into the Temple Mount compound. Goren ordered soldiers to fly the Star of David from atop the Dome of the Rock's golden spire, but Defense Minister Moshe Dayan had it taken down. "I don't want any political problems," he said. While the Israeli government claimed sovereignty over the Mount, Dayan made it clear that day-to-day control would be left in the hands of the Supreme Muslim Council, which prohibited members of other religions from praying there. Israel's two chief rabbis sided with Dayan, upholding the ancient rabbinical ruling that bars Jews from ascending the Mount for fear they would desecrate the holy of holies—the sacred spot where the Ark of the Covenant had been housed, and which could only be entered by the high priest, and only on Yom Kippur, the Day of Atonement. This prohibition has been enforced by the Israeli government until the present day in an effort to soothe Muslim religious sensibilities.

Flouting Dayan's attempts to placate Arab fears, Rabbi Goren marched into the compound in full military gear on August 16, 1967 (the 1,897th anniversary of the sacking of the Second Temple by the Romans) and announced that thanks to recent archeological discoveries, he knew where to tread on the Temple Mount without desecrating the holy of holies. He declared that he would build a synagogue in the courtyard between al-Aqsa and the Dome of the Rock. Panic spread throughout the Islamic world. Arab leaders vowed that streets would flow with Jewish blood if the mosques were disturbed. The Israeli government quickly assured local Arab leaders that Goren would never be permitted to build anything on the Temple Mount compound.

"By what logic," asked Rabbi Goren during an interview at his Jerusalem residence in 1987, "by what justification, can it be that the only place in the world where Jews are not allowed to pray is the Temple Mount? According to Jewish religious law, we are not only allowed to pray on the Temple Mount, we are committed to doing so." Goren, one of the most influential Jewish religious figures in the world, was not troubled that neither of Israel's two chief rabbis would publicly endorse his views. "What do I care what they say?" he said with a tug on his gray beard. "I served as the chief rabbi for eleven years. So I have to listen to what somebody else says?"

Just as communal tensions were beginning to subside in Jerusalem in the wake of Rabbi Goren's inflammatory visit to the Mount in August 1967, an Australian tourist who said he wanted the Second Temple rebuilt, "for sweet Jesus to return and pray in it," torched Al-Aqsa Mosque, then calmly took photographs of the blazing building until police arrived. Jerusalem's Arabs, thunderstruck, rioted. Prime Minister Golda Meir told her Cabinet, "We must condemn this outrage." Menachem Begin, replied, "Yes, of course, but not too much." Jerusalem mayor Teddy Kollek was castigated by right-wing Israelis for apologizing to the Arabs for the disaster.

The firebombing of the mosque was not to be an isolated incident. With an eye toward "liberating" the Temple Mount, Jewish zealots have hatched a number of hair-raising plots to eradicate the Muslim holy places. On May 12, 1980, Rabbi Meir Kahane and Bronx-born Andy Green, a large teddy bear of a man with a scrawny beard and a sly smile, were imprisoned for conspiring to blow up the Dome of the Rock Mosque. They were detained for six months under the 1945 Emergency Powers Law promulgated by the British Mandate in Palestine. The law had been used extensively by Israel against Arab terrorists, but had not been used by Israel against Jews since the early days of the state. Kahane retained New York attorney Barry

Slotnick, who flew to Israel to persuade Prime Minister Begin to release the militant rabbi, arguing that his rhetoric was far worse than anything he might actually undertake. But Begin showed Slotnick incriminating evidence gathered by Shin Bet, and declared that he would not tolerate free-lance terrorism. Two years later, in 1982, Alan Goodman, a young "born again" Orthodox Jew from America, walked onto the Temple Mount with an M-16 and shot to death one Arab and injured another. Kahane paid Goodman's legal fees and made him an honorary JDL member.

On a cold, clear winter evening a few months after Goodman's shooting spree, four Orthodox Jewish youths, wearing knitted prayer caps and armed with Uzi submachine guns and hand grenades, attempted to break into one of the subterranean passageways that wind beneath the Old City of Arab East Jerusalem. Once used by the Romans as an aqueduct, the passageway opens onto the Temple Mount compound. Acting on an informant's tip, Israeli police caught the youths before they could plant their explosives inside the mosques. The police would eventually arrest more than forty people in connection with the plan to blow up the mosques, among them a well-known Orthodox rabbi in whose apartment police found a weapons cache and diagrams of the Muslim holy places.

More recently, on August 9, 1990, Shimon Barda, the leader of a mystical religious cult that lived in caves outside the abandoned Arab village of Lifta near Jerusalem, was arrested for conspiring to blow up the Dome of the Rock after Israeli police discovered a weapons stockpile that included U.S.-made LAW shoulder-held missiles. Six years earlier, in January 1984, the Lifta Gang had been apprehended by police hauling twenty-eight pounds of TNT and fifteen hand grenades over the wall of the Temple Mount. An Israeli court committed several members of the Lifta Gang to mental institutions.

By the mid-1980s, attempts by Jewish extremists to "liberate" the Temple Mount had "emerged from the realm of crackpot utopianism" to occupy a central place in the political agenda of Gush Emunim, wrote Dartmouth professor Ian S. Lustick, an expert on Jewish fundamentalism. Lustick observed that dozens of articles calling for Judaizing the Temple Mount were published in *Nekuda* between 1983 and 1986—a year in which twelve thousand ultranationalist Jews marched from Gush Emunim's stronghold at Yeshiva Mercaz HaRav in West Jerusalem to the Mount of Olives in East Jerusalem to view a sound and light show entitled *The Temple*

Mount Is the Heart of the People. (Recall that as early as 1979, Gush Emunim's Makhteret was already plotting the demise of the Islamic holy places as a way to forestall Israel's scheduled evacuation of the Sinai. Yisrael Medad, a Shiloh resident and Knesset aide to Geula Cohen of the Tehiya party, published an article in *Nekuda* prior to the withdrawal from Yamit, arguing that it could be halted only if the Temple Mount was immediately seized by Israel. The extremity of such an action, reasoned Medad, would be enough to sabotage the Camp David Accords.)

Muslims closely monitored Israel's Temple Mount activities. At a meeting of Arab nations in Morocco in 1986, delegates called for a *jihad,* or holy war, in retaliation for any successful Jewish attempt to destroy the mosques on the Temple Mount. "Muslims will never permit any Jew to pray" on the Temple Mount, vowed Sheikh Saad al-Din al-Alami, the head of the Supreme Muslim Council in East Jerusalem. "The Muslims are prepared to die for this."

No Jewish group has done more to arouse Muslim fury than Gershon Solomon's Temple Mount Faithful, which every Sukkoth like clockwork for the past several years has tried to demonstrate on the Temple Mount.* Solomon's preparations for Sukkoth 1990 began several weeks before the holiday when he distributed thousands of blue-lettered handbills in Jerusalem, calling on Israelis to join his group for a "massive pilgrimage to the Temple Mount on Sukkoth with the knowledge of the security forces and under their protection." In interviews with the Israeli press, Solomon asserted that he would lay the cornerstone of the Third Temple on the Temple Mount compound. In fact, Israeli police officials had told Solomon that no one from his group would be permitted to enter the compound and had informed Arab leaders in Jerusalem accordingly. Unfortunately, the Arabs chose to give more credence to Solomon's boasts.

All during the early morning hours of October 8, 1990, the first day of Sukkoth—the Jewish harvest festival—Islamic sheikhs broadcast appeals through al-Aqsa's loudspeakers, which could be heard throughout much of East Jerusalem, calling on Palestinians to "Come defend the mosques, the Jews are coming!" Thousands answered the call. Sheikhs in white turbans and flowing robes segregated women and men, herding the women into the Dome of the Rock and the men into al-Aqsa's courtyard. Islamic

---

*The Bible commands Jews to make a pilgrimage to the Temple Mount on three holidays, Sukkoth, Passover, and Pentecost.

security police patrolled the crowd that had swelled to some five thousand, trying to maintain order. Israeli police maintained a discreet distance, clustered at several of the exits.

Below, in the Western Wall's vast plaza, tens of thousands of religious Jews prayed, some festively dancing the hora as is customary on Sukkoth. At around 10:00 A.M., about fifty members of the Temple Mount Faithful entered the plaza, where they noisily waved banners and Israeli flags. They attempted to ascend the Temple Mount but were stopped by police. They turned and left the plaza, barely noticed by the huge Jewish crowd, which by 10:15 had already started to disperse.

At about 10:45, an Israeli policeman dropped a tear-gas grenade, which either rolled or was kicked toward the Arab women congregated at the Dome of the Rock. The women started screaming, and in response Arab men hurled grapefruit-sized rocks at Israeli police assembled on the Temple Mount compound. The police opened fire primarily with rubber bullets, as well as with live ammunition fired into the air and at the legs of the demonstrators. Palestinians continued to fling stones at police and onto the Wailing Wall Plaza, which was virtually empty of Jewish worshipers by the time the stoning began. Vastly outnumbered, the police retreated through the Mughrabi Gate, reorganized, then stormed the sanctuary, shooting indiscriminately into the panicking crowd. During the next forty minutes, 17 Palestinians were shot dead, and 150 were wounded. Israeli police killed more Palestinians that afternoon than were killed by the Israeli paratroopers who captured the Temple Mount in the Six-Day War. Not one Israeli was killed, and only a handful of Israeli policemen and Jewish worshipers received minor injuries.

That evening, from my room at the American Colony Hotel, I phoned Solomon to ask if he felt responsible for lighting the fuse that had led to so much bloodshed. He told me that it was a "very sad" day, but only because the blood of Muslim "terrorists and murderers" defiled the site of the Second Temple. "They say we are responsible," Solomon told me, "but I want to tell you that Palestinians want to attack and kill Jews every place in this country."

The Sukkoth Day massacre was a public-relations disaster for the Likud government, although it had only its own shortsighted policies to blame. That Israeli police had permitted the Temple Mount Faithful to march to the Western Wall is inexplicable given communal tensions, which had been roiling since the *intifada* began. Though for much of 1990, the *intifada* had been reduced to a numbing routine of general strikes that turned East Jerusalem into a doleful ghost town, it had exploded anew after Saddam Hussein invaded Kuwait. Suddenly, Palestinian youth, their faces hidden behind masks, began boldly attacking Israeli police stations in East Jerusalem armed with stones and axes. At least nine East Jerusalem Arabs were killed by Israeli troops in the month before the Temple Mount shootings.

That should have been reason enough for Israeli police to keep Solomon indoors on Sukkoth. (The government never had any qualms about imposing curfews on troublesome Arabs.) But as a matter of policy, the Likud government has been intent on allowing Jews the right to live—or march—anywhere in *Eretz Yisrael*. The government reasoned that banning Solomon's march would be taken as a sign of weakness by the Arabs, encouraging them to intensify their resistance to Israeli rule over "unified" Jerusalem.

The government's logic backfired; Solomon's demonstration and the ensuing violence ended up casting the Palestinians in the role of victim. Having, for the most part, successfully delegitimized the PLO as a terrorist organization, Likud leaders suddenly had reason to fear that Israel would be branded an outlaw state following the Temple Mount killings. In a stinging counterattack, Israeli government officials appeared on American television newscasts within hours after the shooting, claiming that the PLO had ordered Palestinians to slaughter Jewish worshipers at the Western Wall, and that Palestinian youths had deliberately provoked Israeli police into shooting them so that they could become martyrs. Several government ministers asserted that the riot was part of a premeditated plot by the PLO to draw the world's attention away from the conflict in the Gulf, in order to relieve pressure on Saddam Hussein and to spotlight the Palestinians' increasingly neglected plight. Arguing that Israeli police had not used unreasonable force to quell the "Arab riot," Deputy Foreign Minister Benjamin Netanyahu said on *Nightline* that Yasir Arafat was responsible for the massacre. He waved a jagged rock in front of the camera for emphasis.

Bowing to pressure brought by Israeli liberals and the U.S. State Department, Shamir appointed a three-person panel headed by Zvi Zamir, a former Mossad spy chief, to investigate what happened on the Temple Mount. After a hasty investigation, the panel found that Palestinians had started the riot by stoning Jewish worshipers in response to "violent and threatening calls" made by Muslim preachers over the mosques' loudspeakers, including exhortations to "slaughter the Jews." The panel's fifty-nine-page report also found that "many in the incited, rioting mob threw stones and metal objects [at Israeli police] from a very short range, some even wielding knives." The report concluded that the police had not overreacted, but instead "were caught in a life-threatening situation" through most of the forty-minute confrontation.

The Israeli right found much comfort in the Zamir report. "The findings of the Zamir Commission . . . confirm [that] the stoning of the police and worshipers at the Western Wall, initiated by incitement through mosque loudspeakers, was unprovoked; the threatened presence of the Temple Mount Faithful was used by the Palestinians leadership . . . as a pretext to recruit and incite," editorialized *The Jerusalem Post,* contradicting the paper's own reporting on the incident.

Many Israelis and Palestinians complained that the Zamir report was little more than a whitewash. The Zamir Commission had not been authorized to subpoena witnesses to give testimony, and most of its information came from Israel's security force, whose testimony was self-serving, critics noted. Furthermore, Zamir heard little evidence from Arab eyewitnesses, whose statements, in any case, were given little credence. The report was extremely vague on what touched off the riot. The central issue of why Israeli police opened fire and whether or not they used excessive force was virtually ignored, as was the question of whether a few or most of the Arab deaths were due to uncontrolled police fire. B'Tselem, an Israeli human-rights group, characterized the report as "extreme negligence."

A U.S.-backed Security Council resolution to send a UN investigative mission to Jerusalem was rejected by the Shamir government, which feared that it would jeopardize its claim that the entire city of Jerusalem was its "eternal capital." "By raising Jerusalem, Washington may have opened a Pandora's box," Harry Wall, the Jerusalem representative of the Anti-Defamation League of B'nai B'rith told *The Washington Post.* The United States, however, has never recognized Israel's annexation of East Jerusalem, which it considers occupied territory. While the Reagan administration conveniently ignored the issue, Bush and Baker have supported Arab claims to the disputed territory. Ironically, just six days before the Temple Mount shootings, Israeli foreign minister David Levy had been in Washington brokering a deal for a $400 million housing loan guarantee for the absorption of Soviet Jews. Baker had exacted a letter from Levy, which promised that the money would not be used to settle Jews beyond the "Green Line," Israel's 1967 border with Jordan. Baker understood the pledge to mean

Soviet Jews would not be settled either in the West Bank or in predominantly Arab East Jerusalem. But even before Levy returned to Israel, housing czar Ariel Sharon had declared that he was preparing to launch an enormous housing project for Soviet Jews in the heart of Arab East Jerusalem. The clear implication, as far as the State Department was concerned, was that Sharon's project was being funded with U.S. money, reportedly causing Bush and Baker to feel cheated.

In order to blunt criticism of the Temple Mount shooting and to divert attention away from Sharon's controversial housing scheme, the Shamir government launched an obstreperous public-relations campaign against the U.S. media's "biased" coverage of Israel. It's a time-honored strategy in Israel, where many government officials have come to believe that a problem hasn't been invented that a little *hasbara,* or propaganda, can't fix.

Reflexively regurgitating the Shamir government's line on the Temple Mount shootings, President's Conference chairman Seymour Reich declared that the Palestinians had perpetrated a "premeditated and unprovoked attack . . . on innocent Jewish worshipers peacefully assembled at prayer in observance of . . . Sukkoth.

"From the safety of the Temple Mount," Reich continued, "a mob of thousands of Palestinian Arabs, spurred on by calls of *jihad,* pelted the unprotected worshipers with rocks, shards of glass and knives. . . . Israeli police offered a deliberately measured response."

AIPAC issued a statement, declaring that the Israeli police on the Temple Mount had been in mortal danger, and added, "The Palestinian attack on the Jewish worshipers was premeditated." The generally more temperate American Jewish Congress issued a press release headlined: AJ CONGRESS OUTRAGED BY DELIBERATE ATTACK ON INNOCENT JEWS IN JERUSALEM. The National Jewish Community Relations Advisory Council sent a public letter to President Bush blaming the violence on the Palestinians.

The Jewish community's strong response seemed to intimidate the media, which with few exceptions followed Israel's interpretation of events. After the initial flurry of press coverage, the story seemed to die until *60 Minutes* aired a stinging segment showing that the Arabs killed on the Temple Mount were the victims of an Israeli police riot. The piece, reported by Mike Wallace, was based on a *Village Voice* investigation by reporter Michael Emery.

The Wallace piece generated intense criticism from right-wing Jewish circles. In the February 1991 issue of *Commentary,* David Bar-Illan, *The*

Jerusalem Post's editorial-page editor and a former speech writer for Israeli deputy foreign minister Benjamin Netanyahu, accused Wallace of accepting "the unadorned Palestinian version of the riot," and compared Wallace to revisionist historians who try to prove the Holocaust never took place. "What CBS did was to give an American stamp of approval to an Islamic fundamentalist blood libel, to the myth that the Jews were provocateurs on the Temple Mount, that what happened there was a massacre initiated by the Israeli police . . . Innocent Jewish victims of Islamic knifers have paid with their lives for this lie."

60 Minutes was also inundated with complaints from mainstream American Jewish organizations and powerful pro-Israel supporters. At a New York dinner party, *60 Minutes* executive producer Don Hewitt got into a shouting match with ABC television's Barbara Walters, the real estate developer and publisher of *U.S. News and World Report* Mortimer Zuckerman, and Mort Janklow, a literary agent, over the Temple Mount segment, causing Hewitt to walk out on his critics. The ADL's Abe Foxman, (an ardent Likud supporter and a former member of Betar, the youth wing of Jabotinsky's Revisionist movement) publicly accused *60 Minutes* of "unprofessional techniques," "bias," and a "prejudicial attitude towards the incident."

A furious CBS chairman Laurence Tisch summoned Hewitt and Wallace to a breakfast meeting to justify their reporting. Tisch is an influential figure in the New York UJA-Federation, which raised more than $1 billion to help settle Russian Jews in Israel. "He [Tisch] felt the piece was unfair," Wallace told me. Armed with notes and documents, Wallace defended his piece point by point. "I said, 'You guys are going to sit here . . . I've heard enough about this now . . . I will demonstrate, if it needs demonstration, that the piece was carefully, thoughtfully, accurately, and faithfully put together.'

"At the end of my presentation . . . Jay Kriegel [Tisch's chief aide] turned to Larry and said, 'Larry, I think they answered every question I had, and I think it was fair.' Well, Larry was not persuaded." Indeed, Tisch later told me that he felt the piece "required more background reporting."

Wallace was fully vindicated in July 1991, however, by Israeli magistrate Ezra Kama, who conducted an exhaustive six-month-long judicial inquest into the massacre. The inquest was begun at the request of the victims' families, in accordance with an Israeli law that allows for investigations into wrongful deaths. Judge Kama determined that the violence began when an

Israeli soldier "accidently" dropped a tear-gas grenade, which "began to roll toward a group of Moslem women." Contradicting the Zamir report in almost every key point, Kama found that the sheikhs did not use the mosque's loudspeakers to incite the Palestinians to riot, and that in fact they tried to calm the crowd; that trigger-happy Israeli police caused the violence, many firing their weapons indiscriminately; that the police were not in life-threatening situations; that there was no evidence that Muslims on the Mount had axes and knives, despite repeated police claims that they were threatened by such weapons; and that by the time the Arabs began to throw stones, virtually all of the Jewish worshipers in the plaza below had dispersed. An Israeli police officer told the court that he saw other police "shoot from the hip" in violation of regulations, while the transcripts show another said he saw police fire on Arabs who had sat down and begun praying. Kama concluded that the Arab deaths were not the result of a PLO plot, but rather of a police riot, adding that both sides allowed a "trivial incident"—plans by the Temple Mount Faithful to pray on the Mount— to get out of hand. However, Kama recommended that no charges be brought against the police.

Judge Kama's report was not without its critics. Skeptical Palestinians questioned Kama's conclusion that the violence began after an Israeli policeman "accidently dropped" a tear-gas grenade, which then "rolled" toward a group of Muslim women clustered at the Dome of the Rock. Joel Brinkley of *The New York Times* noted that "In fact, the women were on a plateau fifty yards away, uphill from where the police were standing." How was the grenade able to roll fifty yards uphill by itself? Palestinians asked incredulously.

Moshe Negby, a legal-affairs columnist for the Israeli newspaper *Hada-shot*, criticized Kama for not pressing charges against Israeli police. "[There] was a lot of material in the [Kama] report justifying, and even compelling, criminal and disciplinary action: illegal use of weapons, break-ing the rules of engagement, and wrongful behavior," he wrote.

Middle East Watch, an American human-rights organization affiliated with Human Rights Watch, argued that Israel's failure to prosecute Israeli police followed "a disturbing pattern in Israel's response to allegations of misconduct by its security forces: truthtelling but without accountability." Middle East Watch noted that in 1987, the government-appointed Landau Commission found that Shin Bet routinely used torture to extract confes-sions from Palestinian security suspects and then routinely lied about it when the defendants challenged their "confessions" in court. Yet the Landau Commisson did not recommend any prosecutions for perjury. In 1982, the Kahan Commission charged that then–Defense Minister Ariel Sharon bore "direct responsibility" for the massacre of Palestinians at Sabra and Shatila. Though Sharon was forced to resign, he was immediately given a Cabinet position and is now a leading contender to replace Shamir as the leader of Likud.

After the release of the Kama report, the ADL's Abe Foxman sent a public apology to Mike Wallace and *60 Minutes.* "The facts are now in regarding the Temple Mount," Foxman wrote. "Judge Kama rejects some of the claims the Israeli officers made and comes closer to some of the conclusions reached by *60 Minutes.*" No other Jewish official apologized to Wallace.

"It's not the end of the world," said Wallace.

I asked him if the criticism was going to prevent him from reporting on Israel.

"Absolutely not," Wallace said stoically. "Not for me it ain't."

"So it's not going to chill you," I pressed.

"Come on," he growled. "I'm an old man."

One of the Temple Mount Faithful's potentially most explosive assaults on the Mount is its ongoing lawsuit against the Muslim Religious Council, or Waqf, which administers the Temple Mount compound. The Faithful sued the Waqf in 1986 for allegedly destroying and damaging important Jewish antiquities on the Mount dating back to the First Temple. The group also sued the Israel Antiquities Authority for failing to enforce the country's laws protecting archeological sites. Israel's high court is expected to rule on the case sometime in 1992.

Solomon is the first to admit that the litigation is meant to weaken the Waqf's hold on the Temple Mount, which is known as Haram al-Sharif, or the Noble Sanctuary, to Muslims. "The point of the suit is to force the government to enforce Israeli law on the Mount and to show the Arabs that the Mount is under our sovereignty," Solomon said. "There is only one Temple Mount. To let them destroy the sacred remains is a sacrilege. It is my duty as a Jew to arouse my people and my country to stop the barbarians from doing these terrible things."

The substance of the lawsuit is based on the research of Dr. Asher S. Kaufman, a historian at the Hebrew University, who claims the Arabs have destroyed critical evidence regarding the location of the First and Second Temples. Some of the damage was caused during laying of utility lines, he said, but in a couple of cases, Jewish remains were deliberately shrouded by gardens or plaster. A garden planted on the northern part of the Mount, he said, was intended to cover stone outcroppings that were part of the inner courtyard of the ancient Jewish temples. Kaufman contends that a total of thirty-five Jewish remains from the temple periods, including rock outcroppings, walls, and mosaics, have been destroyed or covered with dirt or debris since the Six-Day War.

In June 1991, as an expert witness on behalf of the Temple Mount Faithful, Kaufman escorted three Israeli Supreme Court judges to the Temple Mount to explain his assertions with the aid of maps and photographs. Archeologists from the Antiquities Authority who went along told the jurists that they regularly inspect the Mount and that the Arabs have not vandalized Jewish antiquities. According to *The Jerusalem Post,* the Israeli archeologists praised the Waqf for restoration work it has carried out on the ancient Islamic structures in the area. Jerusalem city officials told me that Teddy Kollek does not want archeologists rummaging around the Temple Mount, inflaming passions and making Jerusalem any harder to rule than it already is.

Kaufman, a British-born nuclear physicist with no formal training in archeology, is largely dismissed by scholars who say there are virtually no remnants of the First and Second Temples. "There are cuttings in the bedrock [beneath the Dome of the Rock Mosque] that some say might be related to the temples," Dr. Lawrence Stager, professor of the archeology of Israel at Harvard University, told *The New York Times.* "This kind of evidence is so ambiguous that you can't prove anything one way or another."

Nevertheless, the Washington, D.C.–based *Biblical Archaeology Review* endorsed Kaufman's controversial research—and by extension, seemed to support the Temple Mount Faithful's lawsuit—in a September 1991 article that accused the Waqf of "making changes [on the Temple Mount] that have obliterated evidence critical to continuing scholarly efforts." Arguing that the Israeli government is oversensitive to Muslims' religious sensibilities, the article asked if "the protection of the archeological record on the Temple Mount [shouldn't] override any international outcry that may result?"

The bimonthly publication, which has a circulation of more than 175,000, is read primarily by Christian Evangelicals, said *BAR*'s editor, Hershel Shanks, a former lawyer who does not have a single degree in archeology. Shanks, who takes great pains to distance himself ideologically from the Temple Mount Faithful,* declared, "My interest in this article is archeological." Although few archeologists take *BAR* seriously, its article on the Temple Mount litigation was the subject of a lengthy, uncritical report in a September 1991 Science Section of *The New York Times.*

Gershon Solomon was ecstatic about the favorable press his lawsuit received in *BAR* and *The New York Times.* "Did you see it?" he asked. "Isn't it wonderful? It's helping us to advance our struggle."

As I was to learn, Solomon's family has been struggling against the Arabs for generations. Solomon lives, with his wife and children, near the top of a steep hill in a posh East Jerusalem suburb developed exclusively for Jews after the Six-Day War. His large three-story home resembles a small Crusader castle. It has thick stone walls and parapets. When I called on Solomon a few days after the Temple Mount massacre, his wife was on her hands and knees scrubbing the large black tiles that lined the hallway while listening to classical music that sounded Wagnerian.

I was ushered into Solomon's study, a small, wood-paneled room off the main entrance. An enormous, high-definition aerial photograph of the Temple Mount covered an entire wall; his black-lacquered desk was piled with papers, books in English and Hebrew, a small Israeli flag mounted on a stand, a menorah, and other religious memorabilia. Two large oak bookshelves contained numerous religious works and books about the Kurds and other non-Arab minorities that inhabit the Middle East. "The Arab world will never accept a different political, religious, and cultural entity in its midst," he said softly, pointing to the experience of the Maronite

---

*Shanks is vague and defensive about his politics. He claims he doesn't support any political party in Israel. One has to look at *Moment*, the Jewish monthly magazine he has edited since purchasing it in 1987, to get a sense of where he fits ideologically. One of *Moment's* most controversial pieces was bylined by Shanks himself, attacking Michael Lerner, the editor of *Tikkun*, America's preeminent liberal Jewish magazine of opinion. Shanks asserted that Lerner had grown fat and famous off publishing anti-Israeli polemics during the *intifada.* "[Lerner's] criticism of Israel often seems unrelieved," wrote Shanks in the June 1990 article. "Recently when President Bush objected to Jewish settlements in East Jerusalem, thereby raising a question about Israel's sovereignty over Jerusalem, most Jewish leaders were critical of the President's remarks. . . . The media found in Michael Lerner, however, a Jew who would side with the President."

Shanks had originally assigned Sheldon Teitelbaum, a free-lance writer, to profile Lerner. Teitelbaum's piece was accepted, with kudos from Shanks. But when Teitelbaum got the galleys back, he didn't recognize it. Shanks had rewritten the article himself, deleting most of the positive remarks about Lerner. Teitelbaum subsequently withdrew his name from the piece. "Shanks had an interest in a hit piece," a chagrined Teitelbaum later wrote to Lerner. Shanks maintains the published article was fair and balanced.

state of Israel. "He said explicitly," Solomon said, "that the Messiah and the salvation of the Jews would not come about through a miracle but by the natural acts of man—by the sweat and blood of the Jews. He believed the mystical yearning for the Messiah was a catastrophe. The struggle over the Hurva was like the struggle over the Temple Mount today."

Solomon's parents were disciples of Jabotinsky, and he joined the Irgun terrorist underground, which fought the British and the Arabs during the pre-state period, when he was ten years old. The following year, he was arrested for putting up anti-British posters. A British judge sentenced him to one year in jail. "I'll be here in a year, but you won't," Solomon told the judge. A few days later, the British quit Palestine, and Solomon walked out of prison. Perhaps exaggerating, he said he fought in the Irgun's youth brigade during Israel's War of Independence in 1948, defending the border between East and West Jerusalem from a position in a neighborhood called Katamoun, a neighborhood of graceful, old stone homes that originally belonged to wealthy Arabs.

In 1958, leading an army commando assault inside Syria, Solomon was grievously injured when an Israeli half-track accidently backed over him, crushing his legs. He was hospitalized for more than a year, and today walks with a noticeable limp and the aid of a sleek wooden staff, adding to his prophetic image. "My recovery taught me that I have an important task to play," Solomon explained. "I decided to dedicate my entire life to the land and the people of Israel. I felt I must lead our people to its true destiny."

Solomon took part in the battle for Jerusalem in the Six-Day War and claims he was assigned to guard the Temple Mount the night after the Old City returned to Jewish hands. When Israeli defense minister Moshe Dayan gave the keys to the Temple Mount to its Muslim custodians, Solomon founded the Temple Mount Faithful.

He joined the Herut party in 1969, and served as its representative on the Jerusalem City Council for ten years. Solomon was also a member of Herut's secretariat, and was appointed to head its youth department by his idol, Menachem Begin. He was ecstatic when Begin was elected prime minister in 1977. After years in the political wilderness, the head of the Irgun was now the leader of the Jewish nation. The Labor party may have had doubts about what to do with the occupied territories, but Begin, a man true to Jabotinsky's sacred principles, fervently believed in Greater Israel.

But Solomon's admiration turned to loathing when Begin signed the

Camp David Accords, which promised to return the Sinai to the Egyptians and to work toward Palestinian autonomy on the West Bank and the Gaza Strip. Begin had also accepted UN Resolution 242, which called on Israel to trade land for peace as the basis for negotiations among Israel and its Arab neighbors. While Begin insisted that Jerusalem and the West Bank were nonnegotiable, he also said he would enter into peace talks without preconditions.

On the rainy winter morning that Begin returned from Camp David, in the fall of 1978, Teddy Kollek had organized a ceremony for him at the entrance of Jerusalem. In an emotional speech, Begin said he had "brought peace for my people." Solomon approached the podium, pointed a large black umbrella at Begin, and shouted, "You are the Chamberlain of your people!" It was a blunt reference to Neville Chamberlain, who, after handing Czechoslovakia to Hitler at Munich in 1939, declared that he had achieved "peace in our time." Begin appeared to be momentarily stunned. In a nation that included many Holocaust survivors, Solomon's message was cruelly effective. It was a tactic that Begin, who had tried to turn the legacy of the Holocaust into a sort of secular national religion, might have used himself. "It was not easy to do," Solomon told me. "Begin was the symbol of the *real* Israel. I fought under him in the Irgun. But he was destroying himself and the country."

Solomon started "the Faithful of the Principles of Herut," a group that fought inside Herut to pressure Begin to renounce Camp David. He finally walked out of Herut and merged the Faithful of the Principles of Herut with Banai, a consortium of right-wing groups that accused Begin of betraying Greater Israel. At the prodding of Rav Kook, radicals from Banai and others from Herut, the National Religious party, and Gush Emunim, formed the Tehiya (Renaissance) party on October 8, 1979. Its leaders included Yuval Neeman, the father of Israel's nuclear-weapons program and then chancellor of Tel Aviv University; Geula Cohen, who fought in the Stern Gang with Shamir and was widely known as the Israeli version of the Spanish La Pasionaria; and Gush Emunim's Daniella Weiss, who is even more fiery than Cohen. Many of Tehiya's early meetings were held in Solomon's home.

Tehiya's primary mission was to save the Land of Israel from those who would barter it away for an "illusory" peace treaty with the Arabs. Israel was scheduled to withdraw from the Sinai in April 1982 as part of the Camp David Accords and Tehiya wanted to win enough seats in the 1981 national elections to block the evacuation. It won only three seats, however. Still, it had organized ugly antigovernment demonstrations in Yamit that pitted Rabbi Levinger's Gush Emunim shock troops against Israeli soldiers. The image of Jewish soldiers swinging rifle butts at religious demonstrators on Israeli television traumatized the nation. Any attempt to retreat from the West Bank and the Gaza Strip, Tehiya leaders warned, would end in civil war. Meanwhile, Tehiya successfully prodded the government to build huge housing projects in the occupied territories. Perhaps its greatest achievement was winning passage in the Knesset of its 1980 bill to formally annex Arab East Jerusalem. One year, Tehiya even sponsored Solomon's unsuccessful bid to become Jerusalem's mayor.

By 1992, Tehiya had three seats in Israel's Knesset and a Cabinet position as well as hundreds of activists in key government ministries, making it far from a fringe party. Because of the proportional nature of the Israeli electoral system, which grants a Knesset seat to a party polling a mere 1.5 percent of the vote, small parties have enormous bargaining power. As Labor and Likud had about an equal percentage of supporters throughout the 1980s, small parties were able to tip the balance in favor of one or the other and, in effect, extort prized government posts, cash, and, in the case of the religious parties, virtual control over everything from marriage and divorce to the closing of restaurants on the Sabbath. In the summer of 1991, Tehiya, in alliance with two small right-wing parties, threatened to bring down the Likud government if it traded land for peace with the Arabs at an upcoming Middle East peace conference. Shamir placated the ultranationalist parties by accelerating the pace of West Bank settlements. Several months later, after Shamir said that he would present his plan for Palestinian autonomy at peace talks, Tehiya and "Gandhi's" Homeland party bolted from the government, causing its collapse and setting the stage for Labor's surprising victory in the June 1992 elections.

Tehiya, the most rigidly ideological of all the ultranationalist parties, was severely punished for bringing down the Shamir government. In the June 1992 elections, it failed to win a single seat in the Knesset. Labor, which won 14.8 percent of the settlers' votes, did twice as well as Tehiya in the territories. Many of Tehiya's supporters defected to Likud and the Gush Emunim–dominated National Religious party.

Tehiya has worked closely with Solomon's Temple Mount Faithful. In one prominent example, a delegation of ultranationalist Knesset members led by Geula Cohen and Likud Interior Committee chairman Dov Shilansky held a prayer meeting with Solomon on the Temple Mount, next to the Dome of the Rock Mosque, in January 1986, touching off riots in Arab East Jerusalem. Although key members of Tehiya still support Solomon's group, their backing has become more discreet since the 1990 Sukkoth Day massacre. Neither Tehiya party activists nor Solomon promote the idea of Jewish sovereignty over the Temple Mount because they hope to spur the Messiah's arrival. For them, the Temple Mount Faithful's ideology is profoundly nationalist. "The Temple was more than a religious institution—it was the center of our political and cultural life," Solomon declared. "It is our testimony and license to this land. It's a known fact that whoever controlled the Temple Mount controlled all of the Land of Israel. The Arabs know very well that once we gain control of the Temple Mount, we will close the circle, and the legitimacy of our control over the land will be complete."

Solomon's celebrity has swelled since the Sukkoth Day massacre, helping to draw new converts and funding to his movement. But it is in America where he is attracting his most fervent support—especially from among the 45.5 million-strong Christian Evangelical community. Fundamentalist Evangelicals, who interpret the Bible literally, believe the Jews' return to Israel and the restoration of the Temple will precede the Second Coming of Christ—at which point the Jews will be forcibly converted. Zionist fundamentalists like Solomon accept the Christians' patronage because they are convinced the Messiah will be a Jew. The alliance between Jewish and Christian fundamentalists is perhaps the ultimate marriage of convenience, with the two groups united to bring on the Messiah, and each side convinced the Messiah will be its own.

Israeli ties to Evangelicals in the United States were forged during the early days of Menachem Begin's premiership. The Bible-quoting Begin felt at ease with the Evangelicals, who frequently visited his Jerusalem office, where they reportedly pressed him to rebuild the temple. He developed a particularly close relationship with the Reverend Jerry Falwell, whom he presented with the prestigious Jabotinsky Award for outstanding service to the state of Israel. Their friendship went beyond theology: Begin and Falwell shared the belief that Israel stood as the bulwark against Soviet aggression in the Middle East. Evangelicals became financiers for both the Likud party and the West Bank settlement movement. Begin had been stumping among Evangelicals in the United States in November 1983, when his wife, Aliza, died in a Jerusalem hospital.

Falwell openly supported Likud during the 1984 Israeli elections. "I would sincerely hope no government could be elected in Israel which could freeze the settlements and reverse the trend toward irrevocable control that will come in the West Bank in three to five years," Falwell told several hundred members of AFSI at its annual conference in 1984.

Following AFSI's lead, the ADL, AIPAC, and the American Jewish Committee embraced the Evangelical community. "The rationale wasn't to make Falwell and his cronies into good guys, like AFSI did, but it was a parochial, self-interested move" to gain support for Israel, said Murray Polner, the former editor of *Present Tense*, a liberal magazine of world Jewish affairs published by the American Jewish Committee until it was closed in 1990 for "budgetary" reasons. "They operated under the as-sumption that when you scratch the surface of these guys, there is a lot of latent anti-Semitism."*

So long as there was strong support for Israel, the Christian right's conservative domestic and foreign-policy views didn't seem to matter to these Jewish leaders, even when they went against the Jewish community's long-standing support for civil rights and abortion and opposition to school prayer. "When these issues on which we differ, singly or together, are weighed against our agreement on the prerequisites for the physical security of Israel, they simply do not balance the scale," wrote Nathan Perlmutter, the late director of the ADL. "The fundamentalists' relative religious intolerance can and does coexist with religious and political attitudes sup-portive of Israel's well-being. Fundamentalist intolerance is currently not so baneful as its friendship for Israel is helpful." To Jews troubled by a pro-Israel coalition with the religious right, Perlmutter added, "Praise God and pass the ammunition."

Many liberal Jews denounced this trend. Rabbi Alexander Schindler, the former president of the Presidents' Conference, has said, "When the Jabotinsky Foundation presents its award to Jerry Falwell . . . for his support of Israel, and the Anti-Defamation League offers its platform to Pat Robertson of the Christian Broadcasting Network to speak about Jerusa-

*The American Jewish Committee continues to publish the staunchly pro-Likud journal *Commentary*, the house organ of the neoconservative movement.

lem, it is madness—and suicide. . . . Can someone really be good for Israel when everything else he says and does is destructive of America and undermines the Jewish community? Let us not honor those whose works are anathema to everything for which we stand." Schindler wondered whether Jewish leaders weren't "willing to forgive anyone anything so long as they hear a good word about Israel."

Solomon seemed to benefit from the Jewish establishment's "outreach" to the Evangelicals in America, where he has set up Christian chapters of the Temple Mount Faithful in New York, Florida, Texas, and California. As Solomon made a monthlong whistle-stop tour of the Bible Belt in August of 1991, prominent Christian Evangelical leaders implored him to find a way to build the Third Temple in the here and now. One of Solomon's best-known boosters is Pat Robertson, a Republican candidate for president in 1988, whose *700 Club* talk show is beamed by satellite to more than two hundred U.S. TV stations and syndicated in sixty countries by the Christian Broadcasting Network. Robertson promotes the view that Israel is God's favored nation, and the United States will be blessed if it supports Israel. During Israel's 1982 invasion of Lebanon, Robertson spent several weeks explaining to millions of viewers how Jewish soldiers in Lebanon were fulfilling the apocalyptic vision of the prophet Ezekiel.

Early in August 1991, Robertson hosted Solomon for two days at CBN headquarters in Virginia Beach, Virginia. "We considered him a very important guest," said Susan Norman, a spokesperson for Robertson. "Pat was very favorably impressed with him." Solomon was quartered in the governor's suite of a five-star hotel owned by CBN and was assigned five armed bodyguards to shadow him night and day. "You know," Solomon told me, "my name was ahead of Kahane's on a PLO hit list. Pat was worried about Arab terrorists."

Robertson introduced Solomon on the *700 Club* as the leader of a group fighting for the liberation of the Temple Mount. "We will never have peace until the Mount of the House of the Lord is restored" to Jewish hands, Robertson declared.

Solomon said during his TV interview that his was a historical mission to turn Israel into a kingdom of priests and wise men, "so we will be for all the world a tower of light. . . . I said that God gave us Israel not only for ourselves, but for all humanity. I felt this was the point that would touch Jew and non-Jew alike. I believe that Israel has this mission and must fulfill

it. It's not just a struggle for the Temple Mount, it's a struggle for the
. . . redemption of the world."

The Temple Mount Faithful had languished as a cash-poor adjunct to
Tehiya until Solomon met Monroe Spen, a bald, heavyset seventy-three-
year-old Sarasota, Florida, stockbroker whose instinct for good investments
turned a family inheritance into a fortune. Spen had already helped finance
a number of Israeli right-wing causes, including Meir Kahane's successful
Knesset bid in July 1984. "I always live by the Golden Rule," boasted
Spen. "Whoever has the gold makes the rules. . . . While I am not an
Orthodox Jew, I am an extremely Zionistic Jew and very proud of it, with
no apologies to anyone—Jew or Gentile."

Spen said the call to rebuild the temple came to him "in a vision." He
wrote to Teddy Kollek about his dream, urging him to use city funds to
demolish the Muslim holy places and build in their stead a magnificent
Jewish temple. "According to Jewish tradition," Kollek replied in a letter
to Spen, "the Temple is ready and waiting to descend to its appointed
location together with the coming of the Messiah. No human hands are
allowed to construct it. As far as we are concerned, that makes the situation
very clear."

Spen formally entered the cloistered world of Temple Mount activists on
August 17, 1986, when he assembled a number of radical right-wing
personalities at an expensive Moroccan restaurant inside the newly refur-
bished Jewish Quarter of Jerusalem's Old City. The group, seated around
a table covered with kosher delicacies from North Africa, included Yoel
Lerner, a plump, bearded former Kach party activist who has been imprisoned for conspiring to blow up the Dome of the Rock and, in a separate
case, for plotting to overthrow the government and establish a theocratic
regime; Stanley Goldfoot, a wealthy South African–born Jew and a key link
to U.S. Evangelicals; Peter Goldman, then head of Americans for a Safe
Israel; and Menachem Bar-Shalom, a fund-raiser for Ateret Cohanim.

Meir Kahane attended the summit, as did representatives from the
ultranationalist Tehiya party. Z. H. Hurwitz, adviser on diaspora affairs to
then–Vice Premier Shamir of Likud, which at the time ruled Israel in a
coalition arrangement with the more liberal Labor party, wrote to Monroe
Spen prior to the meeting, "Your sentiments regarding the Temple Mount
coincide with ours." But he warned against rash action: "Those responsible
for the existence and continuation of the reborn Jewish state must proceed

with caution and calculation." The government, Hurwitz explained, cannot take a more active stance on the Temple Mount issue until it gets a directive from the acting chief rabbis.

Spen also invited Yehuda Etzion to the dinner. "Received your dinner invitation, but cannot come as I have been in prison for over two years already for the sin of constant and purposeful loyalty to the Temple Mount," wrote Etzion, the Makhteret's charismatic leader who was then serving a seven-year sentence for plotting to blow up the Dome of the Rock Mosque and for planning car-bomb attacks that injured two Palestinian mayors.

Spen had hoped to unite the disparate Temple Mount groups into an umbrella organization and set up a conduit to fund it. At the outset of the meeting, however, it was obvious that his guests were hopelessly split over tactics. Kach sympathizers like Goldfoot and Lerner advocated stepped-up confrontation with Israeli authorities over their right to worship at the Temple Mount. Gershon Solomon favored a step-by-step approach: first winning the right to pray, perhaps through the Israeli courts, later erecting a small synagogue on the grounds of the Temple Mount, and finally razing the mosques and building the Third Temple. Tensions inside the group flared with Lerner's stinging, sarcastic attacks on Solomon, whom he accused of being a weak, ineffectual leader. Unable to forge a coalition, Spen began funneling tens of thousands of dollars to the various, and often warring, Temple Mount organizations. Tired of the squabbling, Spen eventually gave his full support to Solomon, setting up the tax-exempt Friends of the Temple Mount Faithful in Sarasota. "Gershon is like the prophets of old," Spen said. "He has that magical twinkle in his eye."

Another key link between U.S. Evangelicals and Jewish extremists who have tried to "liberate" the Temple Mount is Stanley Goldfoot. The South African–born Goldfoot, a shrewd, rhetorically gifted former member of the Stern Gang, boasts about his involvement in the 1948 assassination of United Nations mediator Count Folke Bernadotte and his role in the bombing of the King David Hotel, the British headquarters in Palestine during the Mandate period. At his palatial home in Jerusalem, he said he had reached out to U.S. Christians in the early 1980s because the Israeli Temple Mount groups had run out of energy and money. "I put out feelers to certain *goyim* who were looking for some kind of connection" to the Temple Mount, he added.

After forging contacts with several influential Evangelicals, Goldfoot formed the Jerusalem Temple Foundation with Douglas Krieger, a lay minister from Littleton, Colorado, and Terry Risenhoover, an Oklahoma gas and oil millionaire. (In 1987, Risenhoover was sentenced to four years in prison for selling worthless oil-exploration leases in remote sections of Alaska, bilking approximately three thousand investors out of about $25 million. Krieger, an assistant vice president of Risenhoover's company, was not indicted.) The two Americans also set up an affiliated nonprofit, tax-exempt organization called the Temple Mount Foundation, based in Los Angeles. One of their first projects was publishing a detailed map of the Temple Mount, showing the location of the Jewish temples, based on the research of Professor Asher Kaufman.

Krieger and Risenhoover were also deeply involved with the American Forum for Jewish-Christian Cooperation, an ad hoc group that brings Jewish leaders together with a wide range of fundamentalist preachers and political activists. David Ben-Ami, the president of the American Forum and an Orthodox rabbi from Harrisburg, Pennsylvania, chaired the religious committee for President Reagan's 1980 inauguration. Later, the American Forum helped organize a White House meeting where Rabbi Ben-Ami introduced politically conservative Jewish community leaders to Christian fundamentalists. The guests, who included Jimmy Swaggart and leaders of the Lubavitcher Hasidic sect from Crown Heights, Brooklyn, found they shared similar views on homosexuality, civil rights, and the Soviet Union. The meeting featured briefings by national security chief Robert McFarlane, Undersecretary of Defense Fred Ikle, and Ambassador William Middendorf, U.S. representative to the Organization of American States. Risenhoover, known for his beautiful tenor voice, was the evening's featured entertainer.

By the mid-1980s, the Israeli Labor movement's respected newspaper, *Davar*, was reporting that Goldfoot's group had raised $10 million, which it planned to donate to West Bank settlements and use to purchase Arab land in the occupied territories and to help Israelis rebuild the temple. Some money was also transferred to Yeshiva Ateret Cohanim to buy real estate in the Old City near the mosques. According to Krieger, Goldfoot received fifty thousand dollars from wealthy Evangelical bankers in Houston to help pay the legal fees for the yeshiva students caught trying to break into the Temple Mount with explosives in 1983. Risenhoover and Krieger also arranged funding for a full-page ad that appeared in several Israeli newspapers imploring the government to drop the charges against the students. Soon after the ad ran, a Jerusalem judge threw the case out of court, arguing that the students were "amateurs" who had no serious intention of blowing up the mosques.

In 1983, Goldfoot helped to organize a seven-man archeological expedition into one of the underground passageways that snake beneath the Temple Mount. It was led by Lambert Dolphin, a prominent Evangelical who was the head of the radiophysics department at Stanford Research Institute in Menlo Park, California. "What we planned to do," said Dolphin, "was to go into the rabbinical tunnel that starts at the Western Wall and goes back eight hundred or nine hundred feet and look with radar through the Herodian outer wall of the Temple Mount in search of building foundations, temples, storerooms, all of which would have been connected with the First and Second Temples." Goldfoot claims he secured an Israeli Army helicopter and other logistical help for the research team through the good offices of Ariel Sharon. An Arab riot triggered by Dolphin's visit cut short the exploration, however.

The Jerusalem Temple Foundation under way, Goldfoot came to the United States in 1983 to spread the Temple Mount gospel and to help catalyze the movement. "I told the *goyim* in America that the Temple Mount is the highest mountain on the face of the earth because it represents the moral and spiritual Everest of mankind," recalled Goldfoot. "I was astounded by the reception. Not because it was Stanley Goldfoot. It had nothing to do with me as a person. It was because I was somebody from Jerusalem who had come to talk about the temple." Goldfoot larded his speeches with fire and brimstone. "I told the *goyim* that they have a tremendous debt to us Jews. And that I doubt that they can ever repay this debt; that they persecuted us; they murdered us; they've stolen from us for centuries. They have even stolen our religion, which they distorted and called Christianity. But I told them if they make retribution sufficiently, strongly, and long enough, maybe they will be forgiven and accepted in the sight of the Lord. God does not accept you, I told them. But if you help us build the temple, you can be saved. I'm not sure God will forgive you, but you've got to try. They loved it. They cried, 'Hallelujah! Hallelujah!' Then I told them that they have to go immediately and spread propaganda all over America in favor of Jewish sovereignty on the Temple Mount and moving the American embassy to Jerusalem—to put pressure on Congress [and] on the president himself."

Not long after Goldfoot's foray into the Bible Belt, the alliance between Jewish messianics and Christian Evangelicals netted an impressive catch— North Carolina Republican senator Jesse Helms, who has since been installed as minority leader of the Senate Foreign Relations Committee. Helms, long reviled by the pro-Israel lobby for comparing Menachem Begin to Adolf Hitler and for calling on the United States to break diplomatic relations with the Jewish state in the wake of its invasion of Lebanon, became its darling after his sudden and dramatic conversion in 1984. The conversion was abetted by conservative Jews, including Ivan Boesky, the stock swindler, who helped bankroll Helms's costly, bitterly contested 1984 Senate race against former governor Jim Hunt of North Carolina.

In August 1985, Helms made his first visit to the Promised Land, as part of a trip paid for by then-senator Chic Hecht of Nevada, a close friend and ideological disciple of Helms. (During Helms's 1984 Senate race, Hecht had introduced the senator to conservative Jews, including CBS chairman Laurence Tisch. "Larry was very impressed with Jesse," Hecht recalled.) The trip was arranged by Robert Jacobs, a burly, hot-tempered Manhattan real estate developer and accountant, and Peter Goldman, then director of Americans for a Safe Israel. Jacobs, still one of Helms's major Jewish fund-raisers, was responsible more than anyone else for Helms's about-face on Israel. Jacobs introduced Helms to Jews who were as reactionary as the senator himself, even arranging a secret meeting in Washington between the senator and rabble-rousing rabbi Meir Kahane. Indeed, for nearly fifteen years Jacobs had been Kahane's financial guardian angel; he has also raised more than $100,000 for the families of the Makhteret, Gush Emunim's terrorist underground.

In Israel, Helms met with a number of prominent politicians, including Ariel Sharon and Yitzhak Shamir, and toured West Bank Jewish settlements. He also helped dedicate a synagogue and wore a yarmulke to pray at the Wailing Wall, where he apparently had a revelation. "The West Bank is the heart of ancient Israel, the very land that the Bible is all about," he told companions. In a letter to President Reagan, Helms wrote, "We should never pursue any plan that envisions a separation of the West Bank from Israel. . . . Given the deep attachment of the Israelis to Samaria and Judea, they need, from the deepest spiritual motives, free access to those Biblical lands. . . . What we cannot accept is a Soviet-backed PLO state in the heart of the Holy Land." Helms has since introduced legislation to move the U.S. embassy from Tel Aviv to Jerusalem—a bellwether issue for Christian and Jewish fundamentalists who view the city as the coming seat of heavenly power. In response to a request from Monroe Spen that he push for the embassy to be moved, Helms wrote, "Your suggestion certainly appeals to me—but then, I've long been in favor of moving our embassy to Jerusalem. I can't understand the reluctance on the part of the State Department. Let me pass along your suggestion to the president and see how it flies."

So complete was Helms's transformation that he now can count on a steady infusion of conservative Jewish campaign money. In his 1990 race against Democrat Harvey Gantt, for instance, Helms received the maximum individual contribution of one thousand dollars from Mayer Mitchell—the president of AIPAC. Many other pro-Israel supporters followed suit. Jewish donations to the liberal Gantt were noticeably absent, according to the *Jewish Forward*.

If Stanley Goldfoot and Gershon Solomon are the Jewish messianic links to Christian Evangelicals, forty-nine-year-old Douglas Krieger—a lay minister, PR man extraordinaire, and Evangelical jack-of-all-trades—is their mirror image. Krieger, who mixes an apocalyptic rap with a touch of street jive, built a three-thousand-square-foot concert hall at the foot of the Rockies near Littleton, Colorado. "Christian rock is big," he said during construction, while teenage workers with long hair and jeans hammered away to the beat of the Beastbusters, one of Krieger's Christian rock-and-roll discoveries.

Krieger has advised Religious Roundtable founder Ed McAteer on Middle Eastern affairs. The Religious Roundtable was established in 1979 to coordinate the Christian right's agenda; among the Roundtable's influential supporters are Jerry Falwell and Phyllis Schlafly. Krieger also has served as the executive director of the National Prayer Breakfast in Honor of Israel, an annual event sponsored by the National Religious Broadcasters in Washington, D.C. Ed McAteer, who originated the Prayer Breakfast for Israel in 1981, admits he has received "flak" from American Jewish officials who are worried that Krieger wants to "blow up the mosques." When Jeane Kirkpatrick addressed the breakfast one year, a scale model of the Third Temple was prominently displayed in the convention hall.

Krieger denied having any interest in blowing up the mosques, but, like virtually everyone involved in efforts to build the Third Temple, his speech was studded with images of the Apocalypse. In fact, shaping the perceptions of Krieger and his fellow Evangelicals is a belief in the divine scheme of history known as "dispensational premillennialism." They hold that a series of events will occur as history unfolds to its bloody climax, including the Jews' return to Israel, making Jerusalem a Jewish city, and building the Third Temple. They prophesied that these events would set the stage for a nuclear war in which Israel, backed by the United States, would destroy the Soviet Union and its Arab allies, raising Israel to the rank of a world power. Later, according to prophecy, after Christ's return, there would be a second horrific global nuclear showdown at Armageddon, a real place located northwest of Jerusalem where Christ's armies would defeat the antichrist. Two thirds of the Jewish people would be destroyed in the battle, the survivors embracing the Lord Jesus. This view accounts for the Evangelicals' support of Israel and the "New Right" in the United States, which saw the Soviet Union as the "evil empire."

Ronald Reagan himself has been hooked on the Armageddon theory since 1968, when Billy Graham tutored him on the meaning of the End of Days. By 1980, Reagan was proclaiming on the Jim Bakker TV show that "we may be the generation that sees Armageddon." The obsession followed him to the White House. Robert McFarlane told Reagan's biographer Lou Cannon that "Reagan's interest in anti-missile defense was the product of his interest in Armageddon." When, on separate occasions, Frank Carlucci and Caspar Weinberger talked to Reagan about the importance of nuclear deterrence, he gave them a lecture about Armageddon. On May 5, 1989, Reagan told Cannon that Israel's possession of the Temple Mount is a sign that Armageddon is near.

That the Dome of the Rock Mosque will be destroyed and in its place will rise the Third Temple is "preordained," Krieger said, with the destruction probably being caused by an earthquake. But Krieger doesn't discount other possibilities and believes that a nuclear war sparked by clashes between Israel and Syria is imminent. Meanwhile, he refused to say more about joint Jewish-Christian efforts to realize their divine aims: "It's all hush-hush. . . . We don't want to embarrass our friends in Israel," where Stanley Goldfoot and the others are proceeding "underground."

Goldfoot himself is not nearly as cryptic. In a letter to Monroe Spen, he described mounting tensions on the Syrian-Israeli border and added, "We should be running a worldwide propaganda campaign and using clever promotions (like Machiavelli) and preparing public opinion for the day we drop a nuclear device on Damascus—we will have to do it—and time it possibly with another on Libya. The prescription is in *Tanach* [The Bible]: "Behold, Damascus is taken away from being a city, and it shall be a ruinous heap.' (Isaiah 17:1). . . . I am sending you a separate communiqué relating Temple Mount to Syrian situation. We must prepare for this opportunity."

Exactly what Goldfoot had in mind is open to interpretation, but Israeli experts fear that Jewish extremists are planning an incident that could spark an international conflagration. Attempts to establish a Jewish foothold on the Temple Mount could trigger a bloodbath of unimaginable horror. Because the Temple Mount is a focus of Muslim passions, it is an easy political instrument with which to rally the Islamic world to the defense of the faith against the infidels. A successful attack by these zealots for Zion on Muslim holy places could result in a kind of Armageddon—one in which the use of nuclear weapons is not unimaginable.

The possibility of triggering such a catastrophe has not deterred Gershon Solomon. On Sukkoth Day 1991, one year after the Temple Mount massacre, Solomon announced that he would hire a helicopter to airlift the three-ton cornerstone into the Temple Mount Compound. The Israeli police prevented Solomon from doing so, but allowed him to parade around the Old City with his followers. As the Temple Mount Faithful marched with balloons and banners, nearly one thousand Israeli soldiers patrolled Arab East Jerusalem, which remained relatively calm. But on a *moshav* (agricultural cooperative) north of Tel Aviv, a sixty-seven-year-old Jewish man was stabbed to death, apparently by an Arab in revenge for the Temple Mount slayings the year before. Pictures of the Dome of the Rock Mosque were scattered by the body.

CHAPTER 6

Born Again

"We are getting a raw deal," yelled Rabbi Mordechai Goldstein as he squeezed the trigger of a portable fire extinguisher, taking aim at a brushfire that was swiftly spreading toward a large green tank that supplied heating oil to Metzad, a down-at-the-heels religious settlement built in 1984 on a remote plateau in the Judean wilderness. The fire extinguisher was defective; it wheezed and fizzed, and nothing came out. "Look at the junk the government gave us," Goldstein moaned, his white shirt untucked and darkly stained, his half-looped tie flapping, his gray beard and glasses glinting in the sun.

Swarms of small, untidy children, with filthy white shirts and dark pants, their side curls twirling in the wind, fought the fire with brooms and handfuls of dirt. "Rabbi, Rabbi, it's going to the tank," they cried out in Hebrew and English.

A lanky teenager turned on a garden hose, but not enough water dribbled out to fill a drinking glass; there was no water pressure.

"Rabbi, Rabbi, we are going to be incinerated!"

Then the wind changed, and the fire shifted toward a steep ridge and burned itself out. Good fortune had saved Metzad. But Goldstein was still angry. The rabbi complained loudly that from its inception Metzad had been orphaned by the Likud. "We came here when the Likud was trying to push in a *yishuv*" (settlement) on the eve of the 1984 national elections, he said. "They had nobody else so they took us. It's not that we don't love Israel. The RaMBaM says go together into the mountains or desert of

Judea and make your own community. We followed the RaMBaM's advice—we made a community. Now we expect the government to help.

"But because we are mostly Americans here and don't know how to communicate with Israelis, we are easy to push around. Any time we asked for our rights, the government said, 'What are you complaining about?' We had a camp here one summer with one hundred and forty children. The government promised us ten thousand dollars for mattresses, then the ten thousand dollars became eight thousand dollars, and that was a lot, but we still don't have it. We can't get our feet off the ground!"

More forlorn than many Israeli slums I had visited, Metzad is a testament to the fact that not all settlements are created equal. As we shall see, Metzad has suffered because of Goldstein's unconventional religious views and lack of political savvy. The thirty families who have settled in Metzad are *horzim baale teshuvah*, so-called "repentant" Jews who have renounced their secular lives and have embraced the rigors of ultra-Orthodox Judaism. Because the men study in a Jerusalem yeshiva, their families subsist largely on small government stipends that are doled out to all full-time yeshiva students. Eking out a meager existence, Metzad's settlers live in rusted government-surplus trailers, most not larger than seven hundred square feet—though many of the families have ten or more children. Unlike nearby Efrat, a non–Gush Emunim settlement of predominantly modern Orthodox Jews from North America that boasts tennis courts, and a soon-to-be-constructed recreation center that will house an indoor basketball court, and a lavishly equipped gymnasium that would be the pride of any American high school, Metzad has little more in the way of amenities than a tiny hut that has been painted with flowers and converted into a nursery school. "We'd like maybe a prefabricated shed so our kids could have a place out of the wind and the rain," said Shabtai Herman, a South African *baal teshuvah* who gave up a promising career as an economist to study Torah and practice herbal medicine. "In winter it can be sheer hell because the winds blow with such velocity that a child cannot go outside and play. When our kids come home from school, very often they have to go around to the back of the house and climb through the windows because our houses face the wind, and you can't open the door."

There is no commerce or agriculture in this dust-blown corner of Judea. Even grapes from the local vineyards are sour. But if poverty pervades Metzad, so does the fear of Arabs. Once, two goats owned by the settlement were found beheaded. Tracks were discovered leading back to Sair, a neighboring Arab village whose land was expropriated by the government to build Metzad. Another time, a truck delivering a refrigerator was ambushed by rifle fire. During the Gulf War, Metzad's settlers worried that their homes would be overrun by marauding Arabs. "The Israeli Army said, 'Don't worry, we'll come for you with tanks,' " said a settler. "But what if those tanks were stuck on the front lines? How were we supposed to hold back thousands of Arabs with twenty-five men? Our rabbi says the Arabs could squash us like a pimple."

Everyone in Metzad seems to have a story about being stoned by Arabs during the forty-five-minute drive to Jerusalem. Gershon, a pudgy, bearded part-time art dealer originally from Canada, told me about the time he was ambushed while driving a carload of children from Metzad to Jerusalem. He had stopped his white Peugeot along the side of the road near Bethlehem so one of the boys could go to the bathroom. Suddenly, Arabs rose from the hills with a war cry and pelted the car with grapefruit-sized stones. Gershon said he deliberately aimed his Uzi low, spraying bullets several yards in front of the attackers. But the barrage of stones continued. "I trained my gun on the ringleader," Gershon recalled. "I was about to blow his head off when we caught each other's eye. He sensed his time was up, and with a whoop the Arabs withdrew.

"I'm a religious Jew, a God-fearing settler," Gershon continued. "I came to live in a Torah community. But you have to protect yourself from the Arabs. Our army uses tear gas, rubber bullets, plastic bullets—okay, sometimes they demolish a house. But the army is pretty gentle. They hope to wear the Arabs down. It's not the way to handle it. The Arabs don't fear us. The analogy is an easy teacher and one who uses a stick. Who will the kids take advantage of? You need a stick to control the Arabs. They have to live in fear. Gush Emunim wants to be able to go into an Arab village and level it if there is trouble. They understand the Arabs' mentality. If you don't use force, they don't respect you."

The use of physical force is not part of Rabbi Goldstein's repertoire. *Kvetching,* yes. Hysteria, by all means. But he is also a warm, open, caring, charismatic leader, who has formed around him a community that has endured difficult circumstances during difficult times. Rabbi Goldstein is a pioneer, not only in the political sense for having established a settlement,

but also in the religious sense for having created the *baal teshuvah* movement—a revolutionary event in modern Jewish life that has had a profound
effect on Israel and the diaspora Jewish community.

The sixty-five-year-old rabbi grew up in an upper-middle-class home in
the Bronx. His father was the head of the Food and Drug Administration
for the state of New York; his mother was one of the first women to
practice law at the turn of the century. His modern Orthodox parents were
strongly committed to the Zionist experiment in Palestine. "We always
dreamed about and loved Israel," Goldstein remembered. That devotion
was channeled into political activism on behalf of right-wing Jewish causes.
As a teenager, Goldstein joined Betar, whose American director was then
Moshe Arens. When war broke out between the Arabs and the newly
created Jewish state in 1948, many of Goldstein's friends in Betar went to
Israel to fight. Goldstein stayed in New York and joined the Stern Gang,
becoming part of a ring that smuggled weapons to the terrorist group in
Palestine.

Goldstein became an Orthodox rabbi, and in 1964 traveled to Israel with
members of his New York yeshiva for advanced studies in *Halacha* and
business law. He decided to remain in Israel and found a job teaching at
the Hebron Yeshiva, a Haredi, or ultra-Orthodox, religious school that had
moved to Jerusalem in 1936 after vicious programs drove the Jews out of
Hebron.

It was at the Hebron Yeshiva that Goldstein met Eliezer Sachs, a young
American college graduate from Rochester, New York, who had come to
Israel to study Torah. Sachs had been raised in a Conservative home and
had no formal Torah training. The Hebron Yeshiva wasn't set up to teach
beginners, and so its chief rabbi proposed that Sachs hire Goldstein to tutor
him. "I said wonderful," Rabbi Goldstein recalled. "I charged fifteen
dollars an hour in those days. I had a lot of children to feed." An adept
student, Sachs learned the *Gemara* in three months. More importantly, as
far as Goldstein was concerned, Sachs renounced his secular life, donned
the black hat and black coat of the Haredi ultra-Orthodox, and declared his
desire to devote the rest of his life to Torah study.

Goldstein searched for an ultra-Orthodox yeshiva where Sachs could
enroll. But the ultra-Orthodox community is intensely xenophobic and
obsessed with matters of morality and purity. Little girls are taught from
an early age that they are dangerous sexual objects, and Haredi women
shave their heads and wear sacklike dresses that cover them from head to

toe so that they can't lead men into temptation. Sachs may have opened his heart to *Hashem,* and may have been willing to follow the strict religious laws governing what is allowed and what is forbidden, but he had come from a spiritually unclean world that the Haredi believed could infect their entire community.

"He's a wealthy boy, you can charge him a large tuition, he's handsome, smart," Goldstein told the principal of a well-known Haredi yeshiva.

"Listen," said the principal, "we can't accept him. He's a *baal teshuvah.* What will be if he tells the boys in the school about girls?"

"He gave it all up," Goldstein replied. "He's not interested in girls."

In spite of Goldstein's best efforts, not a single ultra-Orthodox yeshiva in Israel would accept Sachs. "The religious schools in those days didn't open their doors for boys who didn't have a pedigree," Goldstein said. "They did not encourage people to come into their circles."

After the bout of rejections, "the boy almost collapsed," Goldstein said. "This is Judaism?" Sachs asked Goldstein.

"So all night long I didn't sleep," Goldstein recalled. "I had taught him that the Torah was true and the best of all worlds." Then the rabbi had a revolutionary idea. In response to the discrimination Sachs had encountered, Goldstein decided to create a yeshiva entirely for *baale teshuvah.* There was nothing quite like it in Israel or the diaspora. "That's how I started the *baal teshuvah* movement," Goldstein said. "We formed a tax-deductible organization, and the boy's father gave us some money."

On a deeper level, Goldstein believed that the time was ripe for a religious renewal within Judaism—and that the movement of Jews away from Judaism that had been going on since the Enlightenment could be reversed. At the same time, he detected a new willingness to explore Judaism, especially among the young, long-haired American Jewish backpackers who came to Israel in great numbers after the Six-Day War, turning the country into a major outpost of the burgeoning counterculture. Whether they had come to live under clouds of hashish smoke in the hippie shantytowns then rising on the outskirts of the Red Sea port of Elat, or to search for their Jewish roots while picking oranges on a socialist kibbutz, they could be the raw material of a Jewish revival, Goldstein concluded.

Goldstein had observed that in many ways, these refugees from the American suburbs were similar to the idealistic youth from Russia and Poland who settled in Palestine in the early twentieth century and built the modern institutions of the Jewish state. The youth of the second and third *aliyah* had come with a deep faith that salvation was possible only in Palestine, that "in Palestine, under socialism, the future would take care of itself and resolve all of Jewry's social and national problems," Amos Elon wrote.

Many American Jews who journeyed to Israel in the late sixties were also in search of salvation. But they were not interested in the great Zionist socialist revolutionaries like Syrkin or Borochov (if they had heard of them at all). Israel, after all, was a *fait accompli*. And with the task completed, Labor Zionism seemed sterile and heavy with bureaucracy. These soft suburban youth were on an inner quest—for truth, clarity of purpose, utopia. Many had experimented with Eastern religions, LSD, transcendental sex. Goldstein told them that they did not have to go to an Indian ashram to find themselves—that truth was in their own backyard. He offered the Torah—a straightforward path without confusion or self-doubt, where one could find community and God.

Goldstein began to teach a small group of American *baale teshuvah* in a room on the top floor of the Hebron Yeshiva. When the number of pupils grew too large for the room, he moved to the Diskin Orphanage, a spacious building in West Jerusalem that also housed a yeshiva run by Rav Shach, a leader of a major wing of the ultra-Orthodox movement in Israel. "God gave me the gift of pedagogical methods," Goldstein said. "Some of the boys started coming from Shach's place to my place." Soon Goldstein had sixty pupils and needed a building big enough to accommodate his growing student body.

In search of additional funding, Goldstein approached Shaul Eisenberg, the richest man in Israel. Born in Galacia, Poland, Eisenberg had escaped from Nazi Europe and spent the war years in Japan, where he reportedly made a fortune, though much mystery surrounds how he was able to do that. After the Six-Day War, Eisenberg moved to Israel, where he became the nation's largest arms merchant. Because most of Eisenberg's family was lost in the Holocaust, he had a genuine sympathy for Goldstein and his mission of Jewish renewal. He made a substantial donation. But more important, he put in a good word for Goldstein with Dr. Kalman Kahane, Israel's deputy minister of education and culture, whose father had been chief rabbi of Warsaw before the Second World War.

Dr. Kahane gave Goldstein a long-term lease on a derelict medieval castle on Mount Zion, overlooking Jerusalem's Old Walled City. Although Mount Zion was within the boundaries of pre-1967 Israel, it was considered a dangerous location prior to the Six-Day War, because it was in easy range of Jordanian sniper fire. Aside from a run-down tourist shop on the mount, there was a *nahal* (paramilitary) post, several churches, and a dilapidated building allegedly holding King David's tomb, as well as the room where the Last Supper supposedly took place.

Goldstein opened the Diaspora Yeshiva in late 1967. "What good is religion if you can't open your doors and help people out?" Goldstein told me. In defiance of Jewish tradition, Goldstein actively evangelized, approaching potential recruits at Jerusalem's Central Bus Station, at the Western Wall, and on the campus of the Hebrew University, where he hung signs in the student center that asked, "How can you understand the Jewish state until you have understood Judaism?" As word spread, the Diaspora Yeshiva became a way station for scores of American Jewish hippies who were searching for God—or for free room and board. They brought with them their guitars, backpacks, and drugs, especially hashish, which was readily available in Israel. "I knew nothing about drugs then," Goldstein said. "I never had heard of hash. I was so naive."

Before long, the Diaspora Yeshiva looked as if it had been invaded by Ken Kesey and the Merry Pranksters, except that the tripsters resembled long-bearded, floppy-hatted Hasids who seemed to be fried on acid. The frenetic tones of the Jefferson Airplane and the Doors echoed from the castle, attracting curious Israelis, who were greeted with shouts of "Come and join us." Goldstein said he started a religious rock band that cut eight albums for CBS records. He also invited assorted Eastern gurus and mystics to live on the mount, confident that Judaism would win out.

There were several suicides on Mount Zion during those first few years. "There were people who died on drugs in my arms," Goldstein told me. "One boy had gotten involved with drugs in America, and his parents didn't know what to do with him, so they shipped him off to Israel. We bar mitzvahed the boy. We tried with all our heart to help him. Then he died on drugs. We can't succeed with everybody." Nevertheless, Goldstein's reputation for working with mixed-up youth grew, and soon more and more well-to-do American Jews were parking their sons with the rabbi, who often took the place of counselor and psychiatrist.

It was Goldstein's belief that these young Americans needed a kind of therapy; that they had to be cured of the ills born of the diaspora. For all of Goldstein's seeming tolerance of the lifestyles of the counterculture, he believed the only way his students could mend was if they rejected virtually everything to do with modern life, and lived according to *Halacha,* a comprehensive code of behavior that has hardly changed since the Middle Ages. His students were required to dress in the black hats and caftans of the ultra-Orthodox; their old identities were slowly stripped away, and they were pressured to conform to the rabbi's desires. Drugs were gradually eliminated, and the yeshiva became more like traditional ultra-Orthodox schools of higher learning. "My approach was, if drugs give you a high, Torah gives you a bigger high," Goldstein said.

What remained unique about the Diaspora Yeshiva was that Goldstein mixed together practices of the two major factions of the Haredi community—Lithuanian and Hasidic. Hasidism began in the eighteenth century as a reaction to the dry, legalistic practice of Judaism that was controlled by a small elite caste of rabbis. Hasidism stressed fervent devotion and intense prayer. The Lithuanians, so named because Lithuania was the center of opposition to Hasidism, emphasized the study of Torah and Talmud. While the Diaspora Yeshiva is Lithuanian, Goldstein adopted many of the devotional dances, prayers, and songs that are typical of Hasidism in order to appeal to students who needed an emotional experience to bind them to Orthodoxy.

Not long after the Diaspora Yeshiva opened, several Israelis asked Goldstein to establish a separate *baal teshuvah* program for native-born Israelis. Goldstein did not have the resources. So he referred them to Rabbi Avraham Ravitz, a Knesset member from the ultra-Orthodox Degel Hatorah party, who, in turn, brought them to Rav Kook, who organized two intensely nationalistic *baal teshuvah* yeshivas. By the early 1970s, a number of *baal teshuvah* yeshivas embracing both the biblical fundamentalism of Gush Emunim and the insular, pre-Enlightenment religious values of the Haredim were established and training thousands of previously secular Israelis.

Goldstein started a women's division in 1971 after Eliezer Sachs, his first student, had difficulty finding a wife. "Rabbi Goldstein realized he was running into a lot of the problems that any innovator or entrepreneur is going to have," said Shabtai Herman. "He had made these men into *baale teshuvah,* but there was nobody for them to marry because the regular Orthodox community looked askance in those days at *baale teshuvah,* and, of course, the boys couldn't return to regular secular life to find wives." So Goldstein designed a program to train women who were Jewish but unfamiliar with Orthodoxy how best to serve their future Torah-scholar husbands and keep a proper Jewish home.

As the Diaspora Yeshiva grew into a full-fledged community with married couples and children, Goldstein decided it was time to build a settlement. "I wanted to build a place behind Hadassah Hospital [in West Jerusalem]," Goldstein told me one day in his cavernous office on Mount Zion. "I talked to city officials. Everybody agreed. I shook their hands. Then I went to America for three months to raise money. When I returned, they said, 'Listen, Rabbi, sorry, the city decided to take over the property and to build who knows what.' Then I tried to make a settlement near Carmel up north near Safed. My son said, 'I'll help you, Dad.' He went to a government minister, a woman. He gave her a box of chocolates. She was nice-looking. He said, 'Put our name down. We have the people who want to make a *yishuv*.' She took his name and told him to move to the next line. He moved from office to office. He talked nicely. He filled out the forms."

For eight years, Goldstein and his son visited government ministries, dispensing chocolates and filling out forms. Finally, on the eve of the 1984 national elections, when the Likud was desperate to create more "facts on the ground," Goldstein was offered a plot of land on a bleak desert plateau where King David is said to have hidden from Saul. "The government pushed us in," Goldstein said. "Nobody else would take it. Nobody else would take it because it's right near [the Palestinian village of] Sair. They are the worst Arabs, the toughest Arabs. Even the Arabs of Hebron are afraid of them."

Initially, Metzad's most pressing problem wasn't Arabs; it was inadequate government funding. Four families quickly left because of the financial strain. "People are only human," Shabtai Herman said. "Some people just couldn't keep it together. It was sad. These were people we loved very much."

It was not as though the Haredi community lacked the political clout to obtain government money. There are several Haredi settlements in the occupied territories, and most enjoy relatively good standards of living. Kiryat Safer has received major donations from the Reichmann family. And Betar, whose land was confiscated from the nearby Arab village of Najilin, has opulent Tudor-style homes and a world-class community center.

Metzad has remained an orphan, in part, because *baale teshuvah* are still discriminated against by mainstream ultra-Orthodox society. But Metzad has also suffered because Goldstein has only nominally aligned himself with one of the four Haredi political parties, which together had 13 seats in the 120-seat Knesset prior to the 1992 elections. Because Goldstein is not part of a larger political network, he cannot easily obtain patronage. As a consequence, Metzad is being financially strangled. "My party is the Po'alei Agudat Yisrael—the Workers of Auguda," Goldstein explained. "They don't help us with a thing. I haven't spoken to the office in six years. They gave us a *Sefer Torah,* and that's about all."

In practice, the ultra-Orthodox parties wield enormous power in Israel, which they have used cynically to extort huge sums of money from Labor and Likud in return for their political backing—essentially determining who forms the government. In 1978, as the price for their political support, the leaders of the ultra-Orthodox parties extracted from Menachem Begin wholesale military exemptions for their students. In early 1990, after the national-unity government was toppled by a vote of no confidence, Shamir and Peres vied for Haredi support with promises of huge cash gifts and even more influence over Israeli public life. Their Rabbinate already controls civil laws governing such things as marriage and divorce and has closed down public transportation and business on the Sabbath; the Haredim would also like to ban all forms of weekend entertainment, including radio and television broadcasts.

In the Haredi view, Zionism is a heresy (the true Jewish state will be created only when the Messiah has arrived), the modern world is evil, and the Jewish people have been on a destructive, downward spiral since the Enlightenment. Rav Shach infuriated secular Israelis when he declared that the Holocaust was God's punishment for sins such as violating the Sabbath and eating pork. "The Almighty keeps a balance sheet of the world, and when the sins become too many, he brings destruction," the ninety-three-year-old Shach said. Following the collapse of the national-unity government in 1990, Rav Shach denounced Labor as the "party of pig and rabbit eaters" in a speech that was carried live over Israeli television. The two ultra-Orthodox parties under Shach's sway lined up behind Shamir, allowing him to form the most extreme right-wing government in Israel's history—a union of Likud, the Haredi parties, and three small ultranationalist lists. The Haredim were handsomely rewarded. Government funds allocated to their educational institutions skyrocketed more than 2,000 percent, from less than $7 million in 1988, to more than $150 million in

1990, according to *Tikkun*. A Haredi rabbi was appointed to head the Ministry of Interior, and the Haredi parties gained control of the Knesset's powerful Finance Committee.

Rabbi Moshe Ze'ev Feldman, the black-robed head of the Finance Committee, left many of his countrymen fuming when he said during an interview on Israeli television in December 1991 that if it were up to him, women would not be allowed to vote. It was not the first time the rabbi's unenlightened views had caused an uproar. When Feldman took over the Finance Committee, he acknowledged that his only economic training was "learning from my mother that two and two equals four."

It's not surprising then that many secular Israelis fear that the Haredim will sweep Zionism away like a roiling black tide and replace it with an austere Torah society. As far as they are concerned, the so-called demographic threat is posed not by the Palestinians but by the Haredim, whose birthrate is five times higher than that of secular Israelis. Resentment of the Haredim, who are so intrusive in public life yet manage to legally dodge military service, exploded during the Gulf War, when large numbers of them fled Israel in fear. "In the past days thousands of Haredi yeshiva *buchers* have left the country," the popular columnist Nachum Barnea wrote in *Yediot Achronot* on the day the war began. "Without shame they stormed airline ticket-sellers, wads of cash in their hands, asking to leave the country at any price."

On the other hand, during the Israeli general elections in 1988, thousands of Lubavitcher Hasidim from Europe and America who held Israeli passports had come to the country to vote for the ultra-Orthodox Agudat Yisrael party in accordance with the instructions of ninety-year-old Rabbi Menachem Schneerson of Crown Heights, Brooklyn. Agudat Yisrael, which won five seats, backed Likud after it allegedly received huge bribes. "Midnight calls were made; millions of dollars changed hands," observed an Israeli politican.

In the end, Schneerson pledged to back Shamir if he accepted the rebbe's view on The Law of Return—that only those who convert to Judaism under traditional orthodoxy can count themselves as authentic Jews. When Shamir acceded, Agudat Yisrael and another religious party sided with Likud, tipping the electoral balance in its favor. While the Knesset subsequently refused to redraft the Law of Return according to Schneerson's wishes, the resulting debate split the Jewish world in two.

Schneerson is a bellicose advocate of "Greater Israel." Other Haredi leaders are more ambivalent about the occupied territories. Rav Shach has stated that he would support territorial compromise if it meant saving Jewish lives. But many of the poor Sephardic Jews who are Shach's disciples support the hard-line views of Kach and Likud—especially those of Sharon. On the question of Greater Israel, Goldstein stands somewhere between the two poles represented by Schneerson and Shach. While Goldstein believes in the totality of the land of Israel, creating a Torah community is his primary goal. "We came here [to the West Bank] without any political aspirations in terms of a bigger picture—advancing the politics of the land of Israel," Shabtai Herman said. "It was simply that beggars can't be choosers."

Morning came with a strong sun, and I sat in a sukkah attached to the side of a trailer in Metzad, listening to Dov, a sinewy, long-haired thirty-five-year-old *baal teshuvah* from America, who talked loudly about the time during his hippie days when he was arrested in Djibouti by the local authorities on suspicion of being a CIA spy. Dov was a real hard-luck guy. On the first day of Rosh Hashanah in 1990, an errant Shabbat candle set fire to his trailer, destroying everything inside, leaving the unemployed father of nine children destitute. Dov had come to Israel in 1972 to work on a kibbutz, having grown weary of the hippie trail. But he said that he was thrown out because he didn't fit in. However, "I wasn't too weird for the Diaspora Yeshiva," he told me, adding that he was approached by Rabbi Goldstein at the Wailing Wall, invited to Mount Zion for a Shabbat meal, and later "indoctrinated."

The sukkah was made of palm fronds, cloth brocades, Navaho rugs, and East Indian tapestries. There were white brocade chairs, a large wooden table fashioned from a telephone spool, a long wooden bench covered with purple quilts and pillows, and fresh-cut flowers. Yehudit, who decorated the sukkah, wore a bouffant wig over her shaved head. She was plump, but not as overweight as some of the other women I saw in Metzad. Yehudit, a Catholic who converted to Judaism, was raised in Bridgeport, Connecticut, where her grandfather, a mafioso from southern Italy, used to give children fifty-dollar counterfeit bills to buy ice-cream cones. "That's how he passed money," she said. She left Connecticut in 1968 for California, where she tried everything from Esalen to *est*. Eventually, she journeyed to Navaho land in Pine Springs, Arizona, to study the art of the Navaho double weave. I had first met Yehudit at the Temple Institute in Jerusalem's

Old City, where she was sitting at a loom in a long white gown weaving a ceremonial curtain that is to hang in the Third Temple. It was Yehudit who had invited me to spend Sukkoth with her family in Metzad.

On Saturday morning, the second day of my visit, Yehudit asked me to help prepare the food for her seventeen-year-old daughter Yael's engagement party. Yael was marrying a bland-looking, twenty-one-year-old Baltimore man, who was planning to take over his grandfather's one-hundred-year-old billboard business. A slim, pretty girl, Yael told me that Metzad was an incredibly boring place to live, and that she would be happy to leave. It's not unusual that the children of *baale teshuvah* are not interested in the lifestyle that their parents chose with so much emotion, Yehudit told me. I made White Russians with cheap Israeli vodka, heavy cream, whole milk, and a little brandy, and carried the pitchers to the *Beit Knesset*, or synagogue, which was actually a converted shed. I placed the drinks on the women's table. Thickly bearded men in black coats and wide-brimmed hats crowded around their own table, devouring tiny slivers of lox on Premium crackers and washing them down with schnapps.

"You don't think we are antediluvian, do you?" Yehudit's husband, Ya'acov, asked me when we were alone in the sukkah after Kiddush. Ya'acov grew up in a traditional Jewish home in London, went to law school, and practiced libel law. One of his clients was *Rolling Stone* magazine. "I was becoming increasingly unhappy with what I was doing," he said. "It's a very hard profession. It takes a lot out of you. I observed that most lawyers are both mean and cynical. And I don't think they started out that way. So something about the practice of law breeds characteristics of cynicism, because people believe that the law should be a system of justice—a system of right and wrong—and in fact it is very seldom that.

"For whatever reason, I was not really very happy about practicing law. Also, I began to grow more and more disenchanted with the English—the society and culture. It was effete and superficial. But I had not seen any alternative. Then, in 1971, I went to visit friends in San Francisco. I enjoyed it very much. I had nothing to lose, so I sold my share in the practice, and I went to live in San Francisco."

After working as a drug-rehabilitation counselor and running a network of halfway houses for recovering addicts, Ya'acov took the California bar exam, which he passed. "I had two possible thoughts," he said. "My wife had studied weaving with American Indians, and I had been on a reservation with her for a week or so. I found the people very sympathetic. Of course, they could always use a lawyer, so I thought perhaps I might go there. The other thought I had was that maybe we'd go to Israel and try a kibbutz. I happened to be reading a book called *The Last of the Just* by a French Jew—a very powerful writer. At the end of that book, the main character goes to a kibbutz. The only thing that ever attracted me about Israel when I was growing up in England was the kibbutz movement. As far as Israel was concerned, I never had any bond or particular closeness to it."

After the Navahos declined Ya'acov's offer, he told Yehudit he wanted to go to Israel. "I was at the point where I felt we had nothing to lose. If we didn't like it [in Israel], I thought we'd go to Japan."

During the next few months, Ya'acov and Yehudit became observant, naively believing that all Jews in Israel were religious. They began to attend a synagogue in the Mission District and started keeping the Sabbath and kosher dietary laws. As they did so, their interest in the counterculture faded. "It would have been difficult to live in San Francisco from 1971 to 1978 without being aware of what was going on at the time in what is generally called the consciousness movement," said Ya'acov. "San Francisco was the motherlode of this activity. But I never found within any of these movements anything of any real interest at all. I looked at them. I read some books. I went to some meetings. I either thought they were all phony, or I thought they were irrelevant, or they were not of any value to me. Of all of the things I looked into, the only one I found interesting was I Ching. But I didn't think I could sit in front of I Ching sticks every day."

When Ya'acov and Yehudit arrived in Israel, the Jewish Agency sent them to a socialist kibbutz, where, to their surprise, no one was religious. Feeling unwelcome, they moved to Tel Aviv, where Ya'acov found a job in a travel agency, studied Hebrew, and took courses to qualify as an attorney. Then Ya'acov discovered the Diaspora Yeshiva, enrolled and, in 1984, moved with his family to Metzad. "In many ways, this was the fulfillment of the dreams that I had when I first came to Israel," he said. "I wanted to do three things: I wanted to be part of a group of people, I wanted to live in the country, and I wanted to feel that I was doing something worthwhile, harnessing whatever talents and energies I have and trying to put them to some value."

Like virtually every settler I met, Ya'acov told me that the *intifada* had interfered with the normal course of his life, making him less sympathetic to the Arabs. "I believe that the Arabs who are living here are exploited by professional politicians who themselves have no interest living in these villages," he said heatedly. "They live in penthouses in Paris and London, and they exploit the local population." He compared Arab rioters to rowdy football crowds in Great Britain. "In the same way that a football crowd expresses anger at the referee or the other team, the Arabs that are throwing stones are expressing their anger and frustrations when they do that. It's very easy to create anger. An Arab may feel full of self-righteous anger and resentment, but that doesn't make the violence right."

Should the Palestinians be accorded political and civil rights? I asked. "They are not Palestinians," he insisted. "They are the Arabs of Israel. Provided they are willing to live in peace with us and accept the seven commandments of Nachmanides, which means they must not worship idols and must comply with certain sexual codes and obey our system of justice—then they have full protection under the Torah. You have to understand that we are in a transitional period on the way to having a full Torah society in Israel. That's the only reason we are here.

"What it will take [to come about] is each person doing what he's supposed to do within his sphere of competence. That means relating to his family, his wife, his children, his parents, the people he eats with, in a way that identifies a high religious standard. And involving himself in study."

If the government evacuated the territories as part of a peace accord but gave the settlers the option of remaining in their homes under a foreign flag, what would he do? "We have a *rosh yeshiva* rabbi [Goldstein] who makes these decisions for us. I can't answer it. I can only say my opinion as I understand it *Halachically* is that the government can't return land. The land doesn't belong to the government. The government is ephemeral. The land is from the Almighty. My first reaction is I'd rather live under King Hussein than under a government that would give up *Eretz Yisrael*.

"On the other hand, anyone who has been in a struggle knows that sometimes there is a time to retreat and a time to advance. If it were a temporary retreat, perhaps I would accept your scenario. I don't think it would be such a terrible thing because I think that if a government gave back the territory and the Syrian armies moved in and put up missiles ten kilometers from Jerusalem, the same government that gave back the land would capture it again, and then they'd never talk about giving it back.

"It's hard to believe that any sensible person would believe that allowing the Arabs to occupy land a few kilometers from the main population centers of Israel is a way to ensure peace. If I was told to leave, I would leave. I didn't come here from England to live in Jordan. I believe with all my essence that every Jew has to find his way to his homeland."

Ya'acov said the biggest threat to Jews comes from other Jews. "To the religious Jew," said Ya'acov "the behavior of nonreligious Jews threatens the survival of the Jewish community more so than the Nazis." It is the secular Jew, he said, who by failing to keep the *mitzvoth* and honoring the Torah and the land, prevents the divine plan from coming about. Suddenly, as our exchange was becoming more heated, a group of men, singing and twirling about, clamored at the entrance of the sukkah, and Ya'acov, who looked at me intently, put on his wide-brim hat and joined his friends outside.

I met Jackie an hour or so before leaving Metzad. Jackie had come to Israel not to find religion but to find a man. She had been a thirtysomething painter in San Francisco, single, and listening to the fearful tick of her biological clock. A demanding, upper-middle-class woman whom some might call a "princess," she had not been, to put it charitably, good at maintaining meaningful relationships with the opposite sex. Now, a *baal teshuvah,* married to a rabbi and with a brood of children, she cooed that Metzad is a utopia so pure that it is like "living in the essence of holiness," where there is a clarity of purpose, no confusion, and absolute faith.

Jackie told me that when she first visited Israel in 1979 on a vacation, she was ready for a radical change. Luckily, she said, she discovered the Diaspora Yeshiva. "I looked around [the yeshiva] and saw a lot of happily married people, families and kids with a support system, a community," she said in a singsong voice as we sat among heaps of children's toys in the living room of her cramped caravan. "I saw religious people for the first time. I had never really seen them. I had heard about them usually in a negative light. But they really didn't seem to me to be so negative. They were very, very nice. They were family-oriented. They had holidays that they celebrated together. There seemed to be depth and meaning in their lives—a purpose. So I thought, Maybe I'll stay a little bit and try it out. I did want to get married and raise a family.

"There was no support system in San Francisco. The women I knew were in their thirties with careers and unmarried. You could get married, but who knew how long a person would stay married. The culture as it stands has a fifty percent divorce rate. It leaves it all to chance. In America, when a person has a marital problem, they say, Let's try to work it out, but if it doesn't work out, we can always get divorced. I wanted to have more emotional security. And I saw in the religious Jewish homelife there was a real effort made. Divorce is a possibility, but it's a minor possibility. Very minor. A last resort.

"My parents were divorced when I was nine. It affected me, certainly. I wanted a secure lifestyle. I think I always wanted the rituals of a religious life; the *Shabbus* candles, the meals, the songs, the prayers, the family life. I never really had it. I was brought up in a Conservative home. Religion was very watered down. But here in Israel I went to a yeshiva. A yeshiva means a place to sit and learn about Jewish customs and laws."

The religious transformation came to her slowly. "I tried keeping *Shabbus*. I tried one thing after another. It seemed very strange at first and didn't make sense. As I tried it, it made more sense. And pretty soon it gave my life a form. It gave it a framework that helped me as a person have meaning in life. My life had a certain meaning, but it was an empty meaning. It was based on superficial things. I'm a deep person. I'm searching for truth. I believe in truth. Being that I'm Jewish, the truth for me is from the Torah, because it fits my soul. My soul was custom-made for the Torah."

Jackie married a man she met at the yeshiva who was studying to become a rabbi. They bought an apartment in Jerusalem, and everything seemed perfect—until Rabbi Goldstein ordered his flock to move to Metzad. "I didn't really want to move to a settlement," she said flatly. "What did I need to move to a settlement for? I was in a little suburb in Jerusalem and happy.

"When we came out here, this place was barren. There was nothing. There were no birds. It was rocks, it was dust, it was wind, high, high, hard, hard wind, like a storm at sea. We lived in one room without a kitchen. The bathroom was outside. I had two children at the time. We lived in one room for a whole winter. Floods of water came in every time we opened the door. Through one whole winter we had no hot water. The whole settlement of eighteen families had one cellular phone. There were no paved roads. There was no bus service.

"I really blossomed here. I painted murals on the children's nursery while I was pregnant. Then I started giving art lessons to the kids. I have six groups of kids that I give lessons to after school. I developed a method of teaching that is very successful. Actually, I'm considering writing a book about it. A book that has to do with Jewish values and art and putting it together.

"I built my own room [an addition to the caravan]. I started sewing. I covered the couch. I never would have done these things someplace else. Metzad gave me the opportunity to use all my different abilities. I started giving talks in America about what life is like on the settlements. American newspapers only cover settlements from a political point of view. Readers wouldn't know that we have close to a hundred-eighty children in Metzad— the whole place revolves around the kids, the beautiful little flowers. They are beaming with life, with Jewish values. They know who they are. They are not confused about their identities. They keep *Shabbus,* they wear yarmulkes, they *doven* [pray] three times a day, they learn Hebrew, they learn about the Five Books of Moses, they learn all the laws of the holidays, they learn about character development, they know they don't eat food that's not kosher because it's not good for the soul. It's not a dietetic reason—it's because the Jewish soul is very special and needs its own kind of fuel."

As for the Arabs, Jackie said, "They are the ones who want to keep the *intifada* inflamed and make it look like Israel is doing them the harm. Like the refugee camps. I always got the impression that the Israeli government wanted to make their lives better. But certain Arabs want to keep them in the camps so it will look like they are oppressed by Israel, which is far from the truth. The Arabs are actually given many opportunities. They have jobs and things. It comes down to one point. They'd rather be oppressed and live in squalor and bad conditions among other Arabs."

"What about political freedom?" I asked. "As an American, you know what that means."

"Political freedom," she said, purring like a kitten. "Political freedom is an issue. But you also have to say if somebody won a war, they won a war. America won a war from the Indians."

But what if the Israeli government said it was time to leave?

"I love it here," she said, a sad look crossing her face. The thought apparently had come to her before, and it was deeply disturbing. "We developed the place. We made it bloom. We planted grass. We planted trees. We made it a nice place. We gave it life. What am I going to do if the government says leave? There is nothing I can do. The Jews were pushed out of this area, and now, as things turn out, the tide of history has brought us back. I feel very honored to be part of this historical movement. I feel that it's a monumental time for the Jewish people, for the whole world."

CHAPTER 7

Rule by the Best

Yoram Hazony was stepping out of the shower as Sabbath arrived in
Eli, a struggling Gush Emunim settlement on a remote hilltop between
Nablus and Ramallah. Standing all of five feet eight, with porcelain skin
and John Lennon glasses, he is a Princeton graduate, a *baal teshuvah*,
and a man with the determined look of the true believer on a sacred
mission. The twenty-eight-year-old Hazony is the leader of a *garin*, a
seed group of twenty families, all friends and Ivy League graduates, who
plan to set up a liberal-arts college in Eli, which they envision becoming
a great university town—the Princeton of Samaria. Just a few years ago,
Yoram was in the United States working on his political-science degree
at Princeton, editing *The Tory*, an off-campus neoconservative journal of
opinion, and playing "Dungeons and Dragons," his favorite pastime.
Now he is playing Napoleon on the West Bank, lording it over the
Palestinians. If Hazony succeeds in bringing Eli to life, he may well
become a prominent West Bank settlement leader. If he and his Ivy
League friends succeed in creating an important religious and educational center in the hardscrabble Samarian hills, he could become a future leader of Israel.

Hazony often has houseguests for the Sabbath, and this chilly November
weekend in 1990 was no exception. He dressed for services, as his wife,
Yael, prepared dinner and fed their two babies. Yael, a Pennsylvania farm
girl who changed her name from Julie after converting to Judaism from
Catholicism, had met Yoram during her freshman year at Princeton. The

couple dated for several years before she adopted Judaism; now she is more observant than he.

Of the four Sabbath guests, all but one were friends from Princeton. Allison, a twenty-three-year-old Oberlin graduate, talked about rampant anti-Semitism on her campus, especially among black students.

They waited for Yoram in the Hazonys' sparsely furnished living room, which had a metal table on wheels and two twin beds that doubled as couches. The walls were bare save for a large illustration of the old French-line ship the *Normandie*. Two half-filled wicker bookshelves in the hallway held several Japanese textbooks that Yoram had studied in college, a Chinese kosher cookbook, and a few dull novels by Leon Uris. The kitchen was small and messy. The refrigerator looked very old, and the stove was a rusty top cooker with two burners. Above the sink, a framed calligraphy poster said, "May the LORD make his face shine on you."

Then Yoram came into the room and led the group to the synagogue, which looked something like a recreation hall in a Catskill Mountains summer camp, with unfinished wood paneling and exposed ceiling beams. Some forty bearded, neatly dressed men prayed on hard benches in the center of the hall. Women, segregated in a back corner of the room, worshiped behind an opaque brown knitted curtain. Several jaunty teenage girls, with young sisters in tow, entered the hall in their Sabbath dresses and Nike sneakers with white lace stockings. Everyone had brought a prayer book. Seth Young, a Princeton graduate a few years younger than Yoram, read from a prayer book filled with instructional minutiae (i.e., "Pronounce this line loudly and intently, thinking of the sovereignty of *Hashem;* pronounce this line quietly"). Seth, who had grown up in a Reform Jewish home in a suburb of Philadelphia, called the book "a *baal teshuvah*'s best friend." He said he became observant after hanging out with Yoram at Princeton. "I was a total ignoramus" about Judaism and Israel before befriending Yoram, he said. An electronical engineer, Seth now studies in a Jerusalem yeshiva for *baale teshuvah;* he plans to move to Eli after he finds a wife. Yoram said that Seth had been, during his senior year, "the main person" at Princeton trying to get people to move to Eli.

As they sat gathered around a small table in the Hazonys' kitchen following services, Yoram elaborately introduced each Sabbath prayer, which everyone enjoyed immensely. The Hazonys' three-year-old daughter, Avital, blue-eyed as both her parents are, sang her very first Kiddush (prayer) with the attentive help of Yoram. It was obvious that Yoram and

Yael were aware of being the "model" settler family, and that everything they did was by way of example. There was a tinge of envy among the others in the room who were also looking for settler bliss—especially among the bachelors, who seemed smitten with Yael. An attractive woman, she wore a pink cotton cardigan sweater buttoned up to the chin with a collar of pale flowers over a white turtleneck and a knitted, black wool skirt. Her blond hair was covered by a white nylon scarf. Yoram's intellectual equal, she said that she would someday like to establish a religious school for women in Eli. In the meantime, she seemed perfectly content to live in her husband's shadow.

The Kiddush, or prayer over wine, was made with grape juice and drunk from little plastic cups; then Yael served heaping portions of pot roast and potatoes, chicken, and three kinds of salads, as Yoram held forth with a discussion about the Bible before veering off into a conversation about what vices ancient Rome symbolized (materialism) in the Torah compared to Persia (sensuality). There was an occasional squabble over some finer point of *Halacha* among these newly awakened Orthodox Jews, but when Yoram and Josh Weinstein, also a *baal teshuvah* and a Princeton graduate, agreed, they whooped and hollered and gave each other the "high five," like football players after scoring a touchdown.

Talk turned to the Soviet Jews, and to Minister of the Interior Yitzhak Peretz, who had just declared that as many as one third of the recent Soviet Jewish émigrés were actually Christian. The Israeli press had also reported that Russian *goyim* were paying up to twenty thousand rubles to marry a Russian Jew so they could immigrate to Israel—the only nation readily granting residence visas to Soviet citizens. Yosha, a Princeton graduate who had emigrated from Moscow to Atlanta as a teenager, and who was then studying in a Haredi yeshiva for *baale teshuvah* in Jerusalem (having deferred for one year admission to Stanford Business School), worried that within a generation, the non-Jews among the Russians would de-Judaize Israel through intermarriage. Yoram disagreed, arguing that anybody who claims to be a Jew must be welcomed. Later, he added that he expected thousands of Russian *olim* to make their home in Eli, although he said there were as yet no specific plans to bring them there. Without a vital transfusion of Russian Jews, he said, Eli would not become a city of one hundred thousand souls. Yael enthused that the Russian *aliyah* made her feel more secure about the future of the settlement enterprise. At the very least, she said, the Russian Jews have created an enormous demand for housing in

Israel proper, impelling many thousands of native Israelis to consider moving to Judea and Samaria. Yael could not have known then that the Russian émigrés, disgusted with the Likud's inability to absorb them, would vote for Labor by a four-to-one margin in the June 1992 elections, helping to topple the Likud government and to jeopardize the Hazonys' sacred mission.

Allison was not as gung-ho about settlement life as the others. Her journey to Israel had begun in the Virgin Islands, where, she said, as a child growing up, she encountered anti-Semitism even though few Jews lived there. Later, at Andover prep school, she said her dark complexion, Jewish features, and brown curly hair made her feel ugly. She turned to Orthodox Judaism at Oberlin because of "all the love and beauty in the Jewish tradition." Although her older sister, Yaffa, had moved to Kiryat Arba, the most militant settlement in the territories, Allison had strong misgivings about how settlers treated Arabs. She talked softly after dinner, away from the others, about riding a public bus into Jerusalem one day after the army had placed the city off-limits to Arabs in the wake of the Temple Mount tragedy. "Soldiers came on the bus, and all the Arabs were taken off," she said. "They were nice about it," but then someone on the bus pointed out an Arab woman they had missed, and when the soldiers took her off too, Allison began to cry. She went straight to the rabbi of the Jerusalem yeshiva where she studied, but nothing he said exorcised the image of the Arab women—their expressions frozen in anger—left standing by the side of the road. Every time Allison was on the verge of going back home to America, Yoram managed to talk her into giving it more time. She likes and respects him and keeps coming to Eli for Shabbat.

After morning prayers on Saturday, lunch was served, and the group conversed about Jewish suffering, the Jewish people's messianic destiny, and about transforming Eli into a city-state ruled by what Yoram called "the best"—men chosen to lead by dint of their superior knowledge of Jewish values. At sunset, Yoram brought everyone outside to revel in the stunning hills and wild gorges. Then, while Yael washed the dishes and the babies played on a rumpled sheet on the living-room floor covered in cookie crumbs that became matted in their hair, Yoram and his friends listened to Elton John records. "I *love* coming out here and *occupying the territories!*" said Josh, ever the smart-ass. "I haven't done it in a while. Someone's got to do it or they're not being occupied, right?"

*

Eli was established by Gush Emunim on a barren mountain ridge mid-way between Nablus and Ramallah on September 11, 1984—just two days before the national-unity government took office. Under the agreement between Labor and Likud in which the two parties would share power until 1988, only three new settlements could be built during the term of the coalition government. So Eli was hastily set up by yeshiva students from neighboring Shiloh who plunked down sleeping bags and tents in an effort to qualify it as an "existing settlement." Three rows of prefab houses were later planted on the hillside, and nine families joined the students.

Named after the last high priest who served at Shiloh during the time of Samuel, Eli was planned to be a mixed religious-secular city of one hundred thousand people, the largest urban center between Ariel in the north and Jerusalem. During Sukkoth of 1985, Gush Emunim brought thousands of prospective settlers to its "Sunrise at Eli" celebration, to inaugurate its home-building campaign. Amana, the settlement arm of Gush Emunim, hoped to sign up at least one hundred home buyers. But fewer than a dozen expressed interest. Eli is more than an hour's drive from either Jerusalem or Tel Aviv—a long commute for aspiring yuppie suburbanites. Israeli construction firms were reluctant to invest their own money in Eli because the market for homes there was soft. So Amana gambled. It contracted for the building of several dozen two- and three-bedroom, southern California tract-style homes with red-tile roofs and small patios, taking out the mortgages and passing the cost on to other Gush Emunim settlements. As of late 1990, many of these homes stood empty. Eli was Gush Emunim's white elephant.

Hazony was determined to change that. He moved to Eli in 1989 and set up a *garin*. His ambition, however, transcended settlement building, which, over the years, has essentially become a routine, bureaucratic process. In 1991, he founded the Israel Academy of Liberal Arts—an eight-week summer program in Jerusalem designed to teach American college students Jewish religious values and Western philosophy within a "politically correct" Zionist environment. He hopes that the academy will be the precursor to a full-fledged liberal-arts college in Eli. "The program's goal is to take the most important Jewish and Western ideas and to take a select group of American students who want to be academic and political leaders and give them a real workout in these sources," Hazony said.

"Part of our aim is to inject Jewish thought into parts of the curriculum where it is absent," he explained. "For example, you can pick up any of the standard political-philosophy texts, and it says political science started twenty-four hundred years ago, when Socrates started talking to Plato. And you say, Gee, where did all these non-Greek ideas like universal brotherhood, absolute justice, or absolute truth, and all sorts of other, much more Jewish ideas, like the Jewish concepts of social equality, come from? So you have a completely de-Judaized view of where our important thoughts come from."

Seminars meet four times a week on subjects such as philosophy, politics, and literature; there is also a workshop on the films of Alfred Hitchcock and nature walks around "Greater Israel." According to IALA's glossy brochure, the courses, taught by a cadre of Princeton graduates, are "designed to meet the needs of intellectually active and morally concerned students who find that their needs cannot be met at university. Like the academies of ancient Greece, Israel, and China, and the humanistic education of Renaissance Europe, the Israel Academy is devoted to the idea that the mind, given a supportive environment of good friends and good conversations, can create thoughts of consequence on important issues."

During the winter months when IALA is not in session, Yoram runs a weekly study group in West Jerusalem. One wet November evening, the group gathered in the home of Josh Weinstein, IALA's education director and the designated director of Yoram's future university. Yoram called Weinstein "our Renaissance man." A former engineering student, Weinstein spent one summer in New Mexico working on SDI-related research projects. He later received a degree in philosophy from Princeton, and was completing a Ph.D. in political philosophy at the Hebrew University. Like the other men from the Eli *garin* at the session, Weinstein wore a neatly trimmed, full black beard, a knitted *kipa*, comfortable old jeans, loafers, and a striped, button-down Oxford shirt. One of the trendier undergrads wore a T-shirt with the slogan HARD ROCK CAFE, JOHANNESBURG splashed across the front.

Weinstein's tiny apartment could have been a grad student's humble digs anywhere in America. The living room was furnished with an old couch, cheap wicker chairs, a world map covering one wall, a glass-topped coffee table with a copy of *Newsweek,* and stacks of books in Hebrew and English such as *Popular Halacha, Zionist Revolution, Gateway to Self-knowledge, Jewish Travel Guide,* and Toni Morrison's *Beloved.* While the bedroom door had fallen off its hinges, there was an expensive, imported tap-water filtering system in the kitchenette.

Josh was a congenial host, working the room before the discussion session began, making introductions, cracking jokes, offering tea and cakes. He made fun of himself for doing a less than sterling job that day giving a lecture on Nietzsche at the Hebrew University. "I said the death of God was only a cognitive experience, and that the emotional part was only correlative. Don't I sound deep and impressive," he said.

Most of the dozen or so students who were not already members of the Eli *garin* had expressed some interest in moving there. But not Avi. A pale, overweight American studying at a yeshiva in Eli, he said, "I want something more adventurous. They just paved the roads at Eli. I'd like to think of myself as a pioneer!"

Gavriel, a classics scholar finishing a Ph.D. in philosophy under Allan Bloom at the University of Chicago's Committee on Social Thought, led the evening's discussion on Aristotle. Gavriel had been raised in an assimilated Jewish home in Montclair, New Jersey; he observed Hanukkah and Passover "every few years," he said, "if someone remembered." He went to a Zionist youth movement meeting when he was fourteen and thought it was stupid. In college, however, he became a *baal teshuvah,* and later, while studying one summer in a Jerusalem yeshiva, met Yoram and Josh, who persuaded him to live in Eli and teach at the academy.

Gavriel began the seminar by comparing Aristotle to Rashi, a prodigious eleventh-century Torah scholar from northern France whose greatest contribution to Jewish life was rewriting parts of the Talmud in the vernacular of the day with great clarity and wit, making it accessible to the average Jew in medieval Europe.

Later, while discussing Aristotle, Gavriel said he agreed with the Greek philospher's idea that friendship among citizens of a state is more important than justice. " 'Friendship,' " Gavriel said, quoting Aristotle, " 'appears to be the bond of the state; and lawgivers seem to set more store by it than they do by justice, for to promote concord, which seems akin to friendship, is their chief aim. And if men are friends, there is no need of justice between them. . . . merely to be just is not enough.' " Ancient Athens, Gavriel explained, derived its political strength, in part, from its homogeneous character. Foreigners were denied citizenship unless they adopted the state religion, as Aristotle himself had done. Athens was not a pluralistic democracy, but rather an oligarchy ruled by the "best."

Friendship was written out of the U.S. Constitution, Gavriel said, in favor of the notion that men of different faiths and beliefs must live together in concord. But democratic pluralism as practiced in America—the notion of one man, one vote, and equal justice under the law—is not a viable option for Israel, he later said. For example, if the two million Arabs of Judea and Samaria had the right to vote for the Knesset, they would no doubt vote out the Jews and attempt to put an end to Zionism. So while it may be "unjust" to deny them citizenship, the alternative is national suicide. Therefore, an Athenian-style democracy in which a homogeneous state is united by common values and ruled by an elite caste is more appropriate for Israel, he said, than a Western-style democracy, which, if extended to the Arabs of Greater Israel, would disrupt the social order.

For this reason, Gavriel said, the Israeli left, with its radical insistence on maintaining a liberal democracy and relinquishing the occupied territories, threatens the nation's existence. "We should take a lesson from the Weimar Republic, which fell to the Nazis," he said after class. "How did that happen? It happened because the liberal state was so liberal, so diverse, so nonnationalistic, so universalistic, so unconcerned with the feelings of its inhabitants, that the people revolted. I think the same thing could happen here if the liberals don't take seriously the Jewish perspective on things. They can't simply be concerned with the Arab perspective."

And just as the Arabs of Judea and Samaria should be denied citizenship unless they adopt Zionism, they should also be denied a homeland on the West Bank because they already have one—in Jordan! "I do not believe it's possible for every nation to have a homeland exactly in the place where they're residing," he said. "For example, the Jews of Russia have a right to a homeland. But no one, to my knowledge, is suggesting that they should have a homeland in Russia—that there should be a small [Jewish] state created in Russia now.

"I think that part of the maturity that's required to really succeed in the modern world in an *adult* way is the willingness to make sacrifices for the things that you want. And I think the Jews have. The Jews moved from many, many lands to come here. These sacrifices shouldn't be underestimated. They're so great that many American Jews today don't want to make them. They'd rather live in the U.S. than make sacrifices to have a homeland. If they want to stay in America, that's their right. But the point is, everyone should have the option, in my opinion, to move to a place that they can consider to be their homeland. Unfortunately, it can't necessarily be exactly where they're living right now. And that's true not just for the [Palestinian] Arabs and the [Russian] Jews, but it's true for the Pakistanis," who were transferred from India during the 1947 partition, and for many other people who were dislocated by historical events.

Yoram Hazony's parents had immigrated to Palestine from eastern Russia in the 1920s. In 1964, the year after Yoram was born, they moved to America, and his father became an engineering professor at Princeton University. Until Yoram returned to Israel, he was a *yored.* It is a derisive Hebrew term used to describe one who leaves Israel. The word, literally, means "one who goes down." To Zionist true believers, it is an apt description, as they consider the modern state of Israel the apogee of the Jewish experience.

The pampered son of well-to-do parents who emphasized classical education and European culture, Yoram, nevertheless, had a deeply troubled homelife. His mother was repeatedly hospitalized for schizophrenia. His parents eventually divorced. "Yoram was quite willing to desert his mother and go to Israel," said a rabbi at Princeton who knew him well. "He needed to get away from her and was worried about his own sanity. He needed a system of right and wrong he could adhere to; he needed a rigid order in his life to keep from going crazy." He found it first in Orthodox Judaism. Although raised in a religiously Conservative home, Yoram became Orthodox in college and started studying in a yeshiva. "He developed an absolute hatred of anything that reminded him of his Conservative background," the rabbi recalled. "He said he felt cheated by a childhood that kept him from experiencing what he called 'authentic Judaism.' "

An aggressive achiever with stratospheric SAT scores, Yoram entered Princeton in 1983. There are no fraternities or sororities at Princeton; instead, upperclassmen join "eating clubs," and social life revolves around meals. Situated along a stately street of towering elms and renovated mansions, the clubs are where students study and party; beer is on tap twenty-four hours a day.

But instead of joining a club, Yoram ate in the kosher dining room at Stevenson Residential Hall, where the Orthodox students formed a small, tight-knit group. "You'd rarely see them at the eating clubs," recalled a former student. "You'd see them at the model UN debates." Yoram, a superb debater, soon gathered around him a circle of followers whom one professor remembered as "a tiny group of political activists. Noisy, conspicuous."

"Yoram was one of the most brilliant minds I met in Princeton," said

Robyn Wagner, Yael's roommate, and later a Ph.D. student at Harvard. "He was an absolutely talented debater. One summer vacation he made a fortune selling Yellow Page advertisements in Boston. He could convince anyone of anything. I found it personally unsettling that he would use his gifts to advance his extremely conservative agenda."

Yoram and his friends, some of whom had previously studied at yeshivas in Israel and on the West Bank, sometimes turned up to heckle campus speakers they deemed anti-Israel. During one Friday night forum held at the campus's Hillel Center, the speaker, Michael Walzer, a member of the faculty of the Institute for Advanced Studies at Princeton and co-editor of *Dissent,* remarked that if the Rabbinate came to power in Israel, the country would become like Iran under the ayatollahs.

"How can you say that about Judaism?" screamed Yoram, who proceeded to tear into Walzer.

"You can grow up to be a dangerous demagogue," Walzer replied.

The Princeton rabbi who has followed Yoram's career in Israel and who attended the forum told me, "I'll never forget how prophetic those remarks were."

Yoram made a name on campus by writing op-ed pieces for the *Daily Princetonian,* a student newspaper whose political bent changed from year to year depending on who was editor. In the winter of 1984, Yoram founded *The Tory,* an off-campus journal of opinion that was a forum for his strident neoconservative views. Its funding was provided by Irving Kristol, who had mobilized an array of conservative business tycoons to put up seed money for right-wing student newspapers across the country. Kristol then helped promising editors obtain internships at the White House or with right-wing think tanks like the Heritage Foundation.

The Tory was not the only right-wing student publication in Princeton. There was also *The Prospect,* then edited by Dinesh D'Souza, who went on to write *Illiberal Education,* which charged that radical, left-wing professors espousing multiculturalism and affirmative action have ruined American higher education. *The Prospect* was not highly regarded, even by serious campus conservatives. It was obsessed with linking the decline of Princeton's football team to the school's going co-ed in the 1960s. "Yoram tried to make *The Tory* more serious, less yellow, more thoughtful" than *The Prospect,* said Leslie Kaufman, the former editor of Princeton's left-wing *Progressive Review.* "*The Tory* was like the *Dartmouth Review* [Irving

Kristol's flagship student newspaper, which at one time was edited by D'Souza], but with more taste."

Kaufman recalled that Yoram, "a peculiar, nebbishy guy with a yarmulke, always wanted to come up to our offices and have serious discussions." Kaufman assiduously avoided him. Another student then involved in campus Jewish affairs and now a Middle East expert in the State Department said that Yoram and his friends "were hostile, defensive and aggressive. . . . They were nebbishy, wimpy Jewish kids from the suburbs—not ethnic Jews from Brooklyn who thought they were Italian. They were the kind of people the football players laughed at."

Yoram's distaste for football players and liberals—and everyone else who did not think or act by his rigid set of rules—was mutual. Princeton may be Ivy League, but to Yoram's dismay, its students partied with the best of the Big Ten. On weekends, the "eating clubs" hosted rowdy drinking games with names like "Viking Night" and "Trees and Trolls," in which short undergrads, or Trolls, would try to fight their way up a staircase past the Trees, usually inebriated jocks. The games had a gladiator-type appeal for those who enjoyed being thrown over a banister and consuming prodigious amounts of alcohol. Josh and Yoram used to monitor the "games," filling out a scorecard on Monday mornings, listing the number of bones broken, students hospitalized, and co-eds raped. "It made us want to become more religious," said Josh. "All these guys did was vomit and rape."

Josh and Yoram's extracurricular pleasures centered around "Dungeons and Dragons," a fantasy-oriented game in which players assume the roles of medieval warriors and pursue complex adventures that can take months—or years—to complete. Josh was the Dragon Master, meaning he ran the game. The pair eventually graduated to war-simulation games, in which opposing "generals" strategically move hundreds of small, numbered cardboard soldiers around a board in mock battles. Josh lamented that the Arab-Israeli war game bored him because Israel always defeated the Arabs. "It was just a question of how fast you won and how many losses you took," he said.

A staunch conservative for as long as anyone could remember, Yoram veered sharply to the far right in the spring of 1984 after Rabbi Meir Kahane spoke on campus—an event Yoram would later describe as one of the most significant in his life. Kahane rose to prominence and a seat in the

Knesset that year by exploiting the basest fears of Jews both in Israel and America. The basis of his popularity was his call to "transfer," or expel, Israel's Arabs—an idea that later would be nourished by the passions unleashed by the Palestinian uprising, or *intifada*. "Yoram became increasingly aggressive after he met Kahane," said Michael Berkowitz, an editor at *The Progressive Review*. "Yoram started quoting Kahane in political discussions, and I was surprised. I saw him as a conservative, not as JDL."

Kahane first gained national attention in the turbulent summer of 1968 when he founded the JDL, declaring it would protect Jews from black street crime and anti-Semitism.* But the militant Brooklyn-born rabbi achieved international celebrity in the winter of 1969 when he seized on an issue largely ignored by the American Jewish establishment—the plight of Soviet Jews. By 1970 the JDL's bombing and shooting attacks against Soviet embassies in America and Europe were so numerous that, according to confidential State Department documents, President Richard Nixon became concerned that Kahane would wreck the Strategic Arms Limitation Talks. The JDL's campaign for Soviet Jewry gained the support of prominent union leaders, politicians, and wealthy Jewish philanthropists. Little did they know that the JDL's guerrilla war against the Soviet Union was orchestrated by right-wing Mossad officers led by Israel's future prime minister Yitzhak Shamir.

The secret relationship was forged in December 1969 when Geula Cohen, who had just been elected to the Knesset as a member of Begin's Herut party, visited Kahane in his cramped JDL office on Manhattan's Fifth Avenue. "Why are you wasting your time fighting the *shvartzers?*" asked Cohen, who had dropped out of Begin's Irgun underground in the 1940s to fight with Shamir's more extreme Stern Gang because she found Begin "too mild."

---

*The JDL had emerged out of the racial tensions generated by the 1968 New York City teachers' strike, which pitted the predominantly Jewish teachers' union against militant black activists who sought greater control of their neighborhood schools. The strike, together with black demands for quotas for civil-service jobs, open admission to city universities, and open housing, drew thousands of Orthodox and working-class Jews from New York's outer boroughs to the JDL, which was at the forefront of the white backlash. Kahane, who was then also the associate editor of the Brooklyn-based Orthodox Jewish weekly *The Jewish Press,* filled the tabloid with lurid stories about anti-Semitic acts of violence by blacks and Puerto Ricans against Jews too old and too poor to leave America's decaying inner cities. The stories further exacerbated racial tensions, while creating a pretext for Kahane to dispatch squads of armed JDL militants to "patrol" mixed Jewish-black neighborhoods. At the same time, Kahane covertly worked with the FBI as an agent provocateur against the Black Panthers in the bureau's infamous COINTELPRO program designed to destabilize black and left-wing political groups. In a few short months, the JDL had helped to polarize New York City almost beyond repair.

During the next few months, Cohen, Shamir, and a group of Mossad officers and Jewish businessmen helped lay the groundwork for the JDL's violent campaign to publicize the plight of Soviet Jewry. Cohen and Shamir calculated that the selective use of violence against Soviet targets in America and Europe would inevitably strain U.S.-Soviet relations. They predicted that rather than risk the breakdown of détente, the Soviet Union would be forced to alleviate the crisis by freeing hundreds of thousands of Jews, who would then be herded to the Jewish state. An influx of Soviet Jews could help redress the demographic imbalance caused when Israel swallowed the occupied territories with its large Arab population. (Since the founding of the state of Israel, one of Mossad's prime directives has been to help bring Jews to Israel. It has operated underground networks in a number of countries, including the Soviet Union and Ethiopia.)

Kahane moved to Israel in September 1971, one step ahead of a federal indictment for his role in a number of violent attacks against Russian diplomats based in the United States, and set up the Kach ["This is the way"] party. He frequently returned to America to raise funds, hold demonstrations, and speak at synagogues and on college campuses, where he dispensed a dangerous brew of hatred and violence.

Yoram was ripe for Kahane's message. "In the spring of 1984," Yoram later recalled in *The Jerusalem Post,* "on a night when most of the university's undergraduates were out drinking and dancing at the annual 'P-Party,' Rabbi Kahane came to Princeton. Two hundred and fifty students, mostly nonobservant Jews, gave up the free beer to go hear what the infamous fanatic, condemned by the Hillel but brought to campus by the debate team, had to say for himself. It was a speech many of us never forgot."

It was vintage Kahane—a combination of Borscht Belt comic and fascist demagogue. "When you have a bar mitzvah where you don't understand a word you read, and the rabbi and the congregation think it's okay because it's a chance to spend ten thousand dollars on shrimp and salmon mousse, that's just idiocy," Yoram recalled Kahane telling the students.

"When millions of Jews sit in America so they can make money, and take part in Israel's fight to survive by turning on the TV and maybe writing a check for a few bucks, that's just cowardice.

"When young American Jews are willing to fight for the Viet Cong, blacks, American Indians, or any other radical-chic flavor of the day, but are unwilling to fight for themselves, that's self-hatred."

A Jewish student challenged Kahane, arguing that Jewish religious law was oppressive and outdated. "What do you know?" Kahane thundered. "What do you know? I'm an Orthodox rabbi. I studied for years and years and years. You don't know a thing about what Judaism is. Why don't you go learn something, so you don't have to be an ignoramus in front of all these people?"

Kahane "mesmerized" the students, Yoram recounted in *The Jerusalem Post.* "Most of my friends, who had never had a conversation with an observant Jew, were astounded that an Orthodox rabbi could be an intelligent person, that he could actually defend his views against a crowd of Princeton students, when we had all thought Judaism had to be something primitive and foolish. We listened in astonishment, and finally in shame, when we began to realize he was right. We did know nothing.

"Rabbi Kahane was the only Jewish leader who ever cared enough about our lives to actually come around and tell us what he thought we could do . . . [to] learn about Judaism, move to Israel, and stand up and fight for what you believe in . . . And his message worked. At least five students who were in the hall that night gradually became observant."

More than that, many of those students later joined the Eli *garin,* a tribute to Kahane's xenophobic brand of militant Judaism in which the outside world is viewed as a bleak panorama of hatred for Jews, and where a Torah in one hand is inevitably supplemented by an AK-47 in the other. "My perception is that the Princeton students who joined Yoram in Eli needed a fixed belief system," said the Princeton rabbi who knew them well. "One in which you are either pro-Israel or an enemy of Israel, in which you are either with us or against us, in which you are either a good Jew or a bad Jew. Now all of that is a psychological splitting off—of not being able to see the world in gray, which, for my money, is what adulthood is about." According to the rabbi, some of them come from troubled homes, "and Kahane's black-and-white views allow them to draw a clear picture of the universe."

Yoram's universe was shaken on November 5, 1990, when Kahane was shot to death in a Manhattan hotel following a public lecture.* Yoram

---

*El Sayyid Nosair, a thirty-five-year-old Egyptian-born Islamic fundamentalist with alleged ties to Middle East terrorist groups, was accused of shooting Kahane in the head with a .357 magnum—a weapon so powerful that it is used by state troopers (a bullet fired from the gun can penetrate the engine block of a moving car and immobilize it). In December 1991, a jury in Manhattan acquitted Nosair in the murder of Kahane, but convicted him on several lesser charges, including criminal possession of the weapon that was used to kill Kahane. In spite of an abundance of physical evidence and testimony of numerous eyewitnesses,

attended Kahane's funeral, which attracted a Who's Who of Israel's radical right. Ex-crony Geula Cohen was there, as was her colleague in the ultra-nationalist Tehiya party Yuval Neeman, the minister of science in the Israeli Cabinet. Rabbi Moshe Levinger, who had only days before completed serving a brief prison sentence for murdering an Arab shoe-store owner, attended, as did Absorption Minister Yitzhak Peretz. More than twenty thousand mourners, many dressed in the long black coats and black hats of the ultra-Orthodox, listened to the first speaker, Sephardic chief rabbi Mordechai Eliahu, praise Kahane's "generosity, his kindness, his politeness. Rabbi Kahane contributed thirty-four thousand dollars to charity just last Rosh Hashanah. He saved many Jewish women from Gentile hands."

Next, Kahane's younger brother, Nachman, an Orthodox rabbi with a synagogue in the Muslim Quarter across the road from Ateret Cohanim, described "Kahaneism" as unabashed love for the Jewish people. Then, under an overcast sky, one Kahane disciple after another called for death to the Arabs. " 'There is a time for love, a time for hate, a time to kill, a time to heal, a time for peace, a time for war,' " said one rabbi quoting a passage from Ecclesiastes. "This is a time for war, for hate, for killing. We must banish the Arabs from our land!"

Thousands of mourners, many of them settlers from the occupied territories who traveled to Jerusalem on chartered buses, accompanied Kahane's cortege to the cemetery. At their head marched two Kach supporters armed with AK-47 assault rifles. Yellow Kach banners—a clenched fist thrust through the Star of David—fluttered nearby.

As Kahane's shrouded body was lowered into the ground, middle-aged matrons wept and young men in Kach T-shirts and bulging muscles hurled stones at journalists. Hundreds of Israeli police backed up by two army helicopters tried to restore order. A Kach leader, handed a powerful megaphone by a police official, tried to quiet the crowd. "Don't touch the photographers," he bellowed. "When you throw stones, it hits people from our own movement. The photographers didn't kill Kahane. Yossi Sarid [a left-wing Knesset member] did. Death to Yossi Sarid!"

Nosair's attorney William Kunstler apparently convinced the jury that Nosair had been framed by Kahane's disciples, who, he claimed, had killed the rabbi in a dispute over money. Following the verdict, mainstream Jewish organizations demanded that Nosair be retried in federal court for violating Kahane's civil rights. "It is easy to dismiss these pleas by saying that occasionally the system does not yield the just result," former U.S. attorney Rudolph Giuliani wrote to Manhattan U.S. attorney Otto Obermaier. "But in this case the result is so jarring that it has tempted people to talk about taking the law into their own hands." Giuliani recommended that the FBI reopen the Nosair investigation.

As dusk was fading over Jerusalem's somber hills, hundreds of Kahane supporters rampaged through the city searching for Arabs, in one of the most frightening outbursts of Jewish fanaticism in Israel's history. The first victim was an Arab employed at a Jewish gas station in West Jerusalem. He was stomped senseless and stabbed in the chest and taken to a hospital in serious condition. Another Arab was attacked and beaten unconscious in front of a West Jerusalem apartment building. Two Israeli soldiers and an armed Jewish settler came to the Arab's aid. "I'm protecting him," yelled the Jewish settler. "I live in Hebron. But this is murder! This is barbarism!" A Kach goon squad then attacked the offices of Israel TV. Mounted police drove the rioters back. Another gang of armed Kahane supporters stormed into the Old City trying to fight their way to the Temple Mount; they were beaten back by Israeli police, but for hours they played cat-and-mouse with Israeli security in the maze of streets in the Old City, torching Arab homes and shops, then darting into an alleyway before the soldiers could come and arrest them.

The day before the funeral, an elderly Arab couple on their way to pick olives was gunned down in a village near Eli in an apparent revenge killing. Three Kach members from the neighboring West Bank settlement of Tapuah were arrested. One was Kahane's twenty-five-year-old son Benjamin; another was David Axelrod, Leon Trotsky's great-great-grandson. (Tapuah was founded by Yemeni Jews who later abandoned the settlement after failing to build a viable community. It was resurrected when a Kach yeshiva moved to the settlement with government approval in 1990.)

Fearing the rising tide of Jewish vigilantism and revenge killings, Israeli peace activists hired bodyguards or briefly went into hiding. *Ha'aretz* reported that senior Kach members had prepared Arab and Jewish "hit lists." In response, the Israeli peace movement, Peace Now, called on the government to outlaw Kach as a terrorist organization.

Three days after Kahane was gunned down in Manhattan, Yoram wrote a remarkably candid tribute to him in *The Jerusalem Post*, where he was an editorial writer under David Bar-Illan—the vituperative hawk who had accused Mike Wallace of crimes against the Jewish people for his report on the Temple Mount massacre. Founded in 1932 as *The Palestine Post*, the paper began as a proud bastion of Labor Zionism. It took a militant role in the battle against British rule, then aligned itself with the Labor government. When the Likud came to power in 1977, the paper became a fierce critic of government policy, prompting Begin to remark that it should change its name back to *The Palestine Post* because of what he perceived to be its pro-PLO bias. "The heart of the *Post*'s argument with the [Likud] government was its policy regarding the West Bank," wrote its co-editor, Erwin Frankel, in a special supplement commemorating the paper's fiftieth anniversary in 1982. "The *Post* contended in numerous editorials that permanent control of the West Bank, the government's chief aim, was, in the editors' views, a serious danger for the Jewish state." Begin was particularly nettled that Israeli-based foreign diplomats religiously read the paper with their morning cup of coffee, and that diaspora Jews got most of their news about Israel from the *Post*'s highly regarded international edition.

In 1989, Koors, the ailing international conglomerate that owned the *Post* (and is a subsidiary of the Histadrut, which is controlled by the Labor party) sold it to Hollinger, Inc., a Canadian newspaper chain, for $20 million. The *Post* was revamped to reflect the new owners' right-wing views; it appointed as its publisher Yehuda Levy, a retired Israeli Army officer who had trained troops for Idi Amin in Uganda and whose only previous experience in journalism was as a spokesman for the Israeli Army in Lebanon after the 1982 invasion. A new editorial board was formed, which included Richard Perle and Robert Maxwell, the late Fleet Street publishing baron who was linked to the Mossad by investigative reporter Seymour Hersh in his book *The Samson Option*. In the wake of the changes, more than thirty journalists quit the paper, which has subsequently drifted to the right of the Likud on many issues. The paper's editor in chief, David Gross, is a Tehiya supporter; Hazony has brought in half a dozen of his extremist friends from Princeton to work there.

In a paper that had been graced by the humanistic elegance of Abba Eban, Golda Meir, and David Ben-Gurion, the *Post*'s devolution was never so apparent as on the day when Hazony memorialized Kahane. "We found ourselves drawn to Kahane," Yoram wrote in a bylined column, "because, unlike any other leader we had ever met, he was willing to say what needed to be said: that an ignoramus was an ignoramus, that a phony was a phony, that there really were things in this world worth fighting for. By coming out and giving Jewish voice to the painful truths about our Jewishness, truths we had previously heard only from those openly opposed to Judaism, he returned to us the belief that Judaism could have truth on its side, that it could be something we didn't have to be embarrassed about, that we should be proud to wear a *kipa* and make our stand on the world stage as Jews."

Although Hazony was never able to reconcile himself to Kahane's predilection for violence, he praised the rabbi for inspiring, cajoling, and shaming tens of thousands of youths into being better Jews and Zionists. Kahane "changed our lives, thrilled and entertained us, helped us grow up into strong, Jewish men and women," he wrote.

The day after his eulogy appeared in the *Post,* Hazony went to Kahane's apartment in Jerusalem to sit *shivah,* or mourn, with the Kahane family. The Hazonys had been personally close to Kahane: "Rabbi Kahane's wife said to me that my article was the only one she read in the press that gave her comfort," Yoram proudly told a colleague at the *Post.* Yet Hazony's impassioned defense of Kahane, which largely ignored his calls for violence against Arabs—not to mention liberal Jews, whose views he detested—seemed like the "famous line that Mussolini was okay because he made the trains run on time," the Princeton rabbi said. "That's what Yoram's arguments [in the *Post*] amounted to."

Kahane's assassination evoked a spate of guilt-ridden accolades from many of the same right-wing politicians who had spearheaded Kahane's banishment from the Knesset in 1988, when it appeared that he was on the verge of forming the third-largest party in Israel. The polls were frightening. On October 2, 1988, a front-page story in *The New York Times* quoted respected Israeli pollster Hanoch Smith predicting that Kahane would win at least three seats, thereby giving him the balance of power between Labor and Likud, which were in a stalemate at the polls. Smith told the *Times* that if Likud didn't invite him into a right-wing coalition, it would be unable to form a government. Other polls predicted Kach would win as many as a dozen Knesset seats, giving Kahane enough clout to demand a Cabinet post. Kahane declared he wanted to become defense minister. The right-wing establishment parties had no intention of sitting back and watching Kach become a right-wing juggernaut. On October 16, 1988, Israel's high court banned Kahane from running for the Knesset on the grounds that his party, Kach, was racist and anti-democratic. Although Yitzhak Shamir and Geula Cohen clearly had much to do with turning Kahane into a potent political phenomenon, they wanted nothing better than to destroy his career and siphon away his tens of thousands of supporters.

Writing in *Hadashot* a few days after Kahane's murder, Uri Elitzur, a prominent Gush Emunim settler from Ofra and the official spokesman for the National Religious party, declared that the rabbi was a Jewish hero who was betrayed by a nation he fought and ultimately died for. "A big part of the violence and hatred expressed by the Kach people at the funeral was a result of this hypocrisy," he wrote. "Rabbi Kahane was a great Talmud scholar, a great student of the Bible and of Jewish history and of Jewish and Western philosophy. He devoted a lot of time and money to charity and a big part of the money he raised in the U.S. was brought to Israel for those purposes. Kahane was the pioneer for the fight for Russian Jews at a time when the Israeli government and the Jewish establishment abroad still thought it was better not to make the Soviet government angry . . . and he saw the first fruits of the struggle that he started almost alone. I'm sorry that I wasn't brave enough to say these things, and others, while he was still alive."

Hazony is certainly not a thug and is quick to decry violence, unlike many supporters of the late Meir Kahane. Yet like nearly all the ultranationalist religious settlers driven by the commandment to build and settle, he blithely ignores the extreme brutality of the occupation and the damage it does to Israel's image as a democracy. But then Yoram did not move to Eli to participate in a Western-style democracy. He believes that Israel is mandated to become a holy nation of priests and wise men, and that the Arabs will learn from the Jews—and be morally elevated in the process. More than that, he says, Jewish ethics demands that Israel retain sovereignty over the West Bank, if for no other reason than to protect the Palestinians from their own odious leadership. Mixing messianism with an old-fashioned paternalism that would not have been out of place in the Deep South one hundred years ago, Hazony declared, "As long as the only leaders that Palestinians have are capricious butchers—then we don't owe them anything. In fact, we owe them the opposite . . . If we understand Arafat to be proposing to set up a [West Bank] state like the one in Syria or the one in Iraq, even if it weren't a threat to our own personal security, we're not allowed to give that state the right to exist. That's not self-determination, but [the Palestinian] people will end up being slaughtered and oppressed [by Arafat], and there's no moral way of justifying such an action. So those of us who set up these Jewish outposts [settlements] understand them to be outposts for democracy.

"The role of the Jews is to build one country that will be, in Isaiah's phrase, 'a light unto the nations.' Then everyone will come to Israel and say, 'How's it done? You've built such a good society.'

"There are certain things that are extremely basic to this project. In Ezekiel there's the famous prophecy that says in order for the Jewish utopia to be established in Israel, first the body has to be built, and then the spirit has to be built. Right now we're at a very material stage where Israeli society has to be turned into something that's capable of surviving first, before it's really going to be possible for it to be something people are going to admire.

"The settlements work on both things simultaneously. You can say they do three things. One, the settlements themselves, the religious ones, are tiny, self-contained, idealistic communities where people strive to implement a Jewish vision of the good society, where people love one another freely, and I don't mean in a sexual sense, but are willing to sacrifice to help one another and be the way people are supposed to be. My wife and I decided years ago we couldn't stand the idea of raising children anywhere else. Eli is just such a good environment. All the problems that plague living in Princeton, New Jersey, just don't exist here. There's no violent crime, there's almost no divorce, no abortions, no drug abuse—alcoholism is basically unheard of. People here have something to live for, something to pull together for, and their children turn out to be straight, powerful people. That's the first thing. We're building the light to the nations within our community.

"The second thing may be a little harder for you to swallow. It has much more to do with building a strong body for Israel. With Judea and Samaria, Israel is fifty miles wide. For us it's completely obvious that with people like Saddam and Assad running around the Middle East . . . Israel should be at least fifty miles wide and not go back to what Abba Eban once called the Auschwitz Line. We're serious about bringing something important into the world with the Land of Israel, and we have to be able to defend ourselves. Jewish ethics demands it.

"Here is the third point. I don't believe and the Torah doesn't believe that there's such a thing as a right for a people to have the freedom to destroy its own members or do any sort of evil. Self-determination in Judaism is discussed in the prophets. Their vision of the future is that every nation will have freedom and peace. But that vision of self-determination is conditional on people being able to govern themselves justly and fairly.

Take Iran—it's a great example. The Ayatollah was elected in a democratic election, one man, one vote, one time. People didn't want the shah. But the ayatollah spent the next decade killing and torturing internal opposition, suppressing thought and religion of anyone he disagreed with, and participating with Saddam in launching a barbaric war that killed a million and one-half people. Judaism doesn't recognize a right to self-determination if you determine that what you should do is slaughter and kill and oppress."

Despite his intellectual pretensions, Yoram has avoided encounters with educated Palestinians. "I don't meet [Arab] intellectuals. I've talked to lots of Arabs on both sides of the Green Line, workers, normal people, the elderly."

"Not your counterparts?"

"What do you mean by counterparts?" he asked.

"Students, doctors, economists?"

"I met some people like that when I was at Princeton and Rutgers [where he worked on a Ph.D.]. But . . . there are two kinds of Arabs. The ones who want to become American . . . don't want to come back to Palestine . . . They're normal people, there's nothing special about them. Then there are, you know, the activists. You can't talk to them. These are people who say, 'I don't care how many die.' Actually, I once talked for hours to one guy at Rutgers who was head of the Palestinian activists [on campus]. He was absolutely against [political] compromise.

"Democracy is a Jewish idea. The respect for individuals, the freedom of conscience, freedom of religion, so long as it holds to minimum ethical norms, are Jewish ideas. The reason Kahane said Zionism and democracy are incompatible is that he had a terribly pessimistic notion of what Jews are capable of creating, which is kind of odd. He thought the Arabs would always have more children than Jews, that the Arabs were completely incorrigible. . . .

"I believe that we Jews are strong enough, have the character, to start having enough children and raising them to want to live in Israel and start building an economy that will make more Jews want to come to Israel and maintain a Jewish society and not have a demographic problem. It essentially comes down to one point: Rav Kahane was not willing to believe Jews could care about having children as much as Arabs do. I believe that they can."

*

POSTSCRIPT: In 1992, Yoram left *The Jerusalem Post* to become "special assistant" to then–Deputy Foreign Minister Benjamin Netanyahu. Following Labor's victory in June 1992, Netanyahu became the leading contender to replace Shamir as head of the Likud party. A Gallup Israel poll published on July 4, 1992, showed Netanyahu with 57 percent support, far ahead of his closest rival, Benny Begin, who had 17 percent. Meanwhile, in a sudden burst of building, Eli has grown by at least 800 percent since December 1990, from fifty-six homes to more than four hundred and fifty.

CHAPTER 8

Gaza

The *intifada* began in Jabalya refugee camp in Gaza on December 9, 1987, when four Arab workers returning from their jobs in Israel were killed in a collision with an Israeli truck. Thousands of mourners from Jabalya marched on an Israeli Army camp, convinced that the accident was deliberate. (Three days earlier, an Israeli merchant had been stabbed to death in Gaza, and Gazans believed that the truck driver was a relative of the merchant intent on avenging his death.) The Israeli Army fired on the demonstrators. Four Palestinians were killed, and the Gaza Strip, a sliver of land crowded with 750,000 inhabitants, exploded with a shower of stones, Molotov cocktails, and burning tires. The rebellion spread to the West Bank, where, as in the Gaza Strip, the refugee camps became the front lines of the *intifada*.

Jabalya continues to be at the forefront of the uprising. The camp is located in a sandy depression about a half-mile inland from the Mediterranean, where more than fifty-five thousand people live packed together in poorly insulated, one- and two-room reinforced cinder-block shelters. A huge pond swollen with raw sewage called Suliman's Pool is situated near one of the elementary schools. I was told that several children walking to school along the pond's banks have fallen in and drowned.

Overcrowding, poor housing, and inadequate sewers and drainage in the camps have resulted in a high incidence of waterborne and respiratory diseases. Dr. Muhammad Abu Sweieh, the head doctor of the camp clinic, said he saw a 20 percent rise in the incidence of clinical depression and schizophrenia, from 189 to 226 diagnosed cases, between April 1989 and February 1990. He attributed the increase to the high number of shootings and beatings by Israeli soldiers and the long curfews designed to keep youths indoors and away from stones. In 1989, Jabalya was for 156 days under a curfew that forbade Palestinians to leave their homes, except for a few hours a day.

In Gaza, where more than half the residents are under age fourteen, children have been the main combatants and the chief victims of the *intifada.* At least ninety-six of Gaza's children have been killed and more than 23,120 wounded since the beginning of the uprising. Amnon Rubin-stein, leader of the liberal Shinui party, called on then–Defense Minister Yitzhak Rabin to investigate the torture of a nine-year-old boy from Gaza's Shati camp, who was said to have been stripped, hung upside down by his feet, and beaten for three hours by Israeli soldiers as an example to young stone throwers. The United Nations Relief and Works Agency (UNRWA), which provides basic services in the refugee camps such as housing, health care, and education, filed a complaint with the Israeli military, but has received no reply.

Every refugee family I met in the occupied territories had at least one son in prison, in the hospital, or dead. Muhammad lives in Rafah with his wife and ten children. Two of his sons were killed in Lebanon fighting with the PLO; two are in an Israeli prison. The day I visited him, his shelter was filled with flowers and boxes of chocolate to celebrate the release of his eldest son from prison. Muhammad had been a policeman working for the Israelis. But when the *intifada* began, the Shabiba—the militant youth organization that runs the camp—told him to quit or he would be executed as a collaborator.

I met "Omar" (not his real name) at Jabalya camp in front of the health clinic, where he said he sometimes goes to help the staff tend to the victims of the ·*intifada*. The walls of the clinic, which were made of cinder block and painted white, were covered with anti-Israeli graffiti, news of upcoming demonstrations, and nationalist slogans. A hand-painted notice signed by Fatah told of an upcoming general strike. A wall slogan declared, "Islamic *jihad* is the vanguard and will hunt down the Jews until victory or martyr-dom." A sign posted by UNRWA warned against gathering in the health center for purposes other than receiving medical treatment. I was told that children sometimes throw stones at Israeli soldiers from inside the clinic's walled-in courtyard.

Omar had spent one year in Ketziot detention center in the Negev. His crime was stoning soldiers. At one time, he worked in Israel as a menial laborer, but since his arrest, the military has forbidden him to leave the Strip, where unemployment is around 40 percent.

Along with his wife, and their eight children, Omar lives with his parents in a tiny two-room hut provided by UNRWA. The children were dirty and appeared to be undernourished. One barefoot child who was naked from the waist up had a surgical scar running vertically up her stomach to her neck. Omar said she had digestive problems, which he claimed were brought on by the *intifada*. The dampness, he said, made it difficult for her to breathe at night, so she slept using an inhalator provided by UNRWA.

Of all the Palestinian leaders, Omar said, he liked George Habash the best. It was a surprising statement because Habash is Christian and Gaza is heavily influenced by Muslim fundamentalists. Both groups, however, oppose Israel's existence. "Habash has principles," Omar told me. "He says what was taken with force will be retaken by force."

Gaza has been tense since 1948, when 180,000 Palestinian refugees poured into the area, engulfing the 160,000 indigenous residents. Palestinian guerrilla attacks from Gaza, which was occupied by Egypt in 1948, were the *casus belli* for Israel's participation in the 1956 Suez War. Israel routed the Egyptian Army and occupied the Strip for about five months before it was pressured to leave by the Eisenhower administration. Israel occupied the Strip again during the June 1967 Six-Day War. Almost immediately, the PLO turned Gaza into a base honeycombed with underground bunkers and safe houses, from which they waged a Viet Cong–style guerrilla war against the Israeli occupation force. General Ariel Sharon was brought in to crush the uprising. He had bulldozers cut open spaces through the densely packed camps so that army jeeps could safely patrol along roadways, which are now known as "Sharon boulevards." The refugees whose houses were destroyed by Sharon were forcibly moved to deserted UN army barracks near the Egyptian border. Between July 1971 and February 1972, Sharon's shock troops killed 104 Palestinian guerrillas and arrested 742 others.

At the same time, Sharon also came up with a plan to stop Palestinian children from stoning Israeli soldiers. "I invited all the Arab parents to meetings in the schools where our policy was explained to them," he wrote in his autobiography, *Warrior*. "The parents were told that if a child was caught stoning a soldier, the child's father or eldest brother would be given a jar of water, a loaf of bread, a head covering, some Jordanian money, and a white flag. We would then transport him to the Jordanian border, point out the direction of the nearest Jordanian town, and send him on his way." As miserable as the camps are, they are part of Palestine and nobody wanted to be forcibly uprooted and separated from friends and family. On two occasions, Sharon reported, he deported about thirty people. "When you walked through the streets of Gaza, you often heard parents disciplining their children vigorously. None of them wanted to end up in Jordan. . . ."

Meanwhile, Sharon devised a master plan to solve the Palestinian refugee problem, which had festered since the end of the 1948 war, when some 600,000 to 760,000 Palestinians had fled or been expelled from Israel. Like refugees in other wars, most Palestinians who left their homes did so to get out of the way of the fighting. Toward the end of the 1948 war, however, as Jewish troops prevailed over the combined Arab armies, Ben-Gurion sought to strengthen Israel's strategic position and expand and secure its highly vulnerable borders by taking more territory and expelling Palestinians from villages—especially near border areas—before a UN-mediated armistice ended the conflict. Dozens of villages were evacuated, often brutally, by Jewish troops. In July 1948, Ben-Gurion approved the largest expulsion of the war from the neighboring towns of Ramle and Lydda. Jewish troops massacred 250 Palestinian civilians after taking Lydda. Both towns had been used as lightly armed garrisons by the Jordanian Arab Legion, the strongest of the Arab fighting forces, and the Israeli command feared that the garrisons posed a threat to Tel Aviv and the Jerusalem–Tel Aviv highway.

Following the killings in Lydda, the 50,000 to 60,000 townspeople remaining there and in Ramle were forcibly expelled. The Israeli Army brought trucks and buses from Tel Aviv to evacuate Ramle's Arabs. In Lydda, the Palestinians left town on Arab buses, trucks, cars, and on foot, carrying with them whatever they could manage.

Lydda and Ramle, like other evacuated areas, were resettled with Holocaust survivors who moved into the vacant Arab houses. Ben-Gurion, who, at the beginning of the war, had said he was surprised by the flight of Arabs from Jaffa (which had been bombarded with heavy mortars of the Irgun and Stern Gang), in July 1948 turned to one of his officers while visiting the newly conquered, largely Christian Arab town of Nazareth and said, "Why so many Arabs, why did you not expel them?"

But whatever the cause of the Palestinians' flight, the Zionist leaders accepted their exodus as good news, or, in Chaim Weizmann's words, "a miraculous simplification of the problem." About one hundred thousand Palestinians remained in the Jewish state, and some sixty thousand slipped back into Israel during the months following the war. As Israeli historian Benny Morris noted, along with the establishment of the state of Israel, the refugee problem was the major political consequence of the 1948 war, and became one of the most intractable components of the Arab-Israeli conflict.

"The essence of my plan," Sharon wrote in *Warrior*, "was to get rid of the Palestinian refugee camps altogether." Sharon proposed to the Golda Meir government that the camps be dismantled, resettling about seventy thousand refugees in towns and cities on the West Bank—and another seventy thousand in Gaza's existing cities. In addition, Sharon recommended resettling 20,000–30,000 Gaza refugees inside the pre-1967 boundaries of Israel

> to show our good will and humane values. The elimination of the camps would be neither easy nor quick; it would take, as I envisioned, ten years or so. Yet I believed that with the help of other countries and international organizations it would be practical for Israel to do it. With such massive new construction [to rehouse the newly evicted refugees] it would have constituted a major spur to the [Israeli] economy.

According to Sharon, the government vetoed his plan for resettlement, fearing it would set a precedent of unilateral concessions, but it approved another of his schemes: the construction of Jewish settlements that would reach out like fingers to divide the cities and camps of the Gaza Strip. Now, thanks in part to Sharon, there are some five thousand Jewish settlers living in nineteen ultranationalist settlements in Gaza that include hothouses and orange groves and a restaurant with a panoramic view of the Mediterranean—all accessible from Israel on roads that bypass Palestinian population centers. A resort hotel catering to American Orthodox Jews was built near Khan Yunis at a cost of $9 million. The hotel's glossy brochure advertised "paradisiacal beaches," where families could frolic "within the framework of traditional Jewish Orthodox values." As a special bonus, hotel guests could "meet the friendly Bedouin living and working as they have for generations." The hotel closed in 1989, then reopened two years later to desultory business.

Zvi Handel, a big, muscular man with a knitted yarmulke and an easy smile, is the head of the Gaza Regional Council, the Gush Emunim–dominated administrative bureaucracy that runs the settlements in the Strip. He invited me to visit him on a warm day in November 1990 at his headquarters in Neve Dekalim, a large settlement that is surrounded by barbed wire, watchtowers, and heavily armed Israeli soldiers. Just across the road is Khan Yunis, where sixty thousand Palestinian refugees live in numbing poverty. Before Handel allowed me to ask him any questions, he insisted that I watch a promotional film in English produced by the regional council to drum up investments and attract prospective settlers from English-speaking countries. The film began as the camera slowly panned across rows of gently sloping, milky white sand dunes as the sound of wind purred reassuringly in the background. An unseen narrator speaking in sonorous tones said that the Jewish settlers had made Gaza, a desert, flourish. Then there were more shots of absolutely pristine wilderness. (I later learned the shots were taken in Gaza's small nature preserve.)

The film cut to thriving Jewish settlements, pulsating with beaming, yarmulke-clad children, smart shops and cafés, and smiling farmer-pioneers proudly showing off an abundance of large, beautiful sun-ripened tomatoes, the settlements' principal crop, earning some $3 million a year. That was followed by motivational testimony from settlers who had moved to Gaza. "Life flows freely here with a dynamic sense of Jewish values and freedom," intoned the narrator. There were no Arabs, let alone a refugee camp, to be seen in the film. The implication, of course, was that Gaza is a virgin land, tamed and redeemed by Jews.

Following the film, Handel, a forty-one-year-old native of Transylvania, Romania, said, "We have two reasons for being here. First, it's our land. Secondly, our presence enhances Israel's security. We are the eyes and ears of the army." Handel reasoned that if Israel left the Strip, the PLO would take over and use it as a base to launch terrorist attacks against Israel. Worse, the various PLO factions and fundamentalist Muslims would compete for the allegiance of the local population by seeing who could murder the most Jews. "The group that says it is the strongest will prove it by killing Jews," he said. "Even if we hermetically sealed the borders, they would still find ways to kill Jews. Whether it wants to or not, Israel must be here!"

Many in the Israeli Army bitterly disagree. In June 1992, thirty-six soldiers from a highly decorated reserve company presented a petition to then–Prime Minister Shamir and Labor party chairman Rabin, calling for an immediate withdrawal of the army from the Gaza Strip. "Our occupation of the Gaza Strip," said the petition, "is unnecessary, destructive to the army . . . of no security value, and above all, a cause of frustration and hatred in a war that has no winners or losers. . . . Our presence there perpetuates a situation that both sides know is to no one's benefit and that is only getting worse."

One of the petitioners recalled the terrible poverty he saw in Gaza in an interview with the Jerusalem weekly newspaper *Kol Ha'ir:* "We had to do guard duty in the observation post overlooking the refugee camp. Every day . . . children would come and start shouting for us to throw them food. At first, we thought this was a game. Later, we saw that they would jump on everything we threw, even if the bread was full of sand. . . . It simply amazed us." Once the soldier saw a group of teenagers kill a pigeon with a slingshot, "and they grabbed it and started arguing about who would get what piece. They ate it raw, left only the feathers, and filled up on the blood. We thought we imagined it."

Even former defense minister Moshe Arens has grown weary of Gaza. Following Likud's loss to Labor in June 1992, a dispirited Arens declared that he was prepared to give up Gaza, a heresy to believers in *Eretz Yisrael.*

Handel claimed that before the *intifada,* the settlers tried to build a "harmonious" life with the Arabs. "There were many good friendships between us and the Arabs" before the *intifada,* he told me. "Once they got to know us, they would say, 'You are not like the other Jews. You are good friends. We have to help each other.' "

I asked Handel for examples. "I have Arab friends in Khan Yunis that I used to visit, and their families have come to my house to visit," he replied rather lamely.

Handel's secretary, who lives in a religious *moshav* in the Strip, where she and her husband own hothouses for growing tomatoes and mint, added, "When I had a bar mitzvah for my son four years ago, I invited our [Palestinian] worker to come with his wife, and when she gave birth, I visited them with presents."

Her example seemed to jog Handel's memory. "When we had a *brit melach* for my son, we invited the mayor of the [Gaza] town of Dir al-Balah," he said. "All his family came. He's dead now. If I tell you the name of someone who is still alive and you publish it, it will be dangerous for him. He could be killed. But even during the *intifada*, I have maintained friendships. I'm sorry I can't take you with me to visit my Arab friends. It would be very real for you to see it. But they are afraid.

"If I go to an Arab market to buy something, it's an opening to a relationship. You start with coffee, and over the course of time they may ask me for a favor. If we live together, we will learn that not all Arabs are killers and not all Jews are soldiers. Therefore, the settlements are important, because you cannot live with Arabs only with guns and soldiers. It's not normal."

Handel claimed that "99 percent" of the Arabs oppose the *intifada*, but they are terrorized into rebelling against Israeli rule by a small number of Palestinian activists. "I saw with my own eyes an Arab child who had his ear cut off [by a Palestinian militant] and another child whose finger was cut off because they went to our soldiers and told them that there were masked youths in their schools.

"When I speak with Arabs privately, they are very angry at *Zahal* [the Israeli Army] for not crushing the *intifada*. They say, 'You are very weak. When Egypt was here, they knew how to deal with this crap.' They are right. We have a saying in Hebrew. 'The person who shows pity to people who are cruel will end up having to be cruel to people who are kind.' Our good Jewish hearts have exacerbated the *intifada*. If we had killed two hundred Arabs at the beginning of the *intifada*, it would be over. If we expel seven thousand troublemakers now, everything would be okay."

After the interview, Handel told his secretary, a small, dour native Israeli, to take me on a quick tour of several nearby settlements. First we stopped for lunch at the tourist hotel near Khan Yunis, which was completely empty. The owner told me that the government pays him to stay open. Because it is extremely dangerous for Israelis to drive into the Gaza Strip, he said the government is considering whether to give him the use of military helicopters so he can fly tourists in and out of the hotel.

After lunch, we drove to Atzmona, a prosperous religious *moshav*, where I was introduced to a small, thin thirty-year-old settler from Chicago, who was the foreman of the settlement's vegetable warehouse. The day before, he said, he had taken a chartered bus to Jerusalem to attend Rabbi Kahane's funeral. "Maimonides said that any Jew who is killed by *goyim* is holy," he said, taking pains to let me know he had studied at Yeshiva Mercaz HaRav, the Gush Emunim stronghold, and was not a disciple of Kahane's. As we spoke, a group of Ethiopian Jews lifted large gunnysacks filled with potatoes onto a truck. I asked if I could speak to them, but he refused, saying curtly, "We are paying them by the hour."

Before the *intifada*, the settlements in the Gaza Strip had employed Palestinian refugees to do most of the manual labor. No longer. The settlers are afraid to allow Palestinians onto the settlements, despite Handel's claims of good fellowship.

Yet Handel was not the only Israeli who asserted that the Palestinians in Gaza are better off living under Israeli rule. In spite of Gaza's wretched living conditions, which are as squalid as any place in the Third World, Israeli government officials claim that the refugees' standard of living in the occupied territories improved markedly after 1967. They have all sorts of statistics to show the rise in the number of television sets and refrigerators and the improvement in health care for the refugees under their aegis. It is true that low-paying jobs as laborers in the construction industry and cleaners and dishwashers in the hotel industry, to name two that employ Palestinians, brought badly needed income to the occupied territories. But in general, the Arabs' living conditions in the territories have actually deteriorated during the occupation. The incipient hardships were the root cause of the *intifada*. "If you take indicators like the number of hospital beds per thousand Palestinians, the length of roads per capita, even the amount of water, the situation is worse" for the Palestinians than before Israeli rule, said Meron Benvenisti, whose study of the occupation, *The West Bank and Gaza Atlas*, was financed by the Ford and Rockefeller foundations. "From land expropriation to . . . the dual system of infrastructure available for Arabs versus Jewish settlers . . . Here you can find the reasons for the *intifada*."

Whatever gains the Palestinians did make have been lost since the *intifada*, as Palestinian society has tried to disengage itself from Israel. Far fewer Palestinians work in Israel, whose products they now boycott. Further, remittances from abroad shriveled after Kuwait expelled three hundred thousand Palestinians following the Gulf War.

Yet as paradoxical as it may seem, young refugees in the Gaza Strip and the West Bank are generally more willing to work out a political settlement with Israel than are their counterparts in Jordan and Syria. Israel isn't an abstraction for them. They are regularly confronted by the awesome power of Israel's army and the vigor of its society. Moreover, the *intifada* and the U.S.-brokered peace negotiations in which Palestinians from the territories represented themselves in talks with Israel have given Palestinians a sense of pride and accomplishment despite their severe hardships. "When a young man goes out of the house to throw stones, he knows he might be killed, but still all young people do it because this is not a decent life we are living," said a woman student at Maghazi camp, which I visited during the dedication of a women's vocational school that had been funded by the Near East Council of Churches.

One result of the refugees' determined stand against the occupation is that for the first time, a broad cross section of refugees has asked UNRWA to improve living conditions. One reason that so many camps are so squalid is that the refugees themselves have vetoed most major camp-improvement projects such as better housing because they don't want anything that looks permanent and might undermine their dream, no matter how improbable, of one day returning to their ancestral homes in Israel. "The *intifada* has cranked up their nationalism to a new level," said a member of a British research team, employed by UNRWA to study ways of improving the camps in Gaza. "They [Gazans] feel they no longer have to walk around in sewage up to their necks. People are ready for improvements. They no longer feel that putting in a sewage-treatment plant means they are surrendering their rights." According to a study commissioned by UNRWA, the estimated cost of installing sewage systems for Gaza's camps is $28 million. The total cost of improving the camps' hygiene, rehabilitating the worst shelters, and building a new hospital, which is planned for Gaza City, is more than $65 million.

The PLO has endorsed the proposed renovation projects, although once there is a peace settlement, it would like to dismantle the camps and place refugees in new housing. "In the next three to five years UNRWA will play an important part," said Muhammad Nashashibi, head of the PLO's economic department in Damascus, who told me that he has discussed with UNRWA officials ways to develop the Palestinian economy in the occupied territories once Israel withdraws. "We want to work with them very closely. We want UNRWA to build infrastructure and improve living conditions." Nashashibi had said that the PLO had at its disposal $100 million, contingent upon the UN's coming up with an equal amount, to spend on industry and agriculture in a future Palestinian West Bank–Gaza Strip state.

UNRWA has recently expanded its activities in the occupied territories in other ways. In February 1988, UNRWA received $21 million in emergency funds authorized by the UN General Assembly to alleviate increased hardship brought on by the *intifada*. Part of the money was used to hire some two dozen refugee affairs officers [RAO], Americans and Europeans who drive around in Volkswagen Pisats, to monitor the camps for human-rights abuses, and in certain instances intervene with Israeli troops to prevent beatings, shootings, and summary arrests. Bernard Mills, a retired major in Britain's Special Forces and former director of UNRWA's Gaza office, said he was mainly responsible for the RAO program. He told me he left UNRWA in the fall of 1989 because "if I had seen another Israeli officer shoot a small child in the stomach, I would have probably grabbed his gun and shot him."

As UNRWA has become a more forceful advocate for the refugees, the Israeli government has begun to bring the organization's activities under close scrutiny. In October 1989, Israeli troops stormed UNRWA head-quarters in Gaza, arresting one local and two international staff members, as well as confiscating documents. The staff members were let go after questioning. In the occupied West Bank, troops raided UNRWA installa-tions at four camps and questioned staff members at each one. According to Reuters, a senior Israel government official said several of the local UN staff who were questioned were suspected of illegally channeling money and jobs to activists in the Palestinian uprising. Margaret Tutwiler, the State Department's spokeswoman, criticized Israel for interfering with UNRWA's operations.

In November 1989, the Permanent Mission of Israel to the United Nations in Vienna, where the agency is headquartered along the banks of the Danube, wrote to UNRWA's commissioner general complaining that the agency had violated its mandate by going beyond its mission of provid-ing relief and economic assistance. Israel specifically criticized the RAO program: "Groups of UNRWA personnel using Agency vehicles and equipment have, for an extended period, been conducting widescale sur-veillance and monitoring of Israeli troop movements and activities in the administered areas," the letter said. "These groups have been tracking, following, and often interfering with Israeli military personnel fulfilling security functions in the areas. Similar activities include random photo-graphing of Israeli troops and systematic maintenance of detailed invento-ries listing troop activities. UNRWA vehicles have been used to block roads and to delay and obstruct IDF patrols in maintaining security in the areas, most frequently in the midst of riots, extreme local disorder and violence.

"The appearance of UNRWA vehicles and personnel at selected locations during such disorders . . . . has served both to increase intensity of the violence on the part of the rioters as well as to enhance the danger to human life both of the Israeli and UN personnel."

In January 1990, UNRWA director Giorgio Giacomelli traveled to Israel, where he discussed these allegations with then–Foreign Minister Moshe Arens, Defense Minister Yitzhak Rabin, and General Shmuel Goren, coordinator of the occupied territories. "I said that we don't go beyond the mandate," Giacomelli told me. "But maybe we should spend some time looking into the mandate. What is the mandate? In my view, the mandate is not cast in bronze. . . . In the beginning, it was providing tents and food and primary medical care, then it was more in the area of work to provide employment, then education and health. . . . Since the *intifada*, what is needed is passive protection for the people."

Giacomelli and other UNRWA officials I talked to said that "passive protection" includes providing emergency rations to refugees under curfew, extending medical and psychological services to victims of shootings and beatings, and, where possible, having RAOs try to defuse tense encounters between soldiers and refugees, preventing the beatings and arrest of children if they can. "While I'm duty-bound to coordinate activities that occur under the aegis of the host government and the occupying power, on the other hand, we have to address the needs of the refugees," Giacomelli said.

Although the relationship between Israel and UNRWA has deteriorated, it is unlikely that Israel will shut down the agency, if for no other reason than that it would displease the United States, UNRWA's single largest contributor. Nor would Israel like the responsibility of caring for an increasingly destitute and hostile refugee population. In the long run, the Shamir government wanted to carry out a version of Sharon's refugee-resettlement plan. In March 1989, Prime Minister Shamir visited the United States seeking $2 billion to dismantle the Palestinian refugee camps and build new housing in order to resettle the refugees permanently in the occupied territories—in effect breaking up the camps and redistributing the people who live in them. The concept was incorporated into Shamir's four-point peace plan. Critics charged it was a callous attempt to save the Israeli construction industry, which, once the money was obtained, could instead build housing for the flood of expected Soviet immigrants. The State Department rejected Shamir's proposal, saying the refugees should be resettled only as part of a comprehensive peace plan.

Brigadier General Fredy Zach, the deputy coordinator of the occupied territories, said during an interivew in his office at Harkirya, Israel's Pentagon in downtown Tel Aviv, that Palestinian hostility toward Israel would be defused if the camps were dismantled and the refugees' economic status improved. He noted that Israel provides small plots of land and small grants to Gaza refugees who want to build homes outside the camps. In return, the refugee has six months to demolish his shelter in the camp and cede the land to Israel. Between 70,000 and 100,000 Palestinians have been resettled in new neighborhoods under the program, in homes that they build and pay for themselves.

When Israel started the program in 1972, according to UNRWA officials, it insisted that refugees sign documents in Hebrew that relinquished their rights as refugees, including their right to receive compensation for property left behind in pre-1967 Israel, but that practice was abandoned after it was condemned by the UN. "We are the only ones in the world who have done anything for these miserable people," Zach said, omitting the fact that during the past twenty years the Israeli treasury has realized millions of dollars in surplus from its taxation of Gaza, while, according to Meron Benvenisti, the former deputy mayor of Jerusalem, it has spent next to nothing on refugee welfare, not to mention Gaza's crumbling infrastructure. But even Zach conceded that in spite of Israel's best efforts at social engineering, the new neighborhoods in Gaza have now become what Bernard Mills accurately described as the "actual hotbeds of unrest."*

Meanwhile, Jewish settlements in Gaza continue to expand on land that could be used to alleviate the refugee camps' crowded conditions. Already, 34 percent of Gaza's land is under exclusive Israeli control, as is more than one third of the underground water, which is used by the Jewish settlements. The Strip's groundwater has become salinated due to overpumping by the settlements, devastating the orange groves, the Palestinians' principal cash crop. "In Gaza," laments Israeli journalist Ari Shavit, "live people whose houses and villages in what is now Israel we took over years ago; and not only did we take their houses, but later, in 1967, we took over their place of refuge too. Not only that, but in those long years of occupation

---

*Suppressing the *intifada* cost the Israeli Army more than $750 million during the first year, according to the head of the IDF's budgetary offices. During the same period, the Israeli economy lost more than half a billion dollars due to the *intifada,* according to a report by the Bank of Israel, which cited a downturn in tourism, construction slowdowns, and fewer Israeli exports to consumer markets in the West Bank and the Gaza Strip.

we turned them into a subproletariat, and we exploited them. Not only did we exploit them, but when they dared to demand their freedom, we put them behind barbed wire. And in Gaza there are no strategic heights, no vital water sources for Tel Aviv. Not even the tombs of our ancestors to which we claim historic rights. In Gaza, indeed, there are no excuses."*

*Ari Shavit wrote about an Israeli prison camp in the Gaza Strip where Palestinians are being held in harsh conditions for *Ha'aretz*. The account was later republished in *The New York Review of Books*.

CHAPTER 9

Peace Now

I first heard of the Israeli progressive movement Peace Now in 1980, when I was a graduate student at the University of Wisconsin at Madison. One evening in a small apartment off campus, Tzali Reshef, then a young reservist in the Israeli Army and a Harvard-educated lawyer, eloquently argued that Israel's occupation of the West Bank and the Gaza Strip was immoral and was eroding the foundations of Zionism and democracy. "People who rule over another people cannot be free," he declared, adding that it was legitimate and necessary to criticize publicly the expanionist policies of the Israeli government. Reshef warned that a government that preferred building settlements across the Green Line to the elimination of the historic conflict with the Palestinians was suicidal.

In 1980, just three years into Menachem Begin's first term as prime minister, Reshef's message was bracing. Begin had already built dozens of ultranationalist settlements in the occupied territories, and most mainstream American Jewish leaders had either embraced the uncompromising policies of the Likud or had been cowed into silence by the Israeli government, which maintained that public criticism of Israel gave aid and comfort to the enemy. In those days, it was important to hear prominent Israelis like Reshef say that the better part of valor was protest and demonstrations, and that American Jews could criticize Israel without being self-hating traitors.

More than a decade later, with the memory of Scud missile attacks still fresh, it appeared that Peace Now had failed to stem the right-wing tide in Israel. Its goal seemed farther away than ever before. Though the movement once marshaled four hundred thousand demonstrators in Tel Aviv to protest the Lebanon war, it could barely muster several hundred people to participate in an antisettlement rally on the eve of the Gulf War.

In recent years, Peace Now's biggest problem has been trying to sell a skeptical Israeli public on the notion that the Palestine Liberation Organization has given up terrorism and is ready to live in peace alongside Israel. Peace Now leaders rejoiced after the Palestine National Council voted in the fall of 1988 to recognize Israel. Following the PLO's diplomatic initiative, Peace Now explicitly called for negotiations with the PLO and the repartition of Palestine into sovereign Jewish and Palestinian Arab states.

At a Peace Now rally in June 1989, Amos Oz, Israel's most acclaimed author and liberal intellectual, cautioned against ignoring a historic opportunity to resolve the Palestinian conflict: "For decades, the Palestinian national movement took a frantic, extreme, and inflexible stance. It was undeterred by any form of slaughter, including the slaughter of its own people, and was not prepared to give up an inch. May God preserve the nation of Israel if it adopts a similar stance, now that the Palestinians are perhaps beginning to shake themselves free of the insane opinions which brought down on them, and upon us, a tragedy that has lasted for eighty years. May God preserve the nation of Israel from stepping straight into the shoes out of which the PLO is trying to step at this very moment."

Much to the consternation of Israeli right-wingers, Peace Now began to hold joint-dialogue groups and press conferences with pro-PLO Palestinian West Bank leaders. Peace Now also brought Palestinians like Faisal Husseini—who is thought to be the PLO's highest-ranking official on the West Bank—to Israeli towns and villages to preach a message of reconciliation.

If these activities helped break down stereotypes among Arabs and Jews, they also deepened the chasm between the right and left in Israel, helping to transform the Jewish state into a bipolar society inhabited by hawks and doves. In blistering disputations, in speech after speech, and in angry manifestos, each side accused the other of leading Israel to Armageddon. The left, however, seemed to be more vulnerable to right-wing charges that it was fostering Israel's demise by naively encouraging peace talks with an organization whose charter still calls for the Jewish state's destruction.

Yet in October 1991, the hard-line government of Yitzhak Shamir sat down with Palestinians at the Hall of Columns in Madrid—the result, partly, of the efforts of Peace Now. By the time the talks began, a slender majority of Israelis were willing to surrender some land for peace, according to public-opinion polls. There was a sudden feeling among the Israeli left that perhaps for the first time since the Zionists had encountered the Arabs while building their initial settlements in Ottoman Palestine, the one-hundred-year war over the Holy Land was coming to an end.

Peace Now was born in the heady days following Egyptian president Anwar Sadat's historic journey to Israel in November 1977. It was a time of great expectations. After all, Egypt had been Israel's most powerful enemy. It had inflicted a frightful toll on Israel in the 1973 Yom Kippur War. Yet Sadat was offering something all Israelis craved. Peace. Not just between Israel and Egypt, but potentially between Israel and much of the Arab world. All Israel had to do was end its occupation of the West Bank, Gaza, and Golan. However, Menachem Begin, the loyal apostle of Jabotinsky, stalled. While he would eventually bribe the Egyptians by giving them the Sinai for a separate peace at Camp David in September 1978, his offer of administrative autonomy for the Palestinians amounted to little more than the freedom to collect their own garbage. The land and the water in the occupied territories would remain under Israeli control; the building of Jewish settlements would continue unabated.

On March 7, 1978, already fearing the worst from Begin, 375 Israeli reserve officers, all Yom Kippur War veterans, wrote to the prime minister, urging him to take the initiative in the quest for peace. "A government that prefers the land of Israel above peace . . . would cause us grave difficulties [of conscience]" and "would raise questions for us about the justice of our course," they wrote. Omri Padan, a paratroop officer in the Israeli Army reserves and one of the authors of the letter, said in an interview some years later that "I felt peace was possible [after Sadat came to Israel] for the first time in seventy years, and Begin was going to blow it. So I got thirty or forty signatures from friends in my army unit, and others did the same."

"The letter became the movement," said Dede Zucker, now a left-wing Knesset member. "After the letter appeared in newspapers, we got more than two hundred thousand calls and letters from around the country. People suddenly found something that expressed their interests. We expected to influence people, but we didn't expect the letter to be so powerful. Three weeks after the letter, forty thousand people demonstrated in the streets in Tel Aviv. It wasn't planned; it was spontaneous. Suddenly, we found ourselves the leaders of a mass movement."

Peace Now's ideology was simple: peace based on territorial compromise that would include stringent security guarantees. Its strategy was equally straightforward: massive protest demonstrations led by popular entertainers and intellectuals, similar to the marches held by the American peace movement during the Vietnam War. Labor party officials, eager to return to the nation's helm, jumped on Peace Now's bandwagon. Cabinet minister Yigal Allon, who had expressed regret for sponsoring Rabbi Levinger's efforts to settle Hebron, and former prime minister Yitzhak Rabin offered their vocal support. "My colleagues and I support them," Abba Eban said on American public television in 1978, "because we would like to include territorial concessions on the West Bank and Gaza . . . and [because] it would present the concept of Israel as a Jewish democratic state endeavoring not to impose its jurisdiction on one million Arabs who do not want that jurisdiction."

Peace Now's early success was sudden, intense, and brief. The movement had a name, an idea, and a following, but it didn't have an organization. Without a bureaucracy to sustain it, Peace Now became dormant shortly after the signing of the Camp David Accords. Slowly, however, in a typically Israeli helter-skelter fashion, the officers forged the infrastructure for a mass organization.

One of Peace Now's most notable early activities focused on Elon Moreh*, a Gush Emunim settlement established on a hilltop south of the West Bank town of Nablus—a center of intense Palestinian nationalism. Peace Now assembled three thousand demonstrators at the site in June 1979, a week after the settlement was founded. Former chief of staff Chaim Bar-Lev, still a potent force in the Israeli Army, attended the rally. One week later, forty thousand people gathered at a Peace Now rally in Tel Aviv to protest Begin's expansionist settlement policy. "We are not protesting one Elon Moreh, but the whole policy of occupation, eviction and coercion," said a speaker.

Elon Moreh was built on an eight-hundred-*dunam* parcel of land that had been expropriated from the village of Rujeb by the Israeli military for "reasons of national security." Encouraged by the debate over Israel's settlement policy initiated by Peace Now, seventeen Palestinian landowners filed suit in an Israeli court, claiming that Elon Moreh had been built on

*The original Elon Moreh settlement, which the newly elected Begin visited in 1977, had been renamed Kedumin.

illegally seized Arab land. An earlier ruling by Israel's high court had established that the expropriation of Arab land could be justified on grounds of national security.

The Elon Moreh case set the stage for a landmark battle over Israel's settlement enterprise. Chief of Staff Rafael Eitan and Agriculture Minister Ariel Sharon submitted statements to the court asserting that Elon Moreh enhanced Israel's security and that the settlers could "assist the IDF in its various tasks" in time of war. But Chaim Bar-Lev, then general secretary of the Labor party, and Matti Peled, a reserve army general and a dovish Knesset member, gave affadavits arguing that during a war the IDF would be tied up protecting settlements like Elon Moreh instead of fighting the enemy army. "The Jewish settlements in the [Arab-] populated areas of Judea and Samaria have nothing whatever to contribute to ongoing security," wrote Bar-Lev. "On the contrary, they interfere with security . . . I absolutely reject the notion that there is any security value in the fact that a few dozen Jewish families live in some settlement outpost in a broad area entirely populated by Arab villagers. They are a target for attack. Any attempt to attribute motives of security to these settlers is misleading and distorted. These settlements are detrimental to security." In defiance of Begin's policy, then–Defense Minister Ezer Weizman attached a letter to Eitan's affidavit asserting that the establishment of Elon Moreh had no security rationale.

Predictably, settlers from Gush Emunim also submitted affidavits, insisting that Israel's messianic destiny transcended security imperatives. The court was not impressed with either Gush Emunim or its hawkish generals. On October 22, 1979, the high court ruled that Elon Moreh must be dismantled, agreeing with Bar-Lev that it was a security liability. "Had it not been for the pressure of Gush Emunim," wrote the court, Elon Moreh would never have been built.

The court's precedent-setting decision threatened to undermine the entire campaign of Jewish colonization in the occupied territories. Peace Now's victory proved to be a hollow one, however. While Gush Emunim, in its typically hysterical fashion, denounced the high court as "a tool in the hands of terrorists," Sharon and Eitan sought to find a way around the ruling. In April 1980, just six months after the Elon Moreh court case, the Israeli Cabinet announced that henceforth any land that had previously belonged to Jordan, or that was unregistered or uncultivated, could be expropriated for the settlers. Security arguments no longer needed to be made to expropriate Arab land. The decade of the great West Bank land grab had begun.

Peace Now continued to protest the Likud's settlement policy at a series of demonstrations and public forums. The movement's high point came in 1982, when it organized a demonstration of some four hundred thousand people in Tel Aviv to protest the massacre of more than one thousand Palestinian civilians at Sabra and Shatila refugee camps in Lebanon. Several months later, an anti–Lebanon War rally organized by Peace Now in front of the Prime Minister's Office in Jerusalem was violently attacked by right-wing thugs wearing knitted yarmulkes and chanting, "Begin, Begin, King of Israel." Women demonstrators were spit upon and told, "You are Arab women! You should have been in Sabra and Shatila." Then a grenade was thrown into the crowd, which included many officers from elite combat units. Emil Grunzweig, a young high school math teacher from Kibbutz Revivim in the Negev, was killed in the blast.* Later, at the hospital, the injured demonstrators were attacked and beaten, as were the doctors, by Jewish extremists screaming, "It's a shame that only one was killed!" Not since the clashes between Begin's Irgun and Ben-Gurion's Haganah in the 1940s had the danger of serious clashes between Jews in Israel seemed so great.

In the months following Grunzweig's murder, prominent liberal Israeli academics, artists, and journalists became targets of right-wing violence. Homes and cars were vandalized and firebombed. In one instance, the apartment of a political pollster who reported that a majority of Israelis were ready to trade land for peace was torched. Peace Now founder Dede Zucker was pummeled outside his Jerusalem home by right-wing toughs. Zucker moved to Tel Aviv. The climate of intimidation and fear was encouraged by government officials like Sharon, who publicly labeled members of Peace Now "defeatists" and "traitors." Kahane did the bellicose ex-general one better by calling on his followers to liquidate liberal Jews whose views he found pernicious.

In April 1986, Peace Now devised a plan that was sure to drive the settlers crazy. It decided to hold a conference with moderate West Bank Arab leaders in Hebron—the first such public meeting between the Israeli peace movement and its Palestinian counterparts. What was worse, from the settlers' perspective, was that the conference would be held in the Park

---

*Israeli police subsequently arrested a right-wing hooligan, who was convicted of Grunzweig's murder.

Hotel, the site of Levinger's historic first Seder, which had taken on a holy significance to the settlement movement.

"The settlers were in a panic," recalled Peace Now leader Janet Aviad, a sociologist at the Hebrew University. "If you want to see the settlers lose their cool and go out of their minds, just have a meeting with the Palestinians on the West Bank. We received threats from them not to go. 'Choose sides,' they said. 'Are you with us or against us?' 'Are you Israeli or not?' "

On the way to the Park Hotel, Peace Now's motor caravan was ambushed by settlers hurling rocks. In Hebron, Yossi Sarid and Hanna Siniora, the mild-mannered editor of the East Jerusalem Arabic-language daily newspaper *Al-Fajr,* were punched in the face and spit at, and then a burly settler threw Siniora into a ditch. The conference, which Aviad chaired, received massive news coverage. The Israeli delegation included members of the Labor party, Ratz, and Mapam. The Palestinian side was represented by Siniora, prominent journalist Ziad Abu Ziad, and Mustafa Natshe, the deposed mayor of Hebron.

The biggest achievement of the meeting was that it took place at all. During the conference, an explosive charge had been placed under the back wheel of one of Peace Now's chartered buses, blowing it off its back axle; as the peace caravan left town under heavy military guard, shots were fired by militant settlers.

Hoping to prevent bloodshed, Ofra resident Yisrael Harel proposed a meeting between Gush Emunim leaders and Peace Now. Peace Now's leadership debated whether to accept the offer. Some felt that to do so would be to grant Gush Emunim legitimacy. Finally, however, it was decided that a meeting would be held in Janet Aviad's West Jerusalem apartment.

It was a historic gathering: Peace Now, the representatives of the liberal, enlightened, secular vision of Zionism, and Gush Emunim, a messianic strain of religious-nationalist Judaism that was nearly extinguished some two thousand years ago only to reemerge after the Six-Day War with a force and fury that seemed to make it unstoppable.

"You crossed our red line by going to the Park Hotel," Harel began. "By meeting with Palestinian leaders in Hebron, you are condoning the killing of settlers by Arab terrorists. We are fighting them, and you are meeting them in the Park Hotel. That discredits us, and in the Palestinian language that is a license to kill. So we'd like you not to cross it again."

But Peace Now had its own red line. "The moment you crossed the

Green Line [Israeli's 1967 border with Jordan], you crossed *our* red line,"
Tzali Reshef declared. "The settlements are endangering Israel's future in
the long run. This is not a gentlemen's debate about ideology. You are
risking my life and my children's lives and perhaps their children's lives by
forcing us to defend the settlements."

Then it was Rabbi Levinger's turn to speak. It was clear from the
deference the other settlers showed him that he was their revered leader.
He began by explaining the religious meaning of Gush Emunim. Next, he
talked about Israelis who lacked religious values. He called them "empty."
"He said that all we [secular Jews] wanted was to go to the beach and have
sex, and that we didn't respect his red line," recalled Yitzhak Galnoor, a
professor of political science at Hebrew University and a member of the
Peace Now delegation.

"As soon as you start this talk about secular Jews being empty, it's
bullshit," Galnoor told Levinger. "I don't have an inferiority complex
vis-à-vis religious Jews. I feel more Jewish than you. I convey the humanistic traditions of Judaism, and you the unpleasant stream of self-destructive
messianism. Your claim is totally lost on us. You are not talking to people
who feel they owe religious Jews anything, particularly to you and to your
twisted view of Judaism."

Gush Emunim leaders asked numerous questions about the politics and
lifestyles of Peace Now's leaders. "We knew more about them than they
knew about us," said Galnoor. "Their world is confined. They are not
intellectuals, but we do read Rav Kook."

Although the talks went badly, Gush Emunim wanted to have further
meetings. Peace Now, however, decided that it had nothing to gain from
them. The split between the two camps only deepened when the *intifada*
began. For the settlers, the *intifada* was an existential threat. For Peace
Now, it gave new meaning to the Green Line, which the settlement
movement was trying so hard to erase: If the Palestinians, in their uprising,
could show the average Israeli that there would be a terrible cost to holding
on to the territories, it would increase dissatisfaction with Likud and
generate a demand to retreat behind the '67 borders.

That was Peace Now's prediction. In reality, the Israeli public quickly
became inured to the uprising, with its tales of extreme cruelty inflicted by
the Israeli Army on the captive population. "This is the worst year ever,"
complained Janet Aviad as we shared a taxi from Tel Aviv to Jerusalem one
day in 1988. "It is worse now than 1982 when we were in Lebanon. The

beatings, the stories of Israeli soldiers burying Palestinians alive. Israelis are growing thick skins. Nobody sees anything. Nobody wants to know what's going on in the territories. Israeli reporters who cover the West Bank are despised. We are becoming good Germans. In Tel Aviv, in the cafés, the *intifada* is derisively called 'the big enchilada.' "

The Palestinian leadership on the West Bank and in Tunis was also alarmed by Israeli apathy. The *intifada* was waged not only to drive the Israelis out of the occupied territories by making their rule untenable, "but to shake the Palestinians out of their passivity and instill the belief that they need not wait for salvation from afar," wrote Danny Rubinstein, *Ha'aretz*'s respected commentator on Arab affairs. But except for the settlers who bore the brunt of the firebombs and stones of the *intifada*, most Israelis reacted to the uprising as if it were taking place far away rather than on roads and in villages a few kilometers from Israel's pre-1967 border. Ironically, if the Palestinians were to achieve recognition for their struggle, they needed to convince the Israelis that they were prepared to be good neighbors once they had their own homeland.

On July 27, 1988, Peace Now held an extraordinary joint Israeli-Palestinian dialogue in Jerusalem, calling on the Israeli government to recognize the PLO as the legitimate representative of the Palestinian people and to accept a two-state solution. Among the Palestinian participants was Faisal Husseini, who spoke publicly to an Israeli audience for the first time. The inclusion of Husseini was particularly significant. His family, said to be descended from the prophet Muhammad, has been at the forefront of the Arab struggle against Zionism since the British ruled Palestine. Haj Amin al-Husseini, the former grand mufti of Jerusalem and the fiery leader of the Palestinian national movement, was dismissed by the British for seditious activity, and fled the country in 1937 for Berlin, where he served the Nazis during the Second World War. Faisal Husseini's father, Abd al Kader al-Husseini, the commander of armed Palestinian opposition to Jewish self-rule, was killed in 1948 in a fierce battle near Jerusalem. Faisal Husseini himself had obtained a high rank in the defunct Palestine Liberation Army (the military arm of the pre-Arafat PLO made up of brigades attached to other Arab armies.)

Faisal Husseini inherited his father's steely determination to fight Zionism, earning him the respect of the Shabiba, as well as of the kaleidoscope of PLO factions. Unlike many Palestinian leaders, he has never been accused of corruption; he began his career humbly as a tractor driver in

Jericho and a door-to-door salesman and is considered direct and hard-working. His ability to communicate with both simple workers and PLO radicals has given him a stature unique in the occupied territories. Yet his anti-Zionist militancy is tempered by a genuine understanding of Jewish history, together with an apparently sincere desire to lead his people into a political settlement with Israel.

Given Husseini's stature, his call for peace with Israel resonated through-out Israel and the territories. "It is only natural that in order to attain this aim [peace], there must be mutual recognition on both sides," Husseini said at the peace forum. "On the Palestinian side, [recognition] of the state of Israel, and on the Israeli side, [recognition] not only of the Palestinian right to self-determination, but of their right to establish their state on their national soil."

Three days after the forum, Husseini was arrested by Israeli police and imprisoned for six months. He was never charged with a crime. Husseini believes, as do many Israelis, that he was being punished by the Likud for his peace initiative.

Not long after the forum, Aviad received an angry phone call from Yisrael Harel. "You crossed the line," the Gush Emunim leader heatedly said. "You met with Faisal Husseini!"

Later, Aviad received a call from Yoel Ben-Nun, the moderate Gush Emunim rabbi from Ofra who had denounced the Makhteret and had unsuccessfully challenged Levinger for leadership of the religious settler movement. Aviad and Ben-Nun had held private talks for several years and had grown to respect, if not like, each other. He told Aviad that he had heard some rough talk coming from radical settlers and warned her that if Peace Now members continued to hold discussions with Palestinians, they would be risking their lives. "We are in a war," he said to Aviad, reminding her that the Palestinian uprising had taken Jewish lives. "If you choose the enemy's side, you will meet our side with guns."

The size of Peace Now's rallies, as well as its effectiveness, diminished during the *intifada*. One reason for its inability to mobilize the nation against the occupation was its failure to build an alliance with Sephardic Jews, who make up 60 percent of Israel's Jewish population and had kept Likud in power. Peace Now is led by Ashkenazi intellectuals who have had little contact with Sephardic Jews in their daily lives. They are more at ease talking to Palestinian intellectuals like the Oxford-educated Sari Nusseibeh, or Faisal Husseini, men who share the vernacular of the Westernized intellectual. Not insignificantly, Nusseibeh, Husseini, and Hanna Siniora, to name three, have European features, with light-colored skin and hair. At a time when it was crusading against the racist rantings of Kahane, who was riding high in the polls during the *intifada*, Peace Now was perceived by many to be too haughty to sit down with Sephardic leaders who had none of the drawing-room charm or "refined" features of their Palestinian interlocutors.

More than that, Peace Now leaders preferred speechifying to research. The settlements had cost the Israeli taxpayer billions of dollars, money that in many cases was taken out of budgets intended for predominately Sephardic "development towns" and slums within Israel. But Peace Now did virtually nothing to explain to working-class Israelis, whatever their background, that they were subsidizing the relatively lavish lifestyles enjoyed by many settlers. For instance, in many new settlements there is one teacher for every five or six children, while in Jerusalem there is one for forty. And funds for Israeli roads, which are notoriously bad and contribute to one of the highest accident rates in the world, have gone to build sleek blacktops on the West Bank, where settlers motor along protected by army patrols. "The Israeli left has never quantified the cost of settlement or made it an effective strategic issue," a U.S. official in Jerusalem told me in December 1990.

Peace Now's constant emphasis on the violations of Palestinian human rights, while virtually ignoring the economic distress of much of the Israeli population, further undercut its credibility with Sephardic Jews, Dede Ben-Shatrit, a liberal member of Jerusalem's city council, a former national soccer star, and one of the few prominent Peace Now personalities of North African heritage, told me. I met Ben-Shatrit in a neighborhood named Garden City, a vast Sephardic slum in West Jerusalem that in December 1990, when I visited, was a damp, dreary concrete canyon of drugs and alcohol. "When I joined Peace Now, the boys in the neighborhood asked me why I was trying to act Ashkenazi," said Ben-Shatrit, whose dark brown face is capped by a thick gray mound of curly hair. "They hate Ashkenazim for a whole host of reasons. So from the early 1980s, I've been saying in Peace Now meetings that we have to go into the [Sephardic] neighborhoods and explain how the settlements hurt their economic interests. Without them [the Sephardim], I said, we will remain a small group. We have to have two banners—peace and social equality."

At Ben-Shatrit's urging, Peace Now printed thousands of bumper stickers that said MONEY FOR THE NEIGHBORHOODS, NOT THE SETTLEMENTS. Ben-Shatrit also sent Ashkenazi speakers into Sephardic neighborhoods. "But it was too little, too late," he said. "When the Jews from the Soviet Union started coming, Peace Now stopped talking about Oriental Jews and how to get them on our side and started grass-roots work among the Russians—the Great Ashkenazi White Hope. I'm afraid our children will be the black* workers of Russian bosses."

Peace Now leaders claimed they hadn't abandoned their efforts to forge a common bond with Sephardim. "We know that the alliance now is with the homeless and the poor," Aviad told me. Still, Peace Now seemed fearful that if it became more than a one-issue group, it would lose support among the Ashkenazi bourgeoisie. "We say without peace, nothing can happen," said Galnoor.

And then Saddam Hussein invaded Kuwait and threatened to "burn half of Israel." Not surprisingly, Peace Now reeled after Palestinians in the territories passionately embraced the Iraqi dictator. Many Israeli doves reacted like spurned lovers. In a fit of political pique, prominent peace activist and Citizens Rights Movement party Knesset member Yossi Sarid told Palestinians that he was not going to talk to them anymore, so they should "forget my number."

"If one can support Saddam Hussein . . . maybe it's not so bad to support the policies of Shamir [and] Sharon . . . In comparison with the misdeeds of Saddam Hussein, the sins of the state of Israel are as white as snow," he wrote in a now-notorious article for *Ha'aretz*. "Now they are up on the roofs," wrote Sarid, "and like lunatics they yell *'Allah akbar'* [God is great] and applaud the terrorist missiles raining down on our heads. . . . After the war, when 'Allah' is less *'akbar,'* don't call me. . . . In the shelter, I don't have a phone . . . and in my gas mask, my breath comes with difficulty and my words are muffled."

After twenty-two years of living under a humiliating occupation, Palestinian behavior may not have been nice, but it was, perhaps, understandable. Arafat embraced Saddam Hussein, in part, because diplomacy had won him nothing—even though he had recognized Israel, renounced terrorism, and accepted the principle of partition. Meanwhile, Palestinians in the territories were clamoring for an end to Israel's military occupation, something the uprising had been unable to accomplish. Saddam held

*In Israel, menial work is called "black" work.

himself out as their savior. Arafat, according to Israeli intelligence sources, felt he had no other choice but to side with the Iraqi strongman.

While Peace Now remained committed to a two-state solution after the war, selling rapprochement with the Palestinians proved even more difficult than before. "Palestinians' support for Saddam Hussein has already made any future negotiating process more difficult," Jonathan Jacoby, the Manhattan-based director of Americans for Peace Now, told me soon after the Gulf War. "It has become harder for Israelis to believe that the Palestinian people are ready to live in peace alongside a secure Israel, and it is important for all of us to consider the implications of the Palestinian response for our work."

By the end of the war, Peace Now was facing irrelevancy. Its peace vigils with Faisal Husseini, who, like most other West Bank Palestinian intellectuals, gave his qualified support to Saddam Hussein, were ineffectual; its polemics were drowned out by the roar of Sharon's bulldozers in the occupied territories. After much debate, the movement reorganized. It set up "Settlement Watch" to monitor settlement activity, compute its cost, which is hidden from Israelis, and distribute its findings to the news media and the U.S. State Department. In late 1991, Peace Now filed a landmark suit with Israel's high court, arguing that settlements are illegal according to international law.

Meanwhile, in the United States, Peace Now increased its budget and membership base and hired professional lobbyists, including David Cohen, the former head of Common Cause.* Under Cohen, Peace Now's Washington office became an important voice on the Israeli-Palestinian problem. Recognizing that the only way President Bush would be able to push Shamir toward political compromise was if there was a significant and vocal Jewish opposition in the United States to Likud's settlement drive, Peace Now publicly endorsed the U.S. policy of linking housing loan guarantees for Soviet Jews to a settlement freeze in February 1992. Without this support, Peace Now reasoned, AIPAC, working through Congress, would continue to paralyze the peace process. As it turned out, this strategy had lethal consequences for the Likud and its vainglorious dream of Greater Israel.

---

*In 1991, Americans for Peace Now, which had a reported budget of more than $1.5 million, increased its membership by eleven hundred to ten thousand.

CHAPTER 10

Debate and Dissent

"It is a very strange experience to read the newspapers from Israel, even those of right-wing orientation, alongside the pro-Israel publications in the United States," Rabbi Arthur Hertzberg, America's preeminent liberal Jewish intellectual and the former president of the American Jewish Congress, has noted. "What everyone in Israel knows as a matter of course is often denounced as false and subversive when quoted in America. . . . Israel is loved and defended in the United States, but the passion often has about it something of the quality of John Donne's outcry to the lady of his dreams: 'For God's sake hold your tongue, and let me love!' "

Enforcing this code of silence during fifteen grim years of Likud party rule was the American Jewish establishment's powerful neoconservative trinity—AIPAC, the ADL, and the Presidents' Conference. The trinity didn't recognize the legitimacy of a "loyal Zionist opposition." As far as it was concerned, all criticism of Israel, whether espoused by anti-Zionist black militants like Leonard Jeffries, American nativists like Pat Buchanan, or left-wing Labor Zionists like Abba Eban, was a threat to Israel, and so had to be discredited. More than believing in a strong Israel, the trinity closely identified with Shamir's colonial vision. Beyond that, it helped to secure financial and political support for Israel, and to demonize the Palestinians and the PLO in order to ensure Israel's control over the occupied territories.

No group or individual that criticized Likud's hard-line policies was spared. AIPAC, which, as we shall see, has a secret unit to gather material on Israel's critics, even maintains files on Woody Allen and Richard Drey-fuss. Allen came under AIPAC's scrutiny after he wrote a *New York Times* op-ed piece condemning the brutal methods Israel used to crush the *intifada*. Dreyfuss's sin was his support for Peace Now. "Believers in Israel who thought the Shamir policy was a betrayal of Zionism and said so found ourselves denounced in vicious terms, as anti-Semites and so on," wrote *New York Times* columnist Anthony Lewis, who was frequently scape-goated by the trinity.*

Peace Now proved to be an especially difficult adversary because it is a Zionist organization with roots in the Labor party. So when Peace Now refused to tone down its activities in America, the "trinity" attempted to dilute its effectiveness by portraying it as a fringe group led by irresponsible leftists. In March 1989, Malcolm Hoenlein, the executive director of the Conference of Presidents of Major American Jewish Organizations, sum-moned representatives of Peace Now to his Manhattan office for a dressing down. Hoenlein was steaming about a widely publicized Peace Now con-ference held at Columbia University, whose speakers included prominent PLO officials and dovish Israeli Knesset members. Hoenlein, a gifted bureaucrat who is close to Likud in policy and temperament, warned Peace Now that its activities were jeopardizing Israel's existence. "Hoenlein was furious with us," said a Peace Now official who attended the meeting. "He told us that we were aiding Israel's enemies and that we would have blood on our hands."

The American peaceniks responded that poll data consistently showed that American Jews were much more dovish and amenable to political compromise than the Likud, and that, besides, open debate is healthy in a democracy. "If your fear is that President Bush will cut back on aid to Israel because of divisions in the Jewish community, let's agree on a consensus position that says Israel's security and continued U.S. aid are bedrock issues that all Jews, left to right, support," a Peace Now official told Hoenlein. "But you have to acknowledge that we are pro-Israel too. We want a broader definition of what pro-Israel means. He wouldn't touch us with a ten-foot pole."

Such attempts to cast American-Jewish doves outside the pale created the climate for more menacing attacks on Jewish liberals. In a speech to the

---

*AIPAC also maintains files on Ed Asner, Vanessa Redgrave, Casey Kasem, Mike Farrell, Peter Yarrow, Peter Jennings, Mike Wallace, and many others, including this author.

Zionist Organization of America's "Gala Tribute Dinner" at the Sands Hotel in Atlantic City on December 3, 1989, Dr. Mordecai Hacohen, then senior vice president of Bank Leumi in New York, called American Jews who advocated territorial compromise "assimilated court Jews, Vichy Jews, *galut* Jews, Kapos, quislings—in short, traitors. They could have served as members of the notorious *Judenrat.* They have to be stamped out from our midst. . . . I appeal to all patriotic Jewish men and women in the United States to stamp their feet on these mischief makers and sowers of disunity wherever they may be found!"

Hacohen, who left prewar Vienna in 1932, fought with the Irgun, and lost many family members in the Holocaust, told me several months after the dinner, "All what I said was an understatement. . . . I can't condemn them strongly enough." As for Rita Hauser and other prominent American Jews who had called on Israel to negotiate with the PLO, he said, they "should be shot at dawn." That same year, a number of critics of Israel's settlement policy, including Rabbi Hertzberg, received death threats from Jewish extremists, and the staff at the Peace Now office in Manhattan was forced to open its mail behind a specially designed bomb-proof screen.

While they would be quick to decry open intimidation and violence, Jewish establishment leaders have long tried to silence their critics with accusations of anti-Israel bias and anti-Semitism. In 1954 AIPAC's forerunner, the American Zionist Council of Public Affairs, was created to counteract anti-Israel sentiment in the Eisenhower administration, and endowed with an annual budget of fifty thousand dollars. From this point on, according to Edward Tivnan in his book *The Lobby,* "No matter how much American Jewish leaders recognized they ought to be more than sworn defenders of all Israeli actions that was what they were on the way to becoming." One of the organization's first tasks was to defend an Israeli reprisal raid on Kibya, a Jordanian village. Led by a young, brash Ariel Sharon, Israeli commandos had dynamited forty-one homes and one school; fifty-three Arab civilians had died. In the aftermath of Kibya, another powerful pro-Israeli group was established: the Conference of Presidents of Major American Jewish Organizations. During this period, the lobby had to explain away a number of Israeli military and political excesses, including the 1956 Suez War, when Israel joined France and Britain in a lightning invasion of Nasser's Egypt following the nationalization of the Suez Canal. Eisenhower forced Israel to withdraw from the

Sinai, threatening to cut off U.S. foreign aid. It was the last time a U.S. president was able to impose his will on Israel.

By 1974, representatives of AIPAC, the ADL, and the American Jewish Committee had created "truth squads" to counter the supposed growth of pro-Arab propaganda, which they felt threatened Israel's lucrative, long-standing "special relationship" with the United States. While vigorously defending Israel's perceived interests, the organizations that created the truth squads turned into a kind of Jewish thought police. Investigators—sometimes overzealous Jewish college students, sometimes sources with access to U.S. intelligence agencies—were used to ferret out critics of Israel, Jew or Gentile, wherever they might be. At ADL and AIPAC, files were opened on hundreds of journalists, politicians, scholars, and community activists. Their speeches and writings were monitored, as were, in some cases, their other professional activities. And they were often smeared with charges of anti-Semitism or with the pernicious label of self-hating Jew. The intention was to stifle legitimate debate on the Middle East within the Jewish community, the media, and academia, for fear that criticism would weaken the Jewish state.

Both the ADL and AIPAC have scoured American college campuses, research foundations, and think tanks for enemies of Israel. In 1983 the ADL sent Jewish academics a 118-page confidential handbook titled *Pro-Arab Propaganda in America: Vehicles and Voices,* listing thirty-four individuals, some of them Jewish professors, who had been critical of certain Israeli government policies. A cover letter from Leonard Zakim, the ADL's New England regional director, alleged that those named were "pro-Arab propagandists" who "used their anti-Zionism merely as a guise for their deeply felt anti-Semitism." Among those on the ADL's blacklist were Dr. Laurence Michalak, coordinator of the Center for Middle Eastern Studies at the University of California, Berkeley, and Professor Israel Shahak, a lecturer in organic chemistry at Hebrew University in Jerusalem and a survivor of the Warsaw Ghetto Uprising. At about the same time, AIPAC circulated another list, even more strident in its accusations, to Jewish leaders around the country. The striking similarity between the language and information in the two groups' handbooks suggested the existence of a central file on opponents of Israel's right-wing policies.

In a two-part column that appeared in *The New York Times* in the winter of 1983–84, Anthony Lewis attacked the ADL and AIPAC's lists, and particularly the inclusion of his friend Harvard professor Walid Khalidi. Noting that Khalidi, a Palestinian, had long argued for a two-state solution based on mutual recognition between Israel and the PLO, Lewis concluded, "Some people see his very moderation as dangerous. He is a Palestinian nationalist after all and one must not allow that idea to have any legitimacy." In response, the ADL reportedly assigned a team of researchers to look through Lewis's columns for evidence of anti-Israel bias.

Meanwhile, AIPAC set up a top-secret research unit, innocuously called Policy Analysis,* to gather information about its political opponents and to distribute unflattering reports about them, often taking statements out of context in order to paint a false portrait of the accused, according to a former AIPAC researcher. In an internal AIPAC memorandum sent to Steve Rosen, AIPAC's foreign-policy issues director, dated August 7, 1990, Michael Lewis† outlined the mandate of Policy Analysis, which he heads: "There is no question that we exert a policy impact, but working behind the scenes and taking care not to leave fingerprints, that impact is not always traceable to us."

One time, however, AIPAC left its prints all over the crime scene. And Mike Wallace was there to report it. In a *60 Minutes* segment, Wallace revealed a November 3, 1987, internal AIPAC memorandum, entitled "News Suggestions for Reporters," that called for helping the media expose then–Democratic presidential candidate Jesse Jackson's purported extramarital affairs and financial irregularities at Operation PUSH in Chicago. Jackson is reviled by the Jewish lobby for his alleged anti-Semitism and hostility to Israel. In the same report, Wallace came up with a second memo, claiming that employees of AIPAC secretly coordinated campaign contributions of pro-Israel PACs in the United States, in apparent violation of U.S. law. AIPAC adamantly denied the charges and was exonerated in a federal investigation. "I think it's disingenuous for AIPAC to say, as for some peculiar reason they frequently do, that they don't direct any money," Rhode Island Republican senator John Chafee later told *The Washington Post*. Chafee, a sometime critic of Israel, was himself targeted

---

*According to Gregory D. Slabodkin, an "opposition researcher" for AIPAC in 1990 and 1991, as part of its intelligence-gathering operation, Policy Analysis created a fictional person and a bogus company to infiltrate opposing organizations by paying membership dues or by making donations to them. "This AIPAC creation is 'Paul Hunt' of 'Paul Hunt & Associates,'" said Slabodkin. "AIPAC rents a post office box on Capitol Hill for Mr. Hunt's mail, and has installed a separate Paul Hunt telephone line in the AIPAC office." Slabodkin's revelations appeared in an August 4, 1992, *Village Voice* article.
†Michael Lewis is the son of esteemed Middle East scholar Bernard Lewis.

by AIPAC in 1988, when his opponent, Richard Licht, received $213,850 in pro-Israel PAC money, according to the *Post.*

One month after the *60 Minutes* story about AIPAC aired, the organization sent a letter to its members charging that the segment "was yet another aspect of an ongoing effort to separate the United States and Israel. It was much more than an attack on AIPAC. It was an attack on the fundamental U.S.-Israel alliance." Asserting that the *60 Minutes* segment should be viewed in the context of "a distinct rise in anti-Semitism at home," the letter, written by AIPAC executive director Tom Dine, urged its members to write their congressmen and newspapers to denounce the CBS program.

"Letters like that," *60 Minutes* chief Don Hewitt wrote Dine, "are no doubt effective in getting money out of your constituents, but hollering 'anti-Semitism' at anybody who has an honest disagreement with you trivializes, demeans and makes a mockery of 'anti-Semitism.' " Hewitt, who is Jewish, told the *Washington Jewish Week* that soon after the program he received numerous letters accusing him of anti-Semitism and self-hate. Many of them used identical language and concluded with a quote from Jewish leader Morris Abram that "anti-Semitism sleeps very lightly in this country."

Another Jewish journalist who drew AIPAC's fire was Larry Cohler, a highly regarded reporter for the *Washington Jewish Week,* who has written several stories critical of the organization. While Cohler was working on an article following up the *60 Minutes* report on AIPAC, his editor received a phone call from Toby Dershowitz, AIPAC's media liaison, who suggested that Cohler be taken off the story. When the editor refused, Dershowitz put AIPAC's legal counsel David Ifshin on the line. According to *The Washington Post,* the attorney warned him that AIPAC would reexamine Cohler's previous stories about the organization, looking for evidence of libel. Nothing ever came of the threat against Cohler, but an AIPAC smear led to the removal of the paper's editor, Andrew Carroll, in June 1992. Ifshin went on to become legal counsel to Democratic presidential candidate Bill Clinton.

After chilling its critics, the lobby's most important mission is delegitimizing the PLO, a task it has undertaken with the fervor of a medieval crusade. No one has worked harder to show that Arafat has remained unchanged in his determination to eliminate the "Zionist entity" than the

ADL's national director Abe Foxman, the former Betarnik and supporter of Jabotinsky, whose framed portrait hangs prominently in his office. In March 1988, Foxman published a letter in the *Times*, charging that those who believed Arafat was ready to make peace with Israel were dupes, making much of the fact that the PLO had never rescinded its National Covenant, which calls for Israel's destruction.

Anthony Lewis, who had just interviewed Arafat for the *Times*, responded in a private note to Foxman, arguing that "there have been numerous signs that the PLO is prepared to negotiate with Israel for a state in the West Bank and Gaza. What Arafat said to me a couple weeks ago was only the latest. Yes, the Covenant remains. It should be noted. But so should Palestinian adjustments to reality. . . . It is necessary to be wary. But surely it is foolish to ignore significant political changes in one's opponent, and even more foolish to take a negative view of everything done by Palestinians of any kind."

On June 17, 1988, after having waited for more than three months for a reply, Lewis sent Foxman another message. "I know you are busy," Lewis wrote, "but I really would like to have your views on the point I tried to make. There *are* Palestinians who earnestly want to negotiate with Israel and who accept a two-state solution. I continue to believe that it would make a great difference if people like you would encourage them instead of reacting to every Palestinian with skepticism or worse."

Four days later, Foxman responded, espousing the Likud party line. "Given the hostility of its neighbors and its narrow margin of security," he wrote Lewis, "Israel does not have the luxury of granting the PLO the benefit of the doubt, as it seems you would have it do. It is fine for Arafat to state in one breath that he would like to negotiate with Israel. But when he states in the next that the banner of Palestine will fly over Jerusalem (Voice of the PLO, December 10, 1987), one is forced to question where his true intentions lie."

On June 27, 1988, an apparently exasperated Lewis wrote Foxman one last time: "You want the Covenant renounced before negotiations. You want Arafat to speak politically to an Israeli constituency exclusively, not to worry about Palestinians who are angry and who may naturally want to hear all-out rhetoric. You want Israel to determine who is 'serious' enough to sit on the other side of the table. That way there can never be negotiations. . . . Unless they [Palestinian moderates] get some response from you and others—something instead of skepticism and rejection—they will get no-where."

Of course, that was the point. Shamir was determined that the PLO never be rewarded for its new moderation. Indeed, within hours after Secretary of State George Shultz announced he was reversing a thirteen-year-old ban on talking to the PLO as its reward for renouncing terrorism and recognizing Israel's right to exist in Geneva in December 1988, stunned Israeli Foreign Ministry officials huddled to plan a counterattack. According to well-placed sources in Israel, the strategy was simple: Paint the PLO as heinous terrorists who would stop at nothing until they occupied the cafés and beaches of Haifa and Tel Aviv. To be sure, there was no lack of PLO atrocities to point to: the brutal killing of wheelchair-bound cruise-ship passenger Leon Klinghoffer, the slaying of eleven Israeli athletes at the Munich Summer Olympics, the massacre of Israeli schoolchildren at Ma'alot. But since 1988, Palestinian terrorist attacks directed against Jew-ish civilians have come from PLO renegades and dissidents, such as Abu Nidal, whose goal was to discredit Arafat as much as it was to hurt Israel.

The Foreign Ministry's point man was Benjamin [Bibi] Netanyahu, the American-born superhawk who has built a career out of demonizing PLO members as Arab Nazis—a surefire way to arouse popular fury and acquire political power. As Israel's ambassador to the United Nations, he tirelessly promoted his theory that the PLO was being manipulated by the KGB in a sinister plot to destroy not only Israel but Western civilization as well. Soon he was a fixture on TV news shows like *Nightline,* where he appeared so often that it sometimes seemed as though his views were the only ones that counted in Israel.

Appearing on the program via satellite from Israel, Netanyahu said the United States was naive if it thought Arafat desired peace with Israel. The "terrorist organization" wants the West Bank as a base to launch its final solution. PLO officials may make noises in English to Western audiences about recognizing Israel, he said, but speaking to their own constituency in Arabic, they are saying something altogether different: that moderation is a ruse designed to liberate the Palestinian homeland. Behind his bald assertions, Netanyahu intimated, was Israel's vaunted national-security ap-paratus, which has eyes and ears in every corner of the Arab world.

Meanwhile, the Foreign Ministry issued position papers outlining the PLO's "nefarious" intentions, which became the basis for assertions of

Foxman and others in Israel's Hasbara, or propaganda network. Netanyahu came to New York in February 1989, pushing the PLO's Covenant—which calls for Israel's destruction—with a vengeance. Abu Nidal himself could not have done any better. Meeting privately with members of the Conference of Presidents of Major American Jewish Organizations, Netanyahu insisted that the PLO's dovish declarations in Geneva, Stockholm, and Algiers did not supersede its Covenant, according to participants. He backed up these allegations with data from Israel's Foreign Ministry. He made much of an interview PLO official Abu Iyad gave to *Al-Yom-Al-Sabi*, a Paris-based Arabic-language weekly magazine that has close ties to Arafat. Abu Iyad told the paper shortly before the PNC meeting in Algiers in November 1988 that the PLO was still committed to the "phase policy," which, according to Netanyahu, culminates in the destruction of Israel.

Abu Iyad, the number-two man in Fatah and the head of the PLO's internal security, was certainly a powerful figure before his assassination in Tunis in 1991. But his opposition to the PLO's officially declared acceptance of a two-state solution was no different from Shamir's and Moshe Arens's opposition to Begin on Camp David. What counts in judging the PLO's real intentions is not what Abu Iyad said to a newspaper, but what PNC resolutions say.

Netanyahu asked the Jewish leaders to press the new Bush administration to end talks with the PLO. He reminded them that Likud could have formed a government with the religious parties in 1985 rather than join a national-unity government with Labor. Likud did not do so, he said, because the religious parties demanded as a price for their support help in passing an amendment to the Law of Return that would have delegitimized conversions by non-Orthodox rabbis. "We could have had our own [right-wing] government," Netanyahu said. "We forged a coalition [with Labor] for you. We blocked 'Who's a Jew' for you. Now it's time for you to do something for us. We need you to support Shamir's peace plan," which was simply a vision of Greater Israel in which Palestinians played the role of hewers of wood and drawers of water.

Netanyahu was being disingenuous about the PLO. An accurate analysis of the PLO's intentions wasn't to be found in the boiler-room propaganda served up by the hacks in the Foreign Ministry, but rather in the classified intelligence estimates prepared by Israel's Military Intelligence, the largest of the Jewish state's four security agencies, which has overall responsibility for preparing Israel's annual national assessments. As Netanyahu well knew, since 1986, Military Intelligence had written a number of classified reports asserting that the PLO was ready to accept a two-state solution and that the Palestinians' quest for self-determination is irreversible and inseparably linked to the PLO.*

But Netanyahu wanted the PLO to be the way it was when it was formed—ontologically opposed to Israel's existence. That way, he undoubtedly reasoned, it would be easier to discredit. As he never tired of pointing out, the PLO was established in 1964 with the declared intention of liquidating Israel and establishing in its place an independent Palestinian state. "Zionism . . . is a racist and fanatical movement in its formation;

*One U.S. Middle East expert warns that journalists should be wary about reporting Israel's propaganda line as if it were objective truth. "There is a conscious effort being made by the Israelis to discredit the PLO," said William B. Quandt, a senior fellow at the Brookings Institution and a senior member of the National Security Council staff from 1972 to 1974 and from 1977 to 1979, when he participated in the negotiations that resulted in the Camp David Accords. Quandt noted that some of the facts in a background report about PLO terrorism sent to journalists by the Israeli embassy in Washington were of "questionable authenticity." "What commentators, journalists, pundits, academics, and American officials should be aware of is that there is a game being played," Quandt said. But isn't the PLO playing its own game by saying one thing to the West and something else for home consumption? "I don't preclude that at all," Quandt said. "Politicians do that all the time. We've just been through a political campaign in which we saw candidates saying quite different things to different audiences. So what else is new?"

No country is better at the game of manipulating public opinion than Israel, where propaganda in the service of policy is a time-honored political tradition. Take the Media Analysis Center in Jerusalem, a propaganda mill run out of the Prime Minister's Office. It provides background reports on the Middle East for the press and diplomats. Backgrounder number 253, a twelve-page report published in December 1988, attempted to prove the PLO's recognition of Israel at the PNC meeting in Algiers was nothing more than "rhetorical ploys targeted at public opinion." But the backgrounder deliberately cooked data and omitted crucial information.

The report employed a kind of perverse Talmudic logic to prove that PLO leaders don't mean what they say—unless Israel can construe what they say as adhering to Israel's preconceived views. The backgrounder failed to mention two crucial points that were *not* made by the PLO in Algiers. Significantly, the resolution passed by the PNC in Algiers was the first one that did not mention armed struggle against Israel. And there was no mention in the resolution of the dread Palestine National Covenant.

The backgrounder inaccurately quoted essays by Palestinian intellectuals written in PLO journals. For example, Jawad al-Bashiti, a senior PLO intellectual, was the PLO's most outspoken advocate of a two-state solution in the late 1980s. Writing in the PLO journal *Falastin Al-Thawra*, he was the first Palestinian Arab to propose that the PLO unilaterally recognize UN Resolution 242. But the backgrounder quoted him out of context in order to make him look like a hard-liner.

The backgrounder performed the same kind of surgery on the writings of Yehoshafat Harkabi, the former head of Israeli Military Intelligence, who advocates negotiations with the PLO. It took a passage from Harkabi's book, *Israel's Fateful Hour*, describing the PLO's old hard-line position, and asserted it was his view as well as the PLO's.

This backgrounder ended by repeating Netanyahu's infamous dictum that "the PLO has been a crucial link in the international terror network, from the Pacific Ocean . . . to Central America. This is even alluded to in the Algiers Political Declaration, which condemns 'American imperialism and colonialism in Latin America.'" But the resolution condemned nothing of the sort. It never used the words "American imperialism" or "colonialism." According to a transcript of the resolution published in the November 1988 issue of the PLO monthly *Sh'un Philastinia*, number 188, the passage reads, "The PNC condemns American attempts to threaten the independence of Central America and to intervene in their internal affairs."

aggressive, expansionist and colonialist in its aims, and fascist and Nazi in its methods," proclaims the PLO's National Covenant. It was the view of the PLO leadership that the creation of Israel was a terrible injustice, and only its annihilation and the return of the Palestinian refugees could restore both their honor and lost homeland. Their call to throw the Jews into the sea was a blatant call for genocide. Never larger than an oversized militia, however, the PLO hadn't the means to do it. So it adopted a policy of trying to draw the Arab states into a regional war with the "Zionist entity." But the PLO's odious dream was thwarted by the Arabs' poor military showing. Israel's victory in the 1967 Six-Day War resulted in even more of the Palestinian patrimony in Zionist hands.

Then, in September of 1970, King Hussein's army moved against the PLO, ejecting it from Jordan, where it was in the process of forming a state within a state, and forcing the organization to take refuge in Lebanon and Syria. The PLO became embroiled in Lebanese politics, fought a shadow war with Mossad in Europe, and attacked civilian targets and hijacked planes, earning the group a measure of fame but not bringing the Palestinians an inch closer to their former homes.

Israel's Military Intelligence first detected a thaw in the PLO's hard line in June 1974, when the PLO announced its intention to establish a state on the West Bank and the Gaza Strip that could be used as a base to liberate the rest of Palestine. Since the PLO's founding in May 1964, its thinking has been dominated by its ultimate goal—"the liberation of Palestine" through "the armed struggle." But between 1974 and 1984, Israeli Military Intelligence chronicled the emergence of a pragmatic wing of the PLO led by Arafat, which prodded the organization increasingly in the direction of restricting itself to a mini-state in the West Bank and Gaza Strip. Ironically, Ariel Sharon's attempt to destroy the PLO in Lebanon in 1982 had more to do with moderating the PLO than almost any other factor. Despairing of ever destroying Israel through armed struggle, Arafat realized that diplomacy was his only recourse if he wanted to gain at least part of Palestine, according to officials in Israeli Military Intelligence.

Though no intelligence agency can work in a vacuum, free of political pressure, Military Intelligence refrained from supporting the political agendas of either Labor, which had sought some kind of territorial compromise to be brokered with King Hussein of Jordan, or Likud, whose vision is Greater Israel. When Shimon Peres was prime minister, Military Intelligence argued that Hussein would not negotiate with Israel without the consent of Arafat, and that the Palestinians in the occupied territories would not accept a substitute for the PLO. In 1986, when Arafat and Hussein signed an accord in Amman that sought a confederation between a PLO-run, West Bank–Gaza Strip entity and Jordan as the senior partner, intelligence analysts argued that Israel should enter into negotiations while it had the strategic advantage, because this was as close to the Jordanian Option as Peres was likely to get. Military Intelligence presented this position to at least one closed session of the Knesset's Foreign Affairs and Defense Committee, chaired by the Labor party's star dove, Abba Eban. But at the time even Eban, who now calls for talks with the PLO, opposed dealing with the organization.

The intelligence estimate that proved most troubling to Netanyahu and the Likud was issued in December 1988, just after the November Palestine National Council meeting in Algiers, and just before then–Secretary of State George Shultz declared that the United States was prepared to talk directly to the PLO. The top secret report concluded that the PLO was ready to accept a two-state solution—a finding that was based on a wide array of evidence gathered from a detailed monitoring of the Arabic and PLO media and public and private remarks of PLO leaders, as well as field reports and electronic intercepts.

Military Intelligence used a number of criteria to support its contention. First, Israeli analysts compared the 1964 Palestine National Covenant (so dreaded by Netanyahu and Foxman) to Arafat's recent declarations. "The PNC declaration speaks of accepting the principle of partitioning Palestine into Jewish and Palestinian Arab states, not of the Covenant," a senior Israeli intelligence official who had worked on the report told me. "The claim that Palestine is 'an indivisible territorial unit' is the backbone of the Covenant. The statement that Palestine can be partitioned, made in their Declaration of Independence,* and which is intended to be authoritative and symbolic, is a denial of the essence of the Covenant."

Using a gamut of monitoring techniques, Israeli intelligence analysts also measured reaction to the new policy of moderation inside the Palestinian rejectionist camp. The Muslim fundamentalists, the various Palestinian rejection groups based in Damascus, and the Syrian government itself condemned Arafat for selling out the Palestinian people. They clearly didn't

*The PLO's Declaration of Independence was signed on November 15, 1988, at the nineteenth PNC in Algiers.

see Arafat's policy as propaganda designed to lull the West into slackening its support for Israel, as the Shamir government insisted. Indeed, several Palestinian rejectionist leaders began to meet in the Bekáa Valley to plan Arafat's assassination as soon as he recognized Israel.

Further, Israel's Military Intelligence painstakingly studied the many publications sponsored by the PLO and its various factions. "The PLO has been building toward a political settlement with Israel for years, and you can detect it in their publications," said the Israeli intelligence official, who added that all their journals talk about a two-state solution with Israel, although they continue to claim East Jerusalem as the future Palestinian capital.

The PLO's declarations were also notable for what they did not mention, the classified estimate said. In the past, PLO officials have not been ambiguous. When they wanted to emphasize the "strategy of stages"—the PLO's euphemism for gaining the West Bank as a base for destroying Israel—they said so in their official resolutions. That rhetoric is no longer in evidence.

The intelligence estimate also analyzed how the *intifada* had helped Arafat break the taboo of recognizing Israel. The uprising, which has pitted Arab youths with slingshots and an occasional firebomb and rifle against the IDF, has given Palestinians a sense of pride and self-confidence after forty years of repeated humiliations at the hands of the Israelis. On the other hand, the *intifada* has shown to the satisfaction of Military Intelligence that the Palestinians will never accept the occupation or abandon the PLO as the embodiment of Palestinian national identity. Even King Hussein of Jordan was compelled to admit this when he was forced to disengage publicly from the West Bank in the fall of 1988. Furthermore, according to a secret Israeli Army report leaked to the Hebrew press early in the *intifada*, senior officers believe the uprising cannot be halted without resorting to unacceptable levels of violence.

Finally, the intelligence estimate noted that Arafat had kept his word and stopped terrorist attacks against Israeli civilians. The report explained, however, that Arafat would not give up violence until he has achieved a political settlement. "Armed struggle is meant to accelerate the political process, not to destroy Israel," said the intelligence source. "The problem is not whether the PLO has really changed, but that the Israeli political establishment has not changed. The problem is that the mainstream of the PLO is ready for partition, and the Shamir government is wed to Greater

Israel. The whole situation has been reversed. The problem is not that the PLO wants to destroy Israel but that they want to coexist. The only one who still believes in the PLO Covenant is Shamir."

Asserting that the Palestinians' quest for self-determination is irreversible and inseparably linked to the PLO, the Military Intelligence estimate concluded that it is an illusion to think that the government can find a "moderate" Palestinian alternative to Arafat. "The report doesn't say talk to the PLO," said a senior Israeli intelligence official who had helped prepare the estimate. "It says you can't have a political process without talking to the PLO. So you can conclude that either the government talks to the PLO or there is no political process. The official view of Israeli Military Intelligence is that the PLO wants peace in return for a state in part of Palestine."

Unfortunately for Shamir, the Israeli intelligence report came at a time when his government was quietly promoting a "peace plan" to key members of the Bush transition team and the American Jewish community that would grant the Palestinians limited autonomy while allowing Israel to control the occupied territories and continue its settlement there. Fearful that news of the intelligence estimate would help legitimize the PLO, Shamir's top aides tried to purge the agency of analysts whose conclusions failed to support Israeli government policy. The witch-hunt went so far as to have the Ministry of Education remove books that present a less than demonic view of the PLO from state-run schools.

The campaign was orchestrated by the director of the Prime Minister's Office, Yossi Ben-Aharon, a soft-spoken, Egyptian-raised career foreign-service officer and lawyer, who was one of the most powerful men in Shamir's inner circle as well as the head of the Israeli delegation to the Middle East peace talks. "We can't negotiate with the PLO because what they want is legitimacy, and if we give them legitimacy, then we have spawned the embryo of a Palestinian state," Ben-Aharon told me in his Jerusalem office in 1989. "And since we are against a Palestinian state west of the River Jordan—there is no purpose in talking. We are not close to dialogue . . . If Arafat thinks he can repeat the Sadat trick and come to Israel and talk peace, he's mistaken. We won't be that gullible and be disarmed by a trick of this sort!

"It's really difficult to comprehend the Arabs' monumental capacity for deception. It is really something the Western mind cannot absorb and appreciate. It is way beyond anything that Goebbels could have conjured up, because for them, lying is second nature. They believe that deception is part and parcel of the art of war."

In January 1989, Ben-Aharon fired off critical letters to the head of Military Intelligence and to Yitzhak Rabin, then minister of defense, in which he argued that the intelligence reports were biased, and if leaked, could be used by the United States to pressure Israel to negotiate with the PLO. He also alleged that the estimate, which recommended that Israel negotiate with the PLO, contradicted an Israeli law that bans talking to the organization. Ben-Aharon intimated in his letter that there should be a housecleaning at Military Intelligence.

However, lawyers for Military Intelligence concluded that the report did not violate Israeli law. Military Intelligence chief Amnon Shahak wrote Rabin affirming that his agency stood by the report. Moreover, no one in Israel's intelligence community wrote a serious refutation of the intelligence estimates.

Shortly after I exposed the controversy about the intelligence estimate in a *Village Voice* cover story in February 1989, the Israeli government threatened to prosecute me for publishing state secrets and breaking censorship laws.* For those in the Shamir government moved by the redemptive rhythms of God and the Zionism of Jabotinsky, no enemy is more insidious than the enemy that dwells within—the unreconstructed Jew of ghetto mentality, the leftists, the Peace Now-niks, the professors, the back-stabbing press, and the Israeli generals who say the *intifada* will sap the army's morale before it can crush the rebellion.

But in May 1990, Palestinian terrorists once again rescued the Likud. Iraqi-backed Palestinian extremist Abul Abbas unsuccessfully attempted to attack Israel using seaborn commandos. Israeli pressure forced the United States to suspend direct talks with the PLO. Soon after, with the pro-Israel lobby's help, Shamir scuttled the 1990 Baker peace plan, which called for direct talks between Israel and Palestinian representatives from the occupied territories, including Arab inhabitants of East Jerusalem, to discuss Palestinian elections. Consequently, Arafat had nothing to show for his dovish diplomacy, setting the stage for the PLO's support for Saddam Hussein.

*

The New York Times published a thinly detailed front-page story about the Israeli intelligence estimate several weeks after my account in the *Voice*.

Flush from its victory over the PLO, the pro-Israel lobby was much in evidence during its bitter battle with the Bush administration over $10 billion in U.S. loan guarantees Israel requested to absorb the vast exodus of Jews from the Soviet Union. Although similar requests for help have been routinely approved by past presidents, Bush did not believe Shamir when he said he would refrain from using the funds in the territories, as the United States has insisted. The Israeli government had made a similar pledge in October 1990, when it received a $400 million loan guarantee, but then never accounted for its expenditure as agreed. A General Accounting Office investigation later found that the money had almost certainly subsidized housing projects across the Green Line. "In other words, receiving written assurances as to how the [loan guarantee] money will be spent, without any accompanying change in Israeli settlement policy, is an exercise in building a paper dam," said Senate Appropriations Committee chairman Robert C. Byrd, a Democrat from West Virginia.

Bush, who linked the loan guarantee to a settlement freeze, "was guided by clear and well-established U.S. policies—the longstanding opposition to Israeli settlements in the occupied territories and the twenty-five-year-old commitment to land for peace, first enunciated in U.N. resolution 242 in 1967," wrote David Ignatius, foreign editor of *The Washington Post*. Given the vast expanse of the settlement enterprise and the billions of dollars Israel has spent on the project since 1967, it was not unreasonable for Bush to be concerned that Shamir would use the loan guarantee to complete his de facto annexation of the occupied territories. Money is the only leverage Bush has over Israel, which subsists to a great extent on American charity. American taxpayers have provided the Jewish state with $50–$60 billion since its establishment in 1948. Though U.S. law bars Israel from spending U.S. aid money in the occupied territories, money is fungible; once it flows into the Israeli Treasury, the government can use the funds any way it likes. Giving Shamir a $10 billion loan guarantee without linking it to a settlement freeze would have made the U.S. taxpayer an unwitting accomplice to apartheid.

The pro-Israel lobby insisted that the loan guarantee was strictly a humanitarian issue and that there was no correlation between U.S. aid money and settlement activity. "The loan guarantee really has to be addressed as a humanitarian issue," Malcolm Hoenlein told me. "You are talking about the absorption of large numbers of refugees. We don't want them to come to the United States. Israel is equipped and ready to accept them and is asking for assistance, not in the form of aid and not in the form of cash from the [U.S.] treasury, but to simply enable it to take on the additional burden."

But if rescuing Soviet Jews was such a pressing humanitarian issue, why did the Israeli lobby urge the United States to limit the number of Soviet Jews allowed to enter America? Until 1989, Jews who could prove they suffered religious persecution in the Soviet Union were allowed to immigrate to the United States after obtaining a visa. At Israel's request, U.S. policy was changed to impose a strict quota on Soviet Jewish immigrants, thereby forcing most Soviet Jews to go to Israel. "The issue [of Soviet immigration] is not an issue of human rights, but the redemption of Jews as Jews," Morris Abram, then chair of the President's Conference, told the Israeli newspaper *Yediot Achronot* in 1989. "They should go to Israel. I didn't see in my whole life a demonstration to let the Jews go to Brighton Beach [a Russian-Jewish émigré community in Brooklyn]."

AIPAC and the Presidents' Conference spearheaded a high-powered campaign to secure congressional support for Israel's request. In June 1991, Thomas Dine, the executive director of AIPAC, declared that the "paramount challenge this year" to American Jews is to persuade Congress and the administration to grant the $10 billion loan guarantees. "We must fight any attempt to imperil this vital program by linking it to the explosive ideological issue of settlement," Dine said during a closed-door meeting with a group of major donors. "Linking absorption guarantees to settlements, or the peace process, is something we must fight with all of our being." Dine said that American supporters of Israel, even those who were unhappy with settlements, should nevertheless "swallow hard, roll up your sleeves, and get to work to fight linkage."

Congress may be sympathetic to Israel, but it is also terrified of AIPAC—without question the most powerful lobby in America. Former Illinois senator Charles Percy,* who had often challenged AIPAC when he was the Republican chairman of the Foreign Relations Committee, was defeated in 1984 after AIPAC directed hundreds of thousands of dollars in pro-Israel PAC money to his Democratic rival. "All the Jews in America, from coast to coast, gathered to oust Percy," Dine declared in a speech

---

*Prominent AIPAC supporter Michael Goland was fined five thousand dollars by the Federal Elections Commission for spending more than $1 million to defeat Percy. FEC rules prohibit a person from donating more than one thousand dollars to a political campaign. Goland was later convicted in a California court for using $120,000 to discredit former U.S. representative Ed Zschau, who lost a close 1986 Senate race against Alan Cranston, one of Congress's strongest supporters of Israel.

after the 1984 election campaign. "And the American politicians . . . got the message." George McGovern told me, referring to his career in Congress, that "it was perceived as a great political risk" not to give Israel everything it wanted: "If you didn't go right down the line [with the pro-Israel lobby], you'd be getting calls from your state within thirty minutes, and those had to be orchestrated out of Washington."

Bush received a similar message early in the summer of 1991 when a wealthy New York real estate developer and major financer of the Republican party brusquely informed the president that he would not receive conservative Jewish money in 1992 if he linked the $10 billion loan guarantee to Israel's settlement enterprise. "There is anger and dismay in Jewish communities over Bush administration policy that is increasingly perceived as one-sided and unfair against Israel," Jesse Hordes, Washington director of the ADL, told *The New York Times*. "I imagine it will be translated into unwillingness to vote for this administration or contribute funds."

New York's intrepid congressional delegation lined up squarely behind AIPAC. "[We] believe very deeply that for many years Israel has been a metaphor for democracy," said an aide to a powerful New York senator who asked not to be identified. "The struggle of Soviet Jewry for freedom was part and parcel of the entire effort to change the Soviet Union to bring the forces of freedom there, and we feel that having got these people to do what they did, it might behoove us to assist. If people are going to be packing millions and millions of dollars of loan guarantees and outright cash to the people who kept them locked up, it's not the end of the world to extend loan guarantees with rigid business restrictions [to Israel]. . . . Israel hasn't defaulted, and they are not about to default."

While it is true that Israel has never defaulted on a loan, that is simply because it uses its annual U.S. aid package to keep up with its debt payments. Of the $3.5 billion Israel receives annually from the United States, about $1 billion flows back to the U.S. Treasury as debt repayment. Under a 1984 law drafted by Senator Alan Cranston of California, U.S. aid is not allowed to drop below the amount Israel owes the United States in repayment for past debts.

Israel desperately needs vast infusions of cash. Israeli economists estimate the country may need as much as $50 billion over the next five years to absorb Soviet Jewish immigrants who have been flooding into the country at the rate of five thousand to ten thousand per month. More than $1 billion has been raised from the world Jewish community, but even with an additional $10 billion in U.S. loan guarantees, that sum doesn't come close to meeting Israel's needs. Even if the Israeli taxpayer foots a major share of the bill, there will still be a huge shortfall. As a result, Israel may be forced to turn to the United States for help in repaying the $10 billion as well as for additional grants.

Even without taking on the additional debt to absorb Soviet Jews, Israel is already considered a poor credit risk by international ratings agencies. Standard and Poor's gives Israel's long-term debt a "BBB-minus" credit rating, its lowest investment grade. The lower a rating, the more likely a country will default on its obligation. According to the magazine *Institutional Investor,* Israel's creditworthiness ranks just ahead of that of Papua New Guinea and just behind Algeria's. The Export-Import Bank gives Israel a "D" rating on a scale of "A" through "F."

"Adding another $10 billion will put them over the edge of insolvency— if not immediately, at least in the near term," a U.S. official told *The Christian Science Monitor.* "Then the question for Israel is, what's going to be the strategy for getting the U.S. to help on debt service. All it's going to take is one security crisis and the U.S. will face . . . pressure to rescue Israel's economy and relieve its debt burden."

According to a State Department report on Israel's economy, the Jewish state will have to establish economic growth rates "approximating those of the Asian Tigers" to prevent a possible economic disaster. State Department economists say that if Israel doesn't dismantle its stagnant socialist economy, it will only compound the country's financial problems, increasing its external debt, which now stands at around $20 billion. And as long as political and economic instability continue to plague Israel, it will be unable to attract sorely needed foreign investment. Dov Frohman, vice president of the California microcomputer company Intel and general manager of Intel Israel, told *New York Times* columnist Anthony Lewis that "people won't send their money to a country that is full of unrest. The idea of attracting investment and at the same time building settlements on occupied land is completely crazy."

Ironically, on the day before the administration asked Congress to delay Israel's request for the $10 billion loan guarantee in September 1991, the Shamir government passed a controversial budget that increased Israel's deficit by $3.7 billion, well beyond the maximum recommended by the Israeli Finance Ministry and the Central Bank. Much of the budgetary increase went to finance Israel's settlement drive. Sharon alone overspent his budget for housing in the territories by $500 million, according to a report by the Finance Ministry. Three left-of-center parties said in a joint statement that Israel could balance its budget if it froze West Bank settlement activity and made modest cuts in defense spending. "This budget will raise doubts as to Israel's future ability to repay the large loans it is requesting, and the repayment will fall on the American taxpayer in this case," the newspaper *Ha'aretz* said.

Implicit in *Ha'aretz*'s warning is that Israel's request for $10 billion in loan guarantees is in fact a camouflaged request for U.S. aid. At a time when many U.S. cities are approaching bankruptcy and the U.S. government is straining to pay the bill for the S&L collapse, should the United States subsidize Israel given the real possibility that it will default on the loan, leaving the American taxpayer with the tab?

As far as the settlers are concerned, the answer is simple. Like the Holy Land itself, American money, they believe, is a divine entitlement. "Bush doesn't make the decisions in America," Rabbi Lowenstein of Eli told me in December 1990. "Congress does. And Congress goes with Israel because Jews give them money. Everything goes with the money there: money and oil. That's why no one here is worried. American Jews are strong, and Congress has to do what they say."

But as of March 1992, Israel's request for the $10 billion loan guarantee was still bottled up in the Senate Appropriations Subcommittee on foreign operations chaired by Patrick Leahy, a democratic senator from Vermont. In September 1991, Leahy had declared publicly that the amount of money Israel spends annually on settlements should be deducted from the amount it had requested. He quietly passed around a proposal to that effect. Some observers believed the dollar-for-dollar amendment could even slip into Israel's annual aid package. "Even as Israel is asking our help [to absorb Russian Jews], it is expanding the construction of the settlements at an unprecedented speed," Leahy wrote in an op-ed piece in *The New York Times* in February 1992. "In so doing, it is ignoring the increasingly blunt criticism by the Administration, which is determined to press the Middle East peace talks to a successful conclusion. Israel wants the guarantees . . . without any conditions, to be used as it sees fit. But this won't happen."

During the first round of Arab-Israeli peace talks in Washington in December 1991, Leahy entertained Hanan Ashrawi, a Palestinian delegate to the talks, in his Washington office. Ashrawi is an articulate, self-assured woman of forty-five who has been compared to Golda Meir. At the end of the meeting, Leahy walked over to a wall and showed Ashrawi a framed photo of his house in Vermont. "My family and I have lived in this house for many years," said Leahy. "My children have derived great pleasure from it. I think I'd be very upset if someone took it away from me, and I couldn't come back. So I understand how you must feel."

Earlier that year, Leahy had visited Israel and the West Bank with his wife. On the way to Jerusalem, after meeting Mayor Elias Freij of Bethlehem, the couple was stopped at an Israeli roadblock. They watched in horror as Israeli troops told a young Palestinian couple that they could not take their sick baby to a hospital in Jerusalem. The couple had passes, which are necessary now for Palestinians to move from one sector of the West Bank to another, but the baby did not. Mrs. Leahy intervened, herself taking the baby to the hospital. It was an experience the Leahys still talk about with anger and sadness.

Although AIPAC targeted Leahy for supporting Bush's policy, he did not appear to be vulnerable to the "Percy syndrome," which has paralyzed many other congressmen. The highly popular senator is an institution in Vermont. Moreover, there are proportionately fewer Jews in Vermont than in Illinois, and the Vermont Jewish community itself is deeply divided on Israel's settlement policy. Nevertheless, Leahy's 1991 pro-Israel PAC money totalled only $13,000, compared to the $85,700 he received in 1986 when he ran for the Senate. "AIPAC has been calling me to do what I can to make sure Senator Leahy is aware of where we stand on the issue," Rabbi Max Wald of Burlington told the *Washington Jewish Week*. Adam Gordon, a Jewish activist and real-estate magnate in Vermont, told the paper, "Leahy has an opportunity to consolidate or obliterate his Jewish support in Vermont in one fell swoop." Following intense pressure from AIPAC, Leahy fashioned an eleventh-hour compromise in which Israel would receive $800 million of the $10 billion in 1992, with the rest being held back to discourage further settlement activity. Bush rejected the plan, saying there were too many "loopholes."

Bush was unflinching in his war of nerves with the lobby, and by the summer of 1991, he had its leaders on the ropes. A sobered Abe Foxman of the ADL wrote an essay in *Yediot Achronot*, warning Israeli leaders that they would have to choose between building more West Bank settlements or getting the $10 billion for Soviet immigrants. "It is not helpful to Israeli leaders to be fed illusions," Foxman wrote in September 1991. "Israeli settlements, coming at a time when Israel desperately needs U.S. guarantees, have a cost." U.S. economic problems, the end of the Soviet threat and Israel's concomitant role as a strategic asset, and Bush's relative popularity, "make it too tempting for the administration to apply leverage" on Israel, he wrote. "To think that the administration and the president, who has always taken personally Israel's continuing settlements, will not use this unique moment to exert their influence is to fool oneself," said Foxman, who had campaigned hard for immediate congressional approval of the loan guarantee.

Astonishingly, even AIPAC begged Shamir to moderate his settlement policy for the sake of the $10 billion at a private meeting in Washington in December 1991. Shamir retorted that Bush would submit to continued pressure from the American Jewish community. The AIPAC people were "aghast" that Shamir had failed to understand how much Israel's support in the United States had eroded, according to a report in the *Washington Jewish Week.*

AIPAC was reflecting not only political realities in Washington, but also the strong, subterranean anti-Shamir, anti-Likud sentiment among American Jews. While Jews were proud to see Shamir in the role of peacemaker in Madrid, his nonstop settlement drive, which accelerated on the eve of the talks, the takeover of Arab homes in Silwan, and the proposed deportation of Palestinian activists disappointed many Jews. According to a poll taken of board members of the Council of Jewish Federations by the Wilstein Institute, a Los Angeles research organization on Jewish issues, an overwhelming number of Federation leaders opposed Shamir's expansionist policies. Eighty-eight percent of the respondents favored land for peace, while 61 percent said they supported negotiations with the PLO if it recognized Israel and renounced terrorism (which it did in 1988, although virtually nobody in the Jewish community believes it thanks to Israel's *hasbara* campaign). Most amazing of all, 79 percent favored the creation of a demilitarized West Bank Palestinian state!

The survey, which was based on 205 replies from 339 council leaders, also revealed that 52 percent believed that Bush administration policies were helpful toward Israel; 75 percent said the United States should keep up the pressure on both sides to be more flexible; and 78 percent said Israel should freeze settlements to get the $10 billion housing loan guarantees.

The respondents were hardly American Jewish leftists. Their median age was fifty-five; their median annual income was more than $200,000. Each respondent contributed more than twenty thousand dollars a year to Israel and considered himself to be middle-of-the road politically.

The survey was made public on November 20, 1991, the day before Shamir was to speak in Baltimore to the Federation's annual General Assembly. "Prime Minister Shamir undoubtedly will receive a standing ovation for his speech," Seymour Martin Lipset, one of the poll's designers and a political scientist at George Mason University, said at a press conference. "We thought it important that he and everyone else should know what his audience really thinks before he speaks—that the ovation is out of respect for his office rather than an expression of support for his policies."

The poll was front-page news in Israel. "Congratulations for the success of Operation 'Welcome,' " wrote Ephram Sneh, the former head of the civil administration for the occupied territories, to one of the poll's sponsors. "Here, at least, it was very effective." In the United States, however, the poll was immediately denounced by officials of the ADL, AIPAC, and the Presidents' Conference as being unrepresentative of the Jewish community, structurally flawed, and politically biased. "This is a calculated effort to ambush the prime minister," railed Foxman. David Harris, a vice president of the American Jewish Committee, wrote a letter to *The New York Times* asserting that American Jews were much more hawkish than the Wilstein poll showed. As proof, he trumpeted the results of an AJC survey that was far more supportive of Shamir's policies. But the AJC poll had been taken soon after the war in the Gulf, when Tel Aviv was under the shadow of Iraqi Scud attacks and when emotions were still running high.

Shamir told the Italian magazine *La Repubblica* that the poll did not reflect the American Jewish community's true feelings about him. After all, he said, "I was received by the U.S. Jewish community with extraordinary enthusiasm. I do not want to exaggerate, but I have never before encountered such enthusiasm." What Shamir didn't say was that Likud advance men packed the halls with loyal Likudniks. "It all added up to a completely cynical exploitation of American Jewish public opinion," said a liberal American Jewish official. A more accurate reading came from Uriel Savir, the Israeli consul general in New York, who warned Shamir that he was putting American Jews in the position of having to choose between America and Israel. "They fear that the nightmare of conflict between two loyalties will come true," Savir said in a diplomatic cable that was published by *Ha'aretz*.

Back at home, Shamir raged at Peace Now, blaming the group for his troubles with the Bush administration. In a December 1991 speech to Likud's central committee that was ugly even by the Israeli right's rabble-rousing standards, Shamir accused the Israeli left of treason: "Legitimate differences of opinion against us cannot be allowed to play into the hands of those who are willing to give away parts of the Land of Israel, who are willing to flee from Judea and Samaria, who are willing to serve in the ranks of foreign and hostile elements. . . . Our so-called fighters for peace do not refrain from collaboration with the Arabs. They collaborate with the most radical of our enemies, those who call for the establishment of a Palestinian state and conspire to take Jerusalem from us; those who use armed terror against Israel. The nation cannot rely on them, on people of the past, on magicians of negativism without spine."

Within hours after Shamir's speech, Peace Now leaders and left-wing members of the Knesset began receiving a flood of anonymous death threats. Peace Now accused Shamir of "preparing the ground for another Emil Grunzweig," a reference to the Peace Now activist killed in a grenade attack on an anti–Lebanon War rally in 1983. Shimon Peres declared that Shamir was guilty of "incitement on a scale previously unknown in the country . . . He treats the Knesset with disdain, divides the country, and incites against half of the nation."

Ultimately, Shamir's divisive tactics and his callous use of downtrodden Jewish refugees from Ethiopia and the former Soviet Union as pawns in the quest for Greater Israel brought Likud's fifteen-year rule to an end. More and more Israelis had come around to Peace Now's view that the country's limited resources were being squandered by fanatical ideologues.

Gush Emunim leader Daniella Weiss, for one, is unfazed by the machinations of the Israeli left and America's hostility to the settlement enterprise. "The soil is holy and belongs to the Jews," she said with messianic self-certainty. Weiss doesn't much care about preserving U.S. aid to Israel if it means that proud, tough Jews like herself have to kowtow to Gentiles. "I despise the president of the United States," she declared, glowering under a flowered scarf, a style favored by Orthodox Jewish women settlers. "I could spit in his face and not feel regret if I lived to be one thousand years old. I'd have one thousand years of continued satisfaction!"

Lords of the Land

Israel is a remarkable achievement. After two thousand years in exile, Jews have returned home to become farmers and soldiers, statesmen and students, poets and zealots. While Israel has not become the exemplary society, or "light unto the nations," its founding fathers and its many friends had hoped, it has become a "nation like any other." In fact, compared to its Arab neighbors—a collection of ruthless dictatorships maintained by coercion and torture—Israel fares much better.

But when Likud came to power in 1977, ending thirty years of Labor party rule, a transformation for the worse occurred in Israel. Two strains of Zionism—the uncompromising, expansionist vision of the secular Jabotinsky, and the militant mystical-messianic settler crusade of the fanatically religious Gush Emunim—joined forces. Suddenly, David became Goliath. Sympathetic Israeli national icons like kibbutzim and Golda Meir were overshadowed by Ariel Sharon, the siege of Beirut, and West Bank settlements. Liberal Jewish peace activists, both in Israel and America, were denounced as traitors, and new alliances were forged with the Christian Evangelical right in the United States. Israel's popular TV advertising slogan, "Come to Israel, stay with friends," was drowned out by Prime Minister Menachem Begin's cry, "We don't care what the *goyim* think!"

Zionism is a pioneering movement, and settlements are its expression. Pre-state Israel was built *dunam* by *dunam*, goat by goat, and paid for in blood and sacrifice. In 1947, when the UN voted to partition Palestine into Jewish and Arab states, Ben-Gurion agreed, the Arabs did not, and as a result of this error hundreds of thousands of Palestinians began a long and painful exile. The Six-Day War brought Israel to the Palestinians' place of refuge, Gaza and the West Bank. The Labor party built sparingly in these areas; the Likud was determined to absorb the territory into Israel, control its land and water, and give the Palestinians there nothing more than the right to administer municipal services like education and health care. Realizing that peace talks could lead to political autonomy for the Palestinians—and eventual statehood—Shamir obstructed their progress while trying to derail them with deliberate military provocations into Lebanon.

Shamir admitted as much in an interview with *Maariv* two days after Labor's surprise victory: "I would have conducted negotiations for ten years and in the meantime we would have reached half a million people in Judea and Samaria. It's very painful to me that in the next four years I will not be able to increase settlement in Judea and Samaria and Gaza, and complete the demographic revolution."

But if the rapid pace of settlement had continued as Shamir intended, an apartheid regime would have resulted, one in which there would be no hope for a solution based on territorial compromise. Conflict would then become a way of life. Israel would be a binational entity without any constitutional arrangement for the Palestinians. Jewish society would rule Palestinian society by force. Israel would be a nation like any other in the Arab Middle East. Palestinian extremists and Islamic fundamentalists would gain ground at the expense of the pragmatists. Diplomacy would be discredited. Arafat, who recognized Israel, renounced terrorism, and accepted a backstage role at the peace talks, would have reached the bottom of his bag. He would have nothing left to surrender and would be replaced by Palestinian radicals. Meanwhile, the Arab population in the territories would continue to grow, as would the call from Jewish extremists to expel them.

Now that Likud has been replaced by a more moderate, Labor-led Zionist coalition, one thing seems certain: Any movement toward peace that challenges the settlements will lead to even greater violence by the settlers who have publicly threatened to sabotage any peace agreement that ends in territorial compromise. Palestinian proposals for elections on the West Bank may, for example, inspire attacks like those by Gush Emunim settlers on two of the pro-PLO mayors elected in 1976. The militant secular settlement leader Eliyakim Haetzni raises the specter of civil war in his book *The Shock of Withdrawal from the Land of Israel,* in which he argues that Jews loyal to "Greater Israel" have the right to overthrow the state if it betrays the dream of Zionism by relinquishing any part of the occupied territories to the Arabs. In 1985, Haetzni succeeded in having the settlers' lobbying group, YESHA, pass a resolution telling then–Prime Minister Peres not to pursue the Jordanian Option: "We warn any regime in Israel which implements such proposals that we will relate to it as an illegal regime as General de Gaulle treated the Vichy regime of Marshal Pétain, which betrayed the French people."

The more apt comparison, however, is between Haetzni,* a former Tehiya Knesset member, and the French officers who conspired to assassinate de Gaulle for ending the French occupation of Algeria and granting it independence. Indeed, just a few days before Haetzni's resolution was passed, an editorial in *Alef Yud,* a settlement newspaper, vowed that the settlers would take up arms against the Israeli government if it tried to trade territory for peace with the Arabs. Later, in a speech to the Knesset, Geula Cohen warned, "Judea, Samaria, and Gaza are not the Sinai. There will be a [civil] war here" if Israel gives up territory (as it did in 1982 in carrying out the Camp David Accords). On June 24, 1992, the day after the Likud government fell, Haetzni told National Public Radio that while he would not personally take up arms against Israeli soldiers, some settlers undoubtedly would.

Hebrew University professor Ehud Sprinzak, an expert on Israeli extremist groups and the author of *The Ascendance of Israel's Radical Right,* is convinced that settlers like Haetzni "will do whatever they can to destroy the peace process." But because *Halachic* injunctions make it difficult for Jews to justify killing fellow Jews, Sprinzak believes that the religious settlers would hesitate to take up arms against Israeli soldiers sent to oust them. Such injunctions, of course, "do not apply to Arabs," he points out. Sprinzak predicts that violence by settlers against Arabs may spiral out of control, and that this could cause some Palestinians to trade their stones for guns, leading in turn to more brutal repression.

The ultimate settler provocation would be blowing up the Dome of the

---

*In Haetzni, one also hears the echo of German ideologues who advocated *Lebensraum,* the Nazi theory that geography, not economics, determines history. The Nazi invasion of Eastern Europe for "living space" and the gassing of the Jews was a result of that theory turned into policy. According to William L. Shirer in *The Rise and Fall of the Third Reich,* Hitler was obsessed with the notion of *Lebensraum* "to his dying breath." Hitler wrote in *Mein Kampf* that the soil of Europe did not belong to any particular nation or race but "for the people which possess the force to take it." And if the possessors object? "Then the law of self-preservation goes into effect; and what is refused to amicable methods, it is up to the fist to take."

Rock Mosque. In view of the the intensity of feeling prevalent on the extreme religious and secular right, the threat of a peace settlement that could destroy their hopes of establishing "Greater Israel" makes it altogether possible that settlers might attempt to blow up the famous mosque. "When you try to think of one single act that could torpedo a peace process—and one that would blow apart the Arab world—it's the bombing of the mosque," said Sprinzak.

Nevertheless, Israel must make a fateful choice: It can remain the lord of *all* the land and never know a day of peace, or it can relinquish political control over the occupied West Bank and Gaza Strip, while maintaining a military presence there sufficient to protect its people. Fortunately, Israelis voted out the heirs of Jabotinsky and the rebels of Masada. By doing so, however, they set the stage for the possibility of civil war with the settlers and their allies. But if they had kept Likud in power, Israel risked becoming another South Africa. That would no doubt jeopardize American aid and political support. Already, the Bush administration has hinted that it may cut aid to Israel, and perhaps turn the Palestinian-Israeli problem over to the UN Security Council, a forum in which Israel will not fare well.

There is a rational way out of this endless conflict. Prime Minister Yitzhak Rabin has proposed an updated version of the Allon Plan, in which Jewish settlements would continue to be built and maintained on the so-called confrontation lines along the Jordan River, the Syrian border, and around greater Jerusalem, while predominantly Arab areas would become part of a self-ruling, autonomous unit linked to Israel in a federation. At the same time, Rabin also said he would freeze the flow of money to "ideological settlements" that were built by Likud in densely populated areas of the West Bank and Gaza. In a June 1992 interview in the magazine *New Outlook*, Rabin said, "Once we reach an agreement over autonomy and implement it—let's try each other out. Maybe new ideas will emerge in which the Palestinians find a solution to their desire for their own entity, not a state—and in which Israel finds a solution to its desire to have access to the entire Land of Israel and, above all, to its security needs."

Doves in the Labor party and the left-wing Meretz bloc are prepared to go much farther. They want to repartition the area into Palestinian and Jewish states, and allow a process of normalization to start. Zev Schiff, the respected military editor of *Ha'aretz*, wrote in a 1989 policy paper for the pro-Israeli Washington Institute that a peace settlement between Israel and the PLO necessarily would include a joint Palestinian-Israeli command to fight terrorism, which Jordan would be invited to join. In Schiff's model, a Palestinian ministate would have a small indigenous police force and no army, and would permit Israel to station troops in strategic areas, away from population centers, during a confidence-building period that would last a number of years until the Arab states bordering Israel signed peace treaties. According to a survey conducted by *Yediot Achronot* in 1988, more than 75 percent of the generals in Israel's General Staff favored ending the occupation, though virtually all wanted to retain an armed presence along the Jordan River (a natural tank trap) so as to deter a possible invasion along the eastern front.*

For an enduring peace, however, all of Israel's Arab neighbors will have to accept its legitimate place among the nations of the Middle East. They have to come to terms with the unique historical role of the Jewish people, who have returned to their homeland. The Palestinians may describe their encounter with Zionism as a catastrophe comparable to the Holocaust, but if they don't accept Israel, their suffering will only worsen. And if Israel doesn't soon end its occupation, Zionism, the national liberation movement of the Jewish people, will be debased by the zealots.

*According to a June 21, 1992, front-page story in *The Jerusalem Post,* a survey of Israel's military elite found that 75 percent of Israel's retired generals and former heads of Mossad and the Shin Bet said that Israel's security can be adequately maintained if the West Bank and Gaza are returned to Jordan or the Palestinians; 83 percent said they believe that continuation of the status quo in the territories is likely to lead to war; 90 percent said they would accept negotiations with the PLO if the PLO recognizes Israel, ceases terrorism, relinquishes its "right of return," and stops the *intifada*. Meanwhile, in August 1992, Prime Minister Rabin agreed to let some ten thousand homes already under construction be completed, which will boost the Jewish population in the occupied territories by as much as fifty thousand.

Index

ABOUT THE AUTHOR

ROBERT I. FRIEDMAN is the author of *The False Prophet: Rabbi Meir Kahane—From FBI Informant to Knesset Member.* He is currently a staff writer for *The Village Voice.* His work has appeared in numerous other publications, including *Vanity Fair, GQ, The New York Review of Books, The Washington Post,* the *Los Angeles Times, Mother Jones, Harper's,* and *The Nation.*

ABOUT THE TYPE

This book was set in Galliard, a typeface designed by Matthew Carter for the Mergenthaler Linotype Company in 1978. Galliard is based on the sixteenth-century typefaces of Robert Granjon, which give it classic lines yet interject a contemporary look.

DATE	ISSUED TO